How to Do *Everything* with Your

Sony
CLIÉ™
Second Edition

S0-BYW-953

How to Do *Everything* with Your

Sony CLIÉ™

Second Edition

Rick Broida
Dave Johnson

McGraw-Hill/Osborne

New York Chicago San Francisco Lisbon
London Madrid Mexico City Milan New Delhi
San Juan Seoul Singapore Sydney Toronto

McGraw-Hill/Osborne
2100 Powell Street, 10th Floor
Emeryville, California 94608
U.S.A.

To arrange bulk purchase discounts for sales promotions, premiums, or fund-raisers, please contact **McGraw-Hill**/Osborne at the above address. For information on translations or book distributors outside the U.S.A., please see the International Contact Information page immediately following the index of this book.

How to Do Everything with Your Sony CLIÉ™, Second Edition

1234567890 CUS CUS 019876543

ISBN 0-07-223074-6

Publisher	Brandon A. Nordin
Vice President	
& Associate Publisher	Scott Rogers
Acquisitions Editor	Marjorie McAneny
Project Editor	Jenn Tust
Acquisitions Coordinator	Tana Allen
Technical Editor	Denny Atkin
Copy Editor	Marcia Baker
Proofreader	Paul Medoff
Indexer	Valerie Perry
Composition	International Typesetting & Composition
Illustrators	International Typesetting & Composition
Series Design	Mickey Galicia
Cover Series Design	Dodie Shoemaker

This book was composed with Corel VENTURA™ Publisher.

Dedication

For my wonderful family: Shawna, Sarah, and Ethan.
—Rick

For everyone who still knows what "Dank Showcase, Cyberspy" is.
—Dave

About the Authors

Rick Broida has written about computers and technology for nearly 15 years. A regular contributor to CNET and *Computer Shopper*, he specializes in mobile technology. In 1997, recognizing the unparalleled popularity of Palm handhelds and the need for a printed resource for users, he founded *Handheld Computing* (formerly *Tap Magazine*). He currently serves as editor of that magazine, which now covers all handheld platforms and devices. Rick also writes the *Tech Savvy* column for Michigan's *Observer & Eccentric* newspapers. He lives in Michigan with his wife and two children.

Dave Johnson is the editor of *Handheld Computing Mobility* magazine and senior editor of *Handheld Computing Magazine*. He writes about digital photography for *PC World* magazine and is the author of the best-selling book, *How to Do Everything with Your Digital Camera*. He's the author of about three dozen books that include *Robot Invasion: 7 Cool and Easy Robot Projects*, *How to Do Everything with MP3 and Digital Music* (written with Rick Broida), and *How to Use Digital Video*. His short story for early readers, *The Wild Cookie*, has been transformed into an interactive storybook on CD-ROM. In his spare time, Dave is a scuba instructor and wildlife photographer.

About the Technical Editor

Denny Atkin has been writing about technology since 1987, and about handheld computers since the Newton's release in 1993. After working with such pioneering technology magazines as *Compute!* and *Omni*, he's now editorial director of *Handheld Computing* and *Mobility Magazine*. Denny lives with his wife and son in Vermont, a state where PDAs are nearly as popular as maple syrup.

Contents at a Glance

Contents

Acknowledgments

The folks at Osborne who back us up throughout the book-writing process—like Jane Brownlow, Tana Allen, Margie McAneny, and Jenn Tust—are simply the best. We can't imagine a better bunch of people to work with. We'd also like to thank tech editor Denny Atkin, who caught and corrected most of the wildly inaccurate things we wrote. Dave would also like to thank Rick for finally turning on his spell checker. Good show, buddy! Rick would like to congratulate Dave for learning to use a second finger while typing.

More thanks to the people at Sony who helped us get what we needed when we needed it. In particular, we're grateful to David Yang—a consummate professional who could teach other PR folk a thing or two.

Finally, thanks as always to our amazingly supportive families, who give us the time and space we need to get the work done without so much as a single complaint.

Introduction

We'll admit it: we're gadget nuts. When PDAs burst onto the scene back in the mid-1990s, we were the first kids on the block to get one. Dave got an Apple Newton MessagePad; Rick got a PalmPilot. In the annals of history, Rick has only been right a few times, and this was one of those occasions—the Newton was discontinued, but Palm licensed the Palm operating system and made it the single most popular kind of PDA in the world today. Sony, of course, has taken the Palm OS and turned it into the coolest family of gadgets you could possibly imagine. Hence this book.

Indeed, Sony's Clié handhelds are such great little devices that any book about them runs the risk of reading like a promotional brochure. We've written thousands of pages about the Windows platform, and half of it always seems to be apologetic. "Computer locked up again? You need to reboot and send $94 in cash to Microsoft. . . ." Books about computers are often more about getting it to work in the first place or explaining why it doesn't work right than about telling you what you can actually accomplish.

Not the Clié, though. It's one of the most forgiving, user-friendly, and non-crashable computers ever created. And because it suffers from so few technical glitches, we were able to devote most of this book to work and play—accomplishing stuff and making your life more fun and efficient.

This book starts at the beginning (unlike that episode of *Seinfeld* that started at the end and went backwards). First we give you some of the history of handheld computers like the Clié (and the Clié itself), then discuss the various models and which one might best suit your needs (in case you haven't purchased one yet). From there, you get a guided tour of your Clié and the accompanying desktop software. We teach you to navigate the core software, to input data, and to share information with your PC as well as other handheld devices.

In Part II, we show you the Clié's core applications and then tell you stuff you'd never think of—like how to get the most out of your Clié when you go on a business trip. Think your new handheld can't take the place of a laptop computer? Think again (and read Chapters 10 and 12).

Part III goes "beyond the box," and that's where things get really interesting. Read those chapters and you learn how to connect to the Internet, manage your finances, track your stocks, and balance your checkbook. We also delve into the arts, with chapters on painting pictures and playing music. You might not think there's a lot to say about playing games, but a whole world of entertainment awaits you—and we show you how to tap into it (pun intended). In fact, you might throw away your Game Boy after reading Chapter 20. And, yes, we said people rarely have trouble with their Cliés, but it does happen occasionally. We have that covered as well.

We wrote this book so you could sit down and read it through like a novel. But if you're looking for specific information, we made it easy to find. Plus, you can find special elements to help you get the most out of the book:

- **How to...** These special boxes explain, in a nutshell, how to accomplish key tasks. Read them to discover key points covered in each chapter.

- **Notes** These provide extra information that's often very important to gain understanding of a particular topic.

- **Tips** These tell you how to do something smarter or faster.

- **Sidebars** Here we address related—and, sometimes, unrelated—topics. Sidebars can be pretty interesting, if only to see us bicker like a pair of elderly muppets.

Can't get enough of Dave and Rick? See the back page of *Handheld Computing Magazine*, where we continue to argue in our lively Head2Head column. You can also send questions and comments to us at *dave@bydavejohnson.com* and *rickbroida1@excite.com*. Thanks, and enjoy reading the book!

Part I   Getting Started

Chapter 1

Welcome to Clié

Imagine this—Stephen King novels, the entire *O Brother, Where Art Thou?* soundtrack, a dozen different solitaire games, a collegiate dictionary, your entire appointment calendar, a guide to more than 10,000 wines, an address book with pictures of every person, episodes of *The Simpsons*—all in your pocket.

It sounds like technology you might see on an episode of *Star Trek,* but you can have it right here in the 21st century. Thanks to remarkable strides in handheld computing, virtually every item in the preceding list can be stored in a single device—a Sony Clié handheld PC. And that's just the tip of the iceberg. These amazing devices can send and receive e-mail, take digital photos, control your home stereo, open and edit Word and Excel files, and a lot more.

In the pages and chapters to come, you'll learn the history of handheld PCs like the Clié, the differences between models in the Clié line, and, of course, everything you need to know about using them.

A Brief History of Handhelds

It all started with a block of wood. In 1994, Jeff Hawkins, founder of a little-known company called Palm Computing, envisioned a pocket-sized computer that would organize calendars and contacts, and maybe let travelers retrieve their e-mail from the road. This idea of a personal digital assistant, or PDA, was by no means new, but previous attempts—like Apple's highly publicized Newton MessagePad—had failed to catch on with consumers.

Hawkins knew he'd have a tough time selling the concept, so he decided to convince himself before trying to convince investors. His device would be roughly the size of a deck of cards— much smaller and lighter than the Newton—and fit in a shirt pocket. But would it be practical at that size? Would it be comfortable to carry around? Hawkins decided to find out. Before a single piece of plastic was molded, before a single circuit board was designed, the Palm Computing Pilot existed solely as a block of wood.

Hawkins cut a piece of balsa wood to the size he'd envisioned for his handheld device, put it in his shirt pocket, and left it there—for several months. He even took it out from time to time and pretended to take notes, just to see if the size and shape felt right. Although he quickly came to realize that such a form factor made perfect sense, doors slammed whenever he showed his "product" to potential investors. "The handheld market is dead" was the mantra at the time.

Fortunately, modem-maker U.S. Robotics didn't think so, and liked the idea of the Pilot so much that it bought Palm Computing outright. In March 1996, the company unveiled the Pilot 1000, and the rest is history.

Flash-forward six years. The Pilot—which would eventually be renamed PalmPilot, and then just Palm—had become the fastest-growing computer platform in history, reaching the million-sold mark faster than the IBM PC or the Apple Macintosh. In the interim, U.S. Robotics had been assimilated into networking giant 3Com, and Palm, Inc., along with it. The Palm line had grown to include a variety of models, and companies like Handspring, IBM, and Sony had adopted the Palm operating system for their own handheld devices.

Today, the *Palm platform* (an umbrella term used to describe not only the actual hardware, but the operating system that drives it) is dominant in the explosive handheld market. The Sony Clié series falls under that umbrella. It's a family of handheld PCs that run the Palm Operating System (OS)—the same OS used in handhelds made by Palm, Handspring, and other companies.

What's an Operating System?

Windows is an operating system. Mac OS X is an operating system. The core software that drives any computer is an operating system. Hence, when we refer to the Clié's Palm OS, we're talking about the software built into the device—the brains behind the brawn. The Palm OS itself not only controls the Clié's fundamental operations, such as what happens when you press a button or tap the screen, but also supplies the built-in applications (the Address Book, Memo Pad, Date Book, and so on—all of which we discuss in detail in later chapters).

The Palm OS is the key ingredient that links the various Palm devices, whether they're manufactured by Palm, Handspring, Sony, or one of the other companies licensed to use the Palm OS.

NOTE   *These "licensees" have been granted permission by Palm, Inc., to use the Palm OS in hardware of their own design. It's kind of like the way you can get PCs from a hundred different companies, yet they all run Windows.*

You can see that a Palm m100 looks quite a bit different from, say, a Sony Clié NX70V (see the Palm m100 and Sony Clié SJ30 in Figure 1-1), but on the inside they're fundamentally the same. They both use the Palm Operating System and, therefore, operate in a similar fashion, each capable of running almost all the same software.

FIGURE 1-1   Palm OS devices don't all look the same and, in fact, can look quite different, but they all use the same core operating system.

The Difference Between a Clié and a Palm

It's easy to get confused by "Clié," "Palm," "PDA," "Palm OS," and other terms we use frequently in this book. Therefore, here's a lexicon to help you understand the basic terminology.

- **Handheld PC**   A portable, pocket-sized computer like the Palm Zire 71, Handspring Treo, and Sony Clié.
- **Operating System**   The core software that makes a handheld PC function.
- **Palm, Inc.**   The company that makes handheld PCs that run the Palm Operating System (OS).
- **Palm OS**   The operating system used in Palm, Handspring, Sony, and many other handheld PCs.
- **Palm Powered**   Denotes a handheld PC that runs the Palm OS. *Palm Powered* is a registered trademark of Palm, Inc.
- **PalmSource**   The division of Palm, Inc., responsible for developing the Palm OS.
- **PDA**   Short for Personal Digital Assistant, a generic term used to describe any handheld PC.
- **Pocket PC**   Microsoft's Windows-like operating system for handheld PCs. Found in devices from Casio, Compaq, Hewlett-Packard, and other vendors. The Pocket PC operating system is not compatible with the Palm OS, though it's possible to exchange certain kinds of information between them.
- **Sony**   Makers of the Clié series of handheld PCs.

Different Versions of the Palm Operating System (Important!)

If you've spent more than a few years using a computer, you've probably transitioned from one operating system to another. For instance, maybe you switched from Windows 95 to Windows XP, or from an earlier version of Mac OS to OS X. Whatever the case, you probably know that operating systems inevitably evolve, and that changes are a part of that evolution. So it is with the Palm OS.

At the time we're writing this book, most Clié models run some variant of OS 4. Indeed, of the seven models currently available for sale from Sony, four employ that version of the OS. However, some of those models will be discontinued by the time you read this. What's more, most of the hot new models—the NX73V, NZ90, and so on—are based on OS 5, which first became available in the fall of 2002. As a result, we've decided to focus this book on OS 5, which is not only rapidly capturing the present, but also sure to occupy the future (at least until OS 6 comes along). Does that mean we're ignoring earlier versions of the Palm OS? Absolutely not! While

1

OS 5 does offer substantial improvements over its predecessors, it's fundamentally quite similar. In fact, using a model like the NX70V (which runs OS 5) is almost identical to using one like the SJ33 (OS 4.1). Rest assured, we're not leaving anybody out. Occasionally we'll pop in with notes or tips that alert you to things that might be a bit different in pre-OS 5 devices.

Here's an example of just such a note. Once again and for the record, whether you own the latest and greatest Clié handheld or one that's four years old, this book has you covered! Okay, end of sales pitch.

Can You Upgrade Your Palm's OS?

Unfortunately, it's not possible to upgrade the OS in any Clié handheld—not at press time, anyway. We won't bore you with the technical details as to why—suffice it to say, if you find yourself yearning for the latest and greatest version of the Palm OS, it's probably time to start thinking about a new handheld.

Understanding Clié Handhelds

Why all the fuss? What makes Palm OS devices like the Clié so special? To answer these questions, we'll first need to look at what a handheld PC is. Put simply, it's a pocket-sized electronic organizer that enables you to manage addresses, appointments, expenses, tasks, and memos. If you've ever used a Franklin Planner or any similar paper-bound organizer, you get the idea.

However, because a handheld PC is electronic, there's no paper or ink involved. Instead, you write directly on the device's screen, using a small plastic stylus in place of a pen. A key advantage here, of course, is that you're able to store all of your important personal and business information on a device that's much small and lighter than a paper planner.

What's more, you can easily share that information with your Macintosh or Windows-based computer. Handheld PCs aren't self-contained: they can *synchronize* with a desktop computer and keep information current on both sides. This is an important advantage, as it effectively turns your handheld into an extension of the computer you use every day. Changes and additions made to your desktop data are reflected in the device, and vice versa (see Figure 1-2).

Saying that a Clié is an extension of your PC is only a half-truth. In reality, it has evolved into a computer in its own right. That's because it's capable of running software written by parties other than Palm, Inc., and those parties (known as software developers) now number in the tens of thousands. There are literally thousands of programs and databases that extend your Clié's capabilities, from spreadsheet managers and expense trackers to electronic-book readers and web browsers. Got five minutes to kill? You can play a quick game of *Bejeweled* (one of our all-time favorites, by the way). Need to check your e-mail while traveling? Just connect your cell phone for wireless connectivity.

While the first several chapters of this book are devoted to the Clié's core capabilities— the things it can do right out of the box—the majority of it focuses on the Clié's extended capabilities—the things that have elevated the device from a basic electronic organizer to a full-fledged handheld PC.

FIGURE 1-2   A Clié connects to a PC via a HotSync cradle, which allows data to be synchronized on both devices.

Above all else, simplicity is a major key to the platform's success. The devices are amazingly easy to use, requiring no more than a few taps of the stylus to access your data and a little memorization to master the handwriting-recognition software. Most users, even those who have little or no computer experience (like Dave), find themselves tapping and writing productively within 20 minutes of opening the box.

An Overview of the Different Clié Models

Whether you're still shopping for a Clié or you've been fiddling with one for a month, it's good to have an understanding of the different models available. In Table 1-1, you can see that in a relatively short period of time, Sony released (and discontinued) quite a number of models. Fear not—even if you own or purchased secondhand a discontinued Clié, much of the material in this book is applicable (and darn useful, if we do say so ourselves). And even if Sony has introduced half a dozen new models by the time you're reading this, well, the same truth applies. A few features might change here and there, but the Palm OS remains.

NOTE   *If you live outside North America, you might encounter Clié models with slightly different numerical designations. In Japan, for instance, the T665C is known as the T650C.*

What's Special about Sony's Handhelds

We're the first to admit it: Sony's first stab at a Palm OS handheld—the PEG-S300—was as dull as dirt. It looked kind of ugly and offered little to distinguish it from Palm's and Handspring's

Model	Memory	Screen	Year Released	Status*
Clié PEG-S300	8MB	Grayscale	2000	Discontinued
Clié PEG-S320	8MB	Grayscale	2001	Discontinued
Clié PEG-S360	16MB	Grayscale	2002	Discontinued
Clié PEG-N610C	8MB	Color	2001	Discontinued
Clié PEG-N710C	8MB	Color	2001	Discontinued
Clié PEG-N760C	8MB	Color	2001	Discontinued
Clié PEG-T415	8MB	Grayscale	2001	Discontinued
Clié PEG-T615C	16MB	Color	200	Discontinued
Clié PEG-T665C	16MB	Color	2002	Discontinued
Clié PEG-NR70/NR70V	16MB	Color	2002	Discontinued
Clié PEG-NX70/NX70V	16MB	Color	2002	Discontinued
Clié PEG-SL10	8MB	Grayscale	2002	Discontinued
Clié PEG-SJ20	16MB	Grayscale	2002	Available
Clié PEG-SJ30	16MB	Color	2002	Discontinued
Clié PEG-NZ90	16MB	Color	2003	Available
Clié PEG-SJ22	16MB	Color	2003	Available
Clié PEG-SJ33	16MB	Color	2003	Available
Clié PEG-TG50	16MB	Color	2003	Available
Clié PEG-NX73V	16MB	Color	2003	Available
Clié PEG-NX80V	32MB	Color	2003	Available
Clié PEG-UX40/50	104MB	Color	2003	Available

*As of July 2003

TABLE 1-1   Sony Clié Models at a Glance

handhelds. But the company rebounded bigtime with a series of models packed with innovative and exciting features. Among the highlights: high-resolution color screens, a Memory Stick expansion slot, the capability to play MP3 music files, a "jog dial" for one-handed operation, and enhanced audio.

In the spring of 2002, Sony really pushed the outside of the handheld envelope with the introduction of the NR70V. It boasted the highest screen resolution of any PDA currently on the market (including Pocket PC devices championed by Microsoft) and offered a wealth of cool features—including a built-in digital camera. Less than a year later, Sony upped the ante even further with the NZ90, which packed in still more features and a higher-resolution camera. By the time you read this, it's possible Sony will have a Clié that can communicate with Saturn. (The planet, not the car company. That wouldn't make sense at all.)

Our Favorite Models

Rick: Well, obviously I'm partial to Charlize Theron, who's an actress now, but did start out as a model, and . . . Oh! Sorry, wrong sidebar. I'm not afraid to say I'm head-over-heels for the NX70V, which has just about everything I want in a handheld PC: loads of memory, a gorgeous high-res screen, an MP3 player, and a built-in digital camera. The latter can't compare with today's multi-megapixel cameras, but it's great for capturing pictures of the kids being silly and other impromptu moments. I liked the NX70V enough to buy it, and I rarely buy anything. For the moment, it satisfies all my PDA needs.

   Dave: This is a bad omen for the first chapter—we never agree on anything—but I, too, love my NX70V. More to the point, I love it with a passion that I usually reserve for Sandra Bullock and Halle Berry. I have loaded it almost exclusively with applications that can take advantage of the 320×480-pixel screen, and use it to watch movies, listen to music, and play games. Oh, yeah—and I use it for work occasionally, too.

What's Important in a Handheld PC?

In the old days, it was pretty easy to differentiate between Palm OS handhelds. For one thing, there weren't that many different models. Plus, they were all pretty similar, save for a few unique features here and there. It's a different story nowadays, what with handheld makers touting things like processor speed, screen resolution, memory capacity, multimedia features, and even wireless connectivity. Let's take a look at a few of these items and how important they are—or aren't—in handheld computing.

- **Speed**   Where handhelds are concerned, speed is a relative issue. Regardless of what processor is inside the device or what version of the Palm OS it uses, it takes but a second to load, say, the calendar program. So why do newer models tout faster processors? Because more advanced features, like watching movies and playing music, do require more horsepower. If you're not interested in those kinds of features, don't worry about processor speed. A "lowly" $129 Clié SJ20 works just as well as a power-packing $799 Clié NZ90 when it comes to scheduling appointments and viewing memos.

- **Memory**   The amount of RAM, or memory, in a PDA is directly related to how much software and data it can store. More is always better, especially when you start loading up on games, electronic books, corporate databases, third-party software, and the like. However, because Cliés are expandable—meaning you can insert memory cards that provide lots more storage space—the amount of internal RAM is less of a factor than it used to be. Sure, your Clié might have "only" 16MB—but slap a 128MB card in there and the sky's the limit!

- **Screen**   While we got along fine for a long while with low-resolution (160×160 pixel) grayscale screens, we definitely prefer the high-resolution (320×320 pixel) color screens common in newer Cliés—and especially the ultra-high-resolution 320×480-pixel screens found in the NR, NX, and NZ series. That's not only because the higher resolution means sharper text and graphics, but also because the color screens are brighter and easier on the eyes. Plus, games and movies look significantly better in color.

Decide How Much RAM You Really Need

Rick and Dave argue constantly about this. Dave complains that he never has enough to space to hold all his applications—despite the fact that he can plug in a memory card and have all the space he'd ever need. Rick keeps the vital stuff in internal memory but stores less-important extras like games, MP3 files, movies, and so forth on a memory card. Problem solved. Dave counters that Clié memory cards are an awkward solution because many applications and their data inevitably take up some space in internal memory, even if stored on a memory card. Worse, you end up losing access to important stuff if you have to swap cards. Why, oh why, Dave asks, couldn't Sony put more memory in the Clié?

Anyway, to answer our own question, the amount of RAM you need depends on the kind of user you are. Most late-model Clié handhelds come with 16MB of internal RAM—enough to hold quite a bit of software. (Note: just because a model advertises 16MB doesn't mean all of it is available to you. For instance, the Sony Clié NX70V comes with 16MB, but 5MB of that are reserved for built-in software. For all intents and purposes, then, it actually has just 11MB.)

Rick maintains that even power users can solve memory-crunch problems via expansion cards and a good memory-managing utility (see Chapter 22). Dave, on the other hand, would like to state here and for the record that if Palm, Sony, or anybody else would please make a handheld with 100 terraquads of internal storage, he'd gladly buy it.

■ **Multimedia**   Speaking of games, movies, and whatnot, certain Cliés fare better than others when it comes to mobile entertainment. Models like the NX70V excel at it, as they come with software for listening to MP3 tunes, watching video clips, and so on. They even have built-in digital cameras.

Where to Find the Best Prices

Everyone likes to save a buck and, with a little smart shopping, you can do exactly that. Even if you're just looking for items like memory cards and, oh, extra copies of this book to give as gifts, it pays to do some research. Below you'll find a few notes regarding where and how to shop, and where to find the best deals.

■ If you're comfortable shopping online, you can find some of the best deals on the Web. We recommend starting with a site called PriceGrabber (**www.pricegrabber.com**), which provides up-to-date price comparisons for most Clié models and many accessories, drawn from a large number of web merchants. It even gives you shipping costs, so you know your out-the-door total before heading to the merchant's site.

- Another worthwhile online destination: web auctions. eBay (**www.ebay.com**) is a treasure trove of new, used, and refurbished Cliés. Just remember to use common sense: sometimes people get caught in a bidding frenzy and wind up paying as much for a used model as they would for a new one. That said, excellent deals can often be had on last year's models.

- Speaking of last year's models, visit Overstock.com (**www.overstock.com**) to find great prices on discontinued and refurbished handhelds. While you're at it, check out ReturnBuy (**buy.returnbuy.com**), another good source for closeouts. This site also gives you the option of purchasing an extended warranty, something to consider given that refurbished models usually come with a short warranty—or none at all.

- Check the Sony web site for package deals and rebates. They often offer bundles (like a handheld with a case and keyboard) that you won't find anywhere else, and at discounted prices. They also sometimes sell refurbished inventory and those deals can be hard to pass up.

 *Auctions can also be a great way to sell your old Clié if you're moving up to a newer one. You can also try a service like SellYourPalm.net (**www.sellyourpalm.net**), which will buy your old handheld outright.*

Where to Find It

Web Site	Address
Sony	www.sony.com/clie

How to ... Decide Which Model to Buy

Sorry, we can't help you with this one. So many great handhelds, so few hands. Virtually every Clié model available today has its merits. The key thing to remember is that right out of the box, every one offers the same great core capabilities: contact and calendar management, easy-to-learn handwriting recognition, seamless synchronization with your PC, and access to a wealth of third-party software. With that knowledge in mind, you can focus on other aspects you might find important: price, memory, screen size, multimedia features, and so on. In the end, you might just have to flip a coin. That's what we do.

Chapter 2

Getting to Know Your Clié

How to…

- Identify the buttons on a Clié
- Identify the infrared transmitter
- Work with the screen and Graffiti area
- Charge the batteries
- Use the Graffiti tutorial
- Reset a Clié
- Configure a Clié's preferences
- Reset the screen digitizer
- Set the time and date
- Work with the operating system
- Check how much memory is left
- Work with Palm Desktop

Okay, enough history—it's time to dive in and start having fun. At the beginning of any lasting and meaningful relationship, you want to get to know the other person as well as possible—find out what makes them tick, what their boundaries are, where they keep their batteries. With that in mind, we tailored this chapter as a kind of meet-and-greet. Reader, Clié. Clié, Reader. Now that we have that out of the way, let's dive in and start having fun!

A Guided Tour of the Hardware

By now, your Clié is no doubt out of the box and getting the once-over. You're seeing buttons, a screen, possibly a keyboard, a little wheel sticking out of the side, and so on. What is all this stuff? What does it do?

 As you learned in Chapter 1, the Clié series includes a couple billion different models. Okay, maybe not that many, but a lot. At press time, Sony's current models included the SJ20, SJ22, SJ33, NX73V, NX80V, and TG50. Although they're the ones we focus on primarily, most of the information in this chapter (and others) applies to older and newer models as well. We just wanted you to be aware that there are some physical differences, so don't be alarmed if something you see in a photo doesn't quite match your handheld. We'll jump in as necessary to let you know when to start worrying.

The Screen

Different Clié models have different kinds of screens. The now-discontinued S320, for instance, employs a grayscale screen with a resolution of 160×160 pixels. At the other end of the spectrum, the NR, NX, and NZ series boast 320×480-pixel screens that can display up to 65,000 colors. In between, the N, SL, SJ, and T series serve up color or grayscale screens with 320×320 resolution.

It's not important that you remember your PDA's resolution; we're just giving you all the facts, ma'am. Sir. Whatever.

When you use a desktop computer, you use a mouse to navigate and a keyboard to enter data. With a Clié, you use a plastic-tipped stylus for both navigation and data entry (unless your Clié has a built-in keyboard, in which case you can use that for data entry as well). That's because the screen is, technically speaking, a *touchscreen,* meaning you interact with it by tapping it and writing on it. If you want to access, say, the To Do List program, you tap the To Do List icon that appears on the screen. If you want to remind yourself to buy milk, you write the words on the screen.

Many novice users think they have to double-tap the application icons, just like double-clicking with a mouse. Not true! A single tap is all you ever need when working with a Clié.

The Difference Between Tapping and Writing

Tapping the screen is the equivalent of clicking a mouse. You tap icons to launch programs, tap to access menus and select options in them, and tap to place your cursor in specific places. Writing on the screen is, of course, like putting a pen to paper. However, most writing you do on a Clié takes place in a specific area of the screen, which we discuss in the next section. But when you're working in, say, a sketchpad or paint program, you can scribble anywhere on the screen, just as though it were a blank sheet of paper.

CAUTION
Don't press too hard with the stylus. The screen is fairly sensitive, and light pressure is usually all it takes to register a tap or stylus stroke. If you press too hard, you could wind up with a scratched screen—the bane of every Clié user.

The Graffiti Area

All Clié handhelds (except the TG50—if you have one, skip ahead to "The Clié TG50 Keyboard") have what's called a *Graffiti area*—a special portion of the screen that's used exclusively for entering text and numbers. *Graffiti* is the handwriting-recognition software that's built into the Palm OS and, therefore, into every Clié. However, different models have different kinds of Graffiti areas. The NR, NX, and NZ series have what we call a "virtual" Graffiti area, meaning that it appears and disappears as necessary. Take a look:

Virtual Graffiti is really slick because it lets you input data when you need to, and then tucks out of the way to give you extra screen estate for icons, text, movies, and so on. Plus, you can install "skins" that give your Clié a personalized, extra-jazzy look. More on that in Chapter 4.

Most Palm OS handhelds, including the Clié SJ series, have a fixed, or "silkscreened," Graffiti area, which looks like Figure 2-1. Regardless of what kind of Graffiti area your handheld has, one thing remains constant: Graffiti makes it possible to enter information using the stylus, but you can do so only within the confines of the Graffiti area (as seen in Figure 2-1).

NOTE *We tell you more about Graffiti—how to use it and alternatives to it—in Chapters 4 and 12, respectively.*

What about those icons on either side of the Graffiti area? They serve some important functions. Here's an overview:

The Home Button Represented by a picture of a house and located in the upper-left corner of the Graffiti area, the Home button is the one you'll tap more often than any other. From whatever program you're currently running, the *Home button* (see Figure 2-1) takes you back to the main screen—"home base," as it were (hence, the house picture).

TIP *When you're using any program, tapping the Home button returns you to the main screen. When you're viewing that screen, however, tapping the Home button cycles through the application categories, which we discuss in the section "The Home Screen".*

The Menu Button Tapping the icon in the lower-left corner of the Graffiti area—aka the Menu button (see Figure 2-1)—gives you access to the drop-down menus that are part of the Palm Operating System. These menus vary somewhat from program to program, insofar as the options they provide, but they're fairly consistent within the core Palm OS applications.

TIP *The Menu button works like a toggle switch. If you accidentally tap it or want to make the drop-down menus go away, simply tap it again.*

FIGURE 2-1 The Graffiti area is where you write data into your handheld and access various options like menus, the calculator, and "home base."

TIP *Another way to access menus is by tapping the title bar in the top-left corner of whatever program is currently running—not unlike the way you use a mouse to access menus on a PC.*

The Calculator Button   Probably the most self-explanatory of all the buttons, *Calc*—located in the upper-right corner of the Graffiti area (see Figure 2-1)—launches the built-in calculator. This functions like any other calculator you've ever used—but you can learn a bit more about it in Chapter 9.

The Find Button   Finally, we get to the little magnifying glass in the lower-right corner. Because a Clié can store such vast amounts of information, and because sifting through all that information to find what you're looking for can be tedious, there's a handy little search feature called the Find button (see Figure 2-1). We talk more about it in Chapter 9.

The *a* and 1 Buttons   In the lower-left corner of the Graffiti area (see Figure 2-1) there's a little *a*. In the lower-right corner, there's a 1. As you'll learn in Chapter 4, these are used to bring up the onscreen keyboards (which serve as alternative input methods). Tapping the *a* launches the QWERTY keyboard, while the 1 brings up the numeric keyboard.

NOTE *You can't access either keyboard unless there's a cursor in a data-entry field. If you're viewing the main screen—the one with all the icons—and tap either keyboard button, you'll just hear a beep. Try starting a new memo, and then tapping one of the two buttons.*

The NR/NX/NZ Keyboard/Graffiti Button   Clié NR, NX, and NZ models have an extra little button just below the Find icon. When you tap it, the virtual Graffiti area changes to an onscreen keyboard. How is this different from the onscreen keyboard discussed in the last section? That keyboard pops up above the Graffiti area, consuming a fair chunk of the main screen. If you have a Clié NR, NX, or NZ, it makes a lot more sense to use the Graffiti-area keyboard than the pop-up keyboard.

What If I Want to Use the NR/NX/NZ Keyboard Instead of Graffiti?

All this talk about Graffiti areas and whatnot—why not just use the physical keyboard that's built into your NR, NX, or NZ instead? Fine with us. That's what it's there for, after all. You can use it for every bit of data you care to enter. However, you still should learn the intricacies of the Graffiti area, such as the functions of the buttons that flank it, the way to make the Graffiti area collapse, and so on. Meanwhile, you can learn more about the keyboard in Chapter 4.

The NR/NX/NZ Graffiti-Go-Bye-Bye Button   As you learned earlier, Clié NR, NX, and NZ models have virtual Graffiti areas that can be made to disappear when not needed. Okay, so how do you work this little magic trick? And, more important, how do you get the Graffiti area back again? The answer to both questions lies in the little blue arrow in the bottom-right corner of the Clié screen (NR models have it closer to the left). Tap it once to make Graffiti disappear, again to make it reappear.

 ——— Graffiti-Go-Bye-Bye
button

You need to know two important things about this button. First, it's not really called the Graffiti-Go-Bye-Bye Button. We made up that name, as we think it sounds cuter than Graffiti Hide/Unhide Button or Graffiti Peekaboo Button. It's not even accurate, though, because it does more than make Graffiti go bye-bye—it makes Graffiti come back, too. Hey, you want perfection, go join a Borg collective.

Second, there might be times when the Magic Graffiti Button appears "grayed out," when tapping it has no effect. That's because not all programs support the virtual Graffiti area, so there might be instances where you just can't make it disappear.

The NR/NX/NZ Status Bar   If you own an NR-, NX-, or NZ-series Clié, you'll notice a row of icons beneath the Graffiti area (see Figure 2-2). This "status bar" duplicates three of the Graffiti-area buttons—Home, Menu, and Find—and supplies a clock, battery gauge, and Memory Stick indicator (a little icon appears when there's a Memory Stick inserted). As you might have figured out by now, the reason for the extra Home, Menu, and Find buttons in the status bar is for when the Graffiti area is minimized—they let you access these features without having to restore Graffiti.

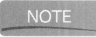 *On the NX and NZ models, you'll also notice a funny-looking little button just to the right of Find. This is the* Silk Plug-In button, *which lets you replace the standard Graffiti area with different "skins." Find out more about this capability in Chapter 15.*

Collapse/Restore
Graffiti area

Menu

Home   Find   Battery gauge

FIGURE 2-2   The NR, NX, and NZ models have this status bar (or a similar one) below the Graffiti area.

The Brightness/Contrast Button   Below the Menu button (see Figure 2-1) resides a little icon that looks like either a starburst or a half moon. Tapping it brings up an onscreen slider that adjusts the brightness of your Clié's screen (if you have a grayscale model, it might adjust the contrast instead). Tap and hold your stylus on the little slider knob, and then drag it left and right until you find a comfortable setting.

TIP   *The brightness setting has a direct impact on battery life. If you travel a lot (meaning you're away from the charging cradle for long periods), try setting the brightness to, say, 50 percent. Your battery will last a lot longer, and you probably won't mind the slightly reduced brightness after you get accustomed to it. Of course, if your Clié spends most of its time in or near the cradle, crank the brightness to maximum. You might as well enjoy what the screen has to offer.*

The Clié TG50 Keyboard

If you own a Clié TG50 (see Figure 2-3) and happened to skim the previous sections on Graffiti, you're probably doing a fair bit of head-scratching by now. The TG50, as you've discovered, has no Graffiti area. Instead, it has a keyboard. There's not much we need to tell you about using it, but you should be aware of a few key differences:

■ The Home and Menu options are accessed via a single round button, which is just above the Q key. Press it quickly for Home, hold it for a second for Menu.

■ On the opposite side, above the P key, there's another round button. Press it quickly to access Graffiti, hold it for a second for Find.

Hey, wait a sec, what? Graffiti? We just said the TG50 had no Graffiti area. Well, just to confuse you as much as possible and make writing this book infinitely more complicated, Sony decided to equip the TG50 with a kind of virtual Graffiti area, one that pops up on the screen.

We suspect you probably won't use this much, as you probably chose the TG50 largely because of its built-in keyboard. But it's there if you need it. See Chapter 4 for more information on using Graffiti—virtual or otherwise.

The Buttons

All Clié handhelds have application and scroll buttons (see Figure 2-4). These are used to instantly launch the core applications (Date Book, Memo Pad, and so forth) and to scroll up and down in screens of data. Let's look at them at little more closely, along with a few other important buttons you'll encounter.

FIGURE 2-3   The Clié TG50 is the only model (so far) with a built-in keyboard instead of a Graffiti area.

Scroll Up button

Memo Pad button

To Do List button

Data Book button

Address Book button

Scroll Down button

FIGURE 2-4   Your model's buttons and Graffiti area might look a bit different than what's shown here.

The Power Button

The Power button is fairly self-explanatory. But it serves another function: to activate (or deactivate) your screen's backlight. If your Clié has a grayscale screen, you'd activate the backlight to make it more visible in low-light situations. With a color screen, you'd deactivate the backlight when venturing outdoors, to maximize battery life. Just hold down the button for two seconds to activate or deactivate the backlight.

NOTE   *Some Clié's have a power "slider" in place of a button. It's usually on the left side of the unit. Sliding it down (and then releasing it) turns the unit on or off. Holding it in the down position for a couple seconds activates or deactivates the backlight.*

TIP   *If you push the power button and your Clié doesn't turn on, it probably means one of two things. First, the battery is dead. Second, you've accidentally engaged the Hold switch (see the upcoming section, "The Headphone Jack"), which can make it seem like the battery is dead. Try sliding it to the off position and see if that resurrects your Clié.*

The Four Program Buttons

So you want to look up a number in your address book. You could turn on your Clié, tap the Home button to get to the main screen, and then find and tap the Address icon. There's a much faster way: simply press the Address button, which is represented by a picture of a phone handset. That serves the dual function of turning on the Clié *and* loading the Address Book program.

The same holds true for the three other buttons (see Figure 2-4), which launch Date Book, To Do List, and Memo Pad. You can use them at any time, whether the Clié is on or off, to quickly switch between the four core programs.

Reprogram Your Handheld's Buttons

Want the Memo Pad button to load your e-book viewer? Or the Calc button to load a sophisticated third-party number-cruncher instead of the built-in calculator? You can reprogram a Clié's four hardware buttons and Calc button to run any installed program. Just tap the Prefs icon, and then select Buttons from the drop-down list in the top-right corner of the Preferences screen. Now, assign your desired applications to the various buttons. That's all there is to it!

The Clié NX73V, NX80V, and NZ90 have a duplicate set of program buttons just below the screen. Why the extras? When you're using the device in "Slate" mode (meaning the screen is all you see—the keyboard and primary buttons are obscured), you can still access the core apps. We sure wish Sony had thought of that when designing our beloved NR70V and NX70V—those models don't have the extra buttons.

The Scroll Buttons

Usually located between the two pairs of Program buttons, the Scroll buttons (or scroll rocker, in the case of some models) are used to cycle through multiple screens of data. If you're looking at, say, a memo that's too long to fit on the screen in its entirety, you'd use the Scroll Down button to move down to the next section—not unlike turning pages in a book. The Scroll Up button simply moves you back a page.

In many programs, onscreen arrows and/or scroll bars serve the same function. Instead of having to press the Scroll buttons, you can simply tap the arrows or slide the bar with your stylus. This is largely a matter of personal preference: try both and decide which method you like better! For the record, we think the scroll rockers on most Cliés are horrendous.

You can skip the scroll buttons/rockers/arrows altogether and just use the Jog Dial (see the next section) to scroll within documents. It's more convenient and usually much more comfortable, and it doesn't require two hands.

The Jog Dial Navigator

A little wheel protrudes from the left-hand side of every Clié. It's called the *Jog Dial* (see Figure 2-5), and it gives the Clié an advantage found in few other handhelds: one-handed operation. Specifically, you can launch programs, navigate menus, and access data just by turning and pushing the Jog Dial. This can come in handy if you have the Clié in one hand and, say, the phone or a live eel in the other.

As with so many aspects of your Clié, the best way to learn the Jog Dial is by experimenting. Turn it a few clicks in either direction and see what happens. Press it directly inward (the wheel doubles as a button) and see what happens. This combination of actions—turn the wheel, press the wheel—is all it takes to navigate your Clié with one hand. However, you'll also want to take advantage of the Back button, which is discussed in the next section. Later in this chapter, in the section, "Setting Clié Preferences," you'll learn how to modify a few Jog Dial and Back button settings.

The Back Button

The Back button (see Figure 2-5) resides right next to the Jog Dial and works in conjunction with it. When pressed, the *Back button* returns you to the previous screen you were viewing. When pressed for two seconds, it enables you to cycle through buttons, menus, and/or options (using the Jog Dial to make your selection). You can also set the Back button to double as a power button, though we don't recommend this (it's too easy to hit by accident).

NOTE   *A few early-model Cliés don't have a Back button, which limits somewhat the functionality and value of the Jog Dial.*

The Headphone Jack

If your Clié came with a pair of headphones, that means it's capable of playing music. Indeed, many Clié models double as damn fine MP3 players. That explains the headphone jack you see on the left-hand side of the unit (see Figure 2-5). We teach you everything you need to know about Clié music in Chapter 18.

Headphone jack

Jog Dial

Hold switch

Back button

FIGURE 2-5   Your model might look a little different, but on the side of your Clié, you'll find items like the headphone jack, Jog Dial, Back button, and Hold switch.

What Is the Hold Switch?

Not far from the headphone jack, you might notice a little switch labeled Hold (see Figure 2-5). This is a staple feature in MP3 players—it effectively locks out all the buttons on your handheld, so you don't accidentally press one while you're jamming. At the same time, it turns off the screen to conserve battery life. Try sliding it to see what happens (you don't need to be listening to music). Your Clié more or less shuts itself off and doesn't respond to any button presses until you disengage the Hold switch.

When the Hold switch is engaged, your Clié appears to be dead. If you find that your unit won't turn on or respond to any button presses, check to make sure the Hold switch wasn't accidentally activated. More often than not, it's the culprit.

The Memory Stick Slot

Every Clié is expandable. If you run out of storage space, you can easily add more thanks to the Memory Stick slot, which you can find at the top of your Clié (or the side, on some models).

Memory Stick refers to a kind of removable storage media created by Sony. True to its name, a Memory Stick (MS for short) is about the size of a stick of gum and provides extra storage space for your Clié—anywhere from 32 megabytes (MB) to 1 gigabyte (GB). You'll find out just how valuable extra memory can be when you get to the chapters on music and movies.

Read more about Memory Sticks—where to buy them, how to use them, and so on—in Chapter 22.

The Back of the Clié

Flip your Clié over. Yes, it's pretty boring back there, but you should know about one important area: the Reset button. Every Clié has a little hole on the back that's used to reset the device. Hey, every computer crashes occasionally, and the Palm OS isn't entirely glitch-free. (We talk more about resetting in Appendix A.)

The Infrared Port

At the top of every Clié, there's a small black-plastic window. This is the *infrared port,* also known as the *infrared transceiver* or *IR port.* It's used to wirelessly beam data from one Clié to another and, if you have a model with "remote" features, to control wireless devices like your TV or stereo (which we discuss in Chapter 19). You learn more about beaming in Chapter 4.

By holding down the Address Book button for two seconds, you can automatically beam your "business card" to another handheld user. In Chapter 6, you learn how to designate an Address Book record as your card.

Clié Can HotSync Wirelessly

If you travel with a notebook PC, one that has an IR port of its own, you can HotSync your Clié to it without the need for a cradle. Learn how in Chapter 4.

The Stylus

Last, but definitely not least, we come to the *stylus*: every Clié has a small plastic or metal pen tucked away inside. What they all have in common is a plastic tip. Under no circumstances should you ever use any kind of ink pen or metal tip on a Clié's screen. That's a sure way to create a scratch, and a scratched screen is a damaged screen.

There's one exception. In a pinch, or if you just don't feel like extracting the stylus, you can use your fingernail for light taps on the screen.

Using Your Clié for the First Time

Now that you're a bit more familiar with the hardware, you're ready to start using it. This means charging the battery, working your way through the startup screens, and checking out the Graffiti tutorial.

Charging the Battery

Most Clié models use a rechargeable battery (the sole exception being the SL10, which uses everyday AAA alkalines). It gets charged and recharged via the same HotSync cradle or cable that links the handheld to your computer.

On several models, it's possible to charge the battery using just the AC adapter—no HotSync cradle required. This makes a handy mobile-charging solution, as it eliminates the need to unplug and bring the cradle with you on road trips. Consult your Clié's documentation to see if your model has this capability. If it doesn't, you can find third-party charging solutions in Chapter 23.

When you first unpack your Clié, it's vital that you fully charge the battery before you start using the handheld. You can do this by plugging the AC adapter into the HotSync cradle or cable, and then connecting your Clié. (The cradle/cable needn't be connected to your PC. In fact, it's probably better that you complete a full charge before going anywhere near your PC.) Let the unit charge for a good four hours. It's a long time to wait, we know, but you can spend those hours reading ahead to some of the more entertaining chapters (namely, the ones Rick wrote).

Never again will you have to wait four hours to fully charge your battery. Most of the time, you'll "top it off" by leaving it in the cradle for a few minutes. Even if the battery dies completely, it should take no more than an hour or so to recharge it.

The Welcome Screens

Once the batteries are in and you turn your Clié back over, you see a "welcome" screen that asks you to remove the stylus and tap anywhere to continue. You're about to undertake a one-time setup procedure that takes all of about 60 seconds. The two key tasks accomplished here are the calibration of the screen digitizer and the setting of the date and time.

What Is Digitizer Calibration?

Put simply, *digitizer calibration* is the process of teaching a Clié to accurately recognize taps on the screen. As you know, the screen responds to input from the stylus, and this calibration process simply ensures the precision of those responses. In a way, it's like fine-tuning a TV set.

Over time, you might discover your screen taps seem a little "off." For example, you have to tap a bit to the left of an arrow for the screen to register the tap. At this point, it's time to recalibrate the digitizer, which you can do in the Prefs menu. We tell you how in the section "Setting Clié Preferences."

Favorite Uses For Our Cliés

Rick: One of the reasons I'm so nuts about the Clié NX70V is its built-in digital camera. Sure, the resolution leaves something to be desired (namely, more pixels), but it's great for grabbing impromptu shots of my little girl, Sarah. It's great for entertaining her, too—when we're on an airplane or waiting for our food at a restaurant, I'll pull out the Clié and let her take pictures of herself. She loves making faces and seeing herself on the screen. I've also discovered some great "edutainment" software that teaches kids to count and identify the alphabet. Yep, my PDA has become my Parental Diversion Assistant.

Dave: I'm embarrassed to say this, but my favorite use for my Clié is *Solitaire*. Yep, you read it right. See, here's the deal: I play *Acid Solitaire* from Red Mercury, and it's a colorful, full-screen program for the NR70's 320×480-pixel mode. With the virtual Graffiti area minimized, you can fit a whole game of *Solitaire* on the screen. Whenever I sit down with a spare minute, I invariably open *Acid Solitaire*. I'd love to tell you that I read a book with Palm Reader or compose solutions to world hunger in Quickword, but the truth is that it's, um, *Solitaire*.

Setting the Date and Time

The last stage of the welcome process is choosing your country and time zone, and then setting the date and time. To set the time, you simply tap the box next to the words Set Time, and then tap the up/down arrow keys to select the current time (don't forget to specify A.M. or P.M.). Tapping the box next to Set Date reveals a calendar. Again, a few strategic taps is all it takes to select today's date. (Be sure to choose the year first, then the month, and then the day.) When you've done so, tap the Today button.

NOTE *If you find yourself in a different time zone and need to change your Clié's clock, you needn't repeat the whole "welcome" process to do so. The date and time settings can be found in the Prefs menu, which we discuss in the section "Setting Clié Preferences."*

If you want your Clié to automatically adjust for Daylight Saving, tap the little arrow that appears next to that field and select On.

The Graffiti Tutorial

On the last screen of the welcome wagon, you're given this option: "To learn about entering text on your handheld now, tap Next." Doing so takes you to a brief but helpful tutorial on using *Graffiti*, the Clié's handwriting-recognition software. If you'd rather jump right into using your handheld and learn Graffiti later, tap Done instead of Next. You can revisit the Graffiti tutorial at any time, just by finding and tapping the Graffiti icon in the Home screen.

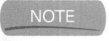

At press time, the two newest Cliés—the NX73V and NX80V—had adopted a newer version of Graffiti called, simply enough, Graffiti 2. Find out all about the differences in Chapter 4.

Why Use the Tutorial?

Mastering Graffiti is arguably the most difficult aspect of using a Clié because it requires you to learn and use a special character set. Thus, you should definitely spend some time with the tutorial. That said, most users can gain a working knowledge of Graffiti in about 20 minutes. And, after a few days' practice, you should be writing quickly, accurately, and effortlessly. We show you the ins and outs of Graffiti in Chapter 4.

You might have discovered a Graffiti cheat-sheet sticker among the materials that came with your handheld. However, the Palm OS has a built-in cheat sheet of its own. Just draw a line from anywhere in the Graffiti area all the way to the top of the screen. Presto—a diagram of all the Graffiti characters!

What to Do If You'd Rather Not Use Graffiti

Psst! Don't tell anyone we told you this, but you don't have to use Graffiti at all. As you learned a few pages back, the Palm OS gives you an out, a way to enter data without drawing a single character. It's the built-in keyboard, which appears when you tap the little *a* in the lower-left corner of the Graffiti area. As you work your way to Chapter 4, which discusses Graffiti in much greater detail (the keyboard, too), you might find it's easier to enter data with the keyboard.

Getting to Know the Operating System

We aren't exaggerating when we say working with Cliés is roughly eight gazillion times easier than working with traditional computers. Although they're plenty powerful, Cliés are just a lot less complicated. There's no confusing menu system to wade through, no accidentally forgetting to save your document. Here we've highlighted some of the fundamental—but still important—differences between a Clié and a PC:

- When you turn on a PC, you have to wait a few minutes for it to boot up. When you turn on a Clié, it's ready to roll instantaneously. Same goes for shutting it off: just press the power button and the screen goes dark. There's no lengthy shutdown procedure.

- On a PC, when you're done working with a program (say, your word processor), you must save your data before exiting that program. On a Clié, this isn't necessary. Data is retained at all times, even if you, say, switch to your to-do list while in the middle of writing a memo. When you return to Memo Pad, you find your document exactly as you left it. This holds true even if you turn off the Clié!

- In that same vein, you don't "exit" a Clié program so much as switch to another one. This is a hard concept for seasoned computer users to grasp, as we've all been taught to shut down our software when we're done with it. There's no exit procedure on a Clié, and you'll rarely find that word in a drop-down menu. When you finish working in one program, you just tap the Home button to return to home base, or press one of the program buttons.

NOTE   *We strongly encourage experimentation. Whereas wandering too far off the beaten track in Windows can lead to disaster, it's virtually impossible to get "lost" using a Clié. So tap here, explore there, and just have fun checking things out. Because there's no risk of losing data or running too many programs at once (impossible in the Palm OS), you should have no fear of fouling anything up. Play!*

The Icons

Icons are, of course, little pictures used to represent things. In the case of the Palm OS, they're used largely to represent the installed programs. Thus, on the Home screen, you see icons labeled Address, Calc, Date Book, and so on—and all you do is tap one to access that particular program.

NOTE *Say, didn't you just learn that tapping a button in the Graffiti area is the way to load the calculator? And that you're supposed to press a button to load Date Book? In the Palm OS, there are often multiple ways to accomplish the same task. In this case, you can load certain programs either by tapping their onscreen icons or using their hardware-button equivalents.*

The Menus

As in most computers, *drop-down menus* are used to access program-specific options and settings. In most Clié programs, tapping the Menu button (or the title bar at the top of any running program) makes a small "menu bar" appear at the top of the screen. You navigate this bar using the stylus as you would a mouse, tapping each menu item to make its list of options drop down, and then tapping the option you want to access.

The Home Screen

On a Clié, the *Home screen* (the screen you see when you tap the Home button) displays the icons for all the installed programs. (It also shows you the time and a battery gauge, as the following illustrates.) We occasionally refer to this as the applications screen as well.

How to ... **Find Out How Much Memory Your Handheld Has Left**

As you start to add records and install new software on your Clié, you might wonder how to check the amount of memory that's available. From the Home screen, tap Menu | App | Info. The screen that appears shows the total amount of memory on your device and how much of it is free. Notice, too, the other options that appear when you tap Menu | App. There's Delete (used to delete third-party programs), Beam (used to beam third-party programs), and Copy (used to copy programs to a Memory Stick—but we recommend using one of the methods discussed in Chapter 22.

NOTE   *If your Home screen doesn't look like the screen shown here, it's probably because it's running Sony's Clié Launcher instead (see Figure 2-6). As you can see, it looks quite a bit different from the standard Home screen, as it was designed to take advantage of the Clié's Jog Dial. Thus, you spin the wheel to choose the program you want to run, and then press the wheel to run it. However, because the majority of Cliés don't have Clié Launcher, and because we're not big fans of it (much better launchers are out there—see Chapter 13), we're going to ask that you not use it for now. To exit the launcher and return to the Standard View (the one represented by most of our screenshots), tap Menu | Options | Go to Standard View.*

FIGURE 2-6   This is the Clié Launcher found in some Clié models. While it looks cool and enables one-handed operation, we think most users will be better off with Standard View—or a third-party launcher.

In the upper-right corner of the screen, you'll also notice a small arrow next to the word "All." What this means is the Home screen is currently showing you all the installed programs. If you tap the arrow, you see a list of categories (see Figure 2-7) into which you can group your programs.

Why Use Categories?

The use of categories is entirely optional. They're intended solely to help you keep your applications organized. See, as you install more software, you wind up with more icons. Right out of the box, a Clié has only about a dozen of them—a manageable number. But, suppose you install all the bonus software that came with the Clié, plus a few third-party games, an e-book reader, and some spreadsheet software. Now things are getting a little cluttered, icon-wise.

Categories offer you a way to minimize the clutter. As you saw in the drop-down list, the Clié comes with a number of categories already created. You can use them if you want or create your own.

How to Create and Modify Categories   Look again at the drop-down list in the upper-right corner of the applications screen (see Figure 2-7). Notice the last option: Edit Categories.... Tapping this takes you to a screen where you can add, rename, and delete categories. To rename or delete one, first select it by tapping it with the stylus (you see it becomes highlighted). Then, tap the appropriate button.

NOTE   *If you have a Memory Stick inserted, Edit Categories won't be the last item in the list. It will be Card. In fact, you can't categorize programs stored on a Memory Stick, which is one reason we recommend the use of a third-party launcher. Find out more in Chapter 13.*

To create a new category, tap the New button, and then write in the desired name. That's all there is to it!

FIGURE 2-7   In the applications (Home) screen, categories can be used to organize your programs.

How to Assign Programs to Categories   Once you tailor the categories to your liking, you must next assign your programs to them. This isn't difficult, but it might take you a few tedious minutes to complete. Here's how:

1. In the applications screen, tap the Menu button, and then select Category....

2. Identify any one program you want to assign (you might have to scroll down the list, which you can do by using on the onscreen arrows or scroll bar, or the scroll buttons), and then tap the little arrow next to it.

3. The list of categories appears. Pick one by tapping it.

4. Repeat the procedure for the other programs you want to assign.

5. Tap Done to return to the applications screen.

Now, when you tap the category arrow in the corner and select one, you see all your reassigned icons have been placed in the respective screens.

TIP   *One way to change the displayed category is to tap the aforementioned arrow. However, there's a quicker way: if you tap the Home button repeatedly, the Clié cycles through the categories that have programs assigned to them. Again, the Clié offers us two ways to accomplish the same goal.*

Setting Clié Preferences

What would a computer be without a control panel where you can tweak the settings and customize the machine? The Palm OS has one, called *Prefs*. Find the Prefs icon in the applications (you know, Home) screen, tap it, and meet us at the next paragraph.

Divided into several different sections (all of them accessible by tapping the arrow in the upper-right corner of the screen), Prefs is the place to reset your Clié's digitizer, change the date and time, input any necessary modem settings, and more. In listed order, here's the scoop on each individual Pref.

Depending on which Clié model you have, the Prefs options might be a bit different than what we have listed here. Most of the options are pretty self-explanatory, though, so not to worry.

Bluetooth

At press time, the NZ90 and TG50 were the only two Clié models to feature built-in *Bluetooth*— a wireless "personal area networking" technology that enables the Clié to communicate with similarly equipped cell phones, computers, PDAs, and other devices. Thus, they're the only two models to have Bluetooth as the first Prefs option.

When the Bluetooth option is set to Enabled, that activates the Clié's built-in Bluetooth radio. (To learn when and why you'd want to do this, see Chapter 11.) The following options appear:

- **Device Name** This is usually your HotSync ID, which you'll choose the first time you HotSync your Clié with your PC (see Chapter 4). If you want to change the Device Name for some reason, tap the box.

- **Allow Device To Be Discovered** This enables the Clié to be "found" by other Bluetooth-equipped devices within range. You still have to manually accept a connection, however, so don't worry about someone sneaking into your Clié's innards without your knowledge (not that Bluetooth makes that possible anyway). Be default, this is set to Yes—you should probably leave it that way.

- **Allow Wake Up** This feature lets one Bluetooth device—say, your mobile phone—wake up your sleeping Clié via Bluetooth if something important happens. Right now, there aren't a lot of reasons why you'd want to set this to Yes, but we can envision a time in the near future when your Bluetooth-enabled Alien motion sensor might need to trigger an alarm on your Clié so you can ready the flame thrower.

- **Trusted Devices** Any devices that are formally "paired"—that is, you have permitted them to communicate with each other—will appear in the Trusted Devices list. Your mobile phone, for instance, should be a trusted device if you want your Clié to use it for e-mail and Internet access.

Even if you use Bluetooth a lot, you can save a lot of battery life by disabling the Bluetooth radio when it's not needed.

Buttons

As we explained earlier, a Clié's four program buttons are used to quick-launch the four main Palm OS programs (Date Book, To Do List, and so forth). However, it's possible to reassign these buttons to launch other programs instead. If you find you rarely use, say, To Do List, but you use Audio Player all the time, it might make sense to reassign the To Do List button accordingly.

After selecting Buttons from the drop-down menu in the Prefs screen, you see an icon that corresponds to each button. (You can also customize the Calc button, except on the TG50, which doesn't have one.) All you do to change the function of any given button is tap the little arrow next to it, and then select the desired application. The buttons can launch any installed application—you're not limited to just the core Clié apps.

Notice, too, the three options at the bottom of the Buttons screen:

- ■ **Default**   Restores the button assignments to their original settings.
- ■ **Pen**   Lets you choose what happens when you drag the tip of your stylus from the Graffiti area to the top of the screen. (This action can be made to load the built-in Graffiti help screens, invoke the onscreen keyboard, turn on backlighting, or one of several other options.)
- ■ **HotSync**   Enables you to reprogram the HotSync button on your docking cradle—something we don't recommend doing.

Connection

The *Connection* screen, shown next, lets you set up whatever modem you might be using with your Clié, or choose to HotSync via the unit's IR port (instead of using the cradle). You probably won't need to fiddle with the modem settings.

Date & Time

Flying into another time zone? Hit this screen to change your handheld's internal clock (an important thing to remember so you don't miss your alarms!). You can also change the date, if necessary, and set the Clié to automatically adjust for Daylight Saving.

 Instead of adjusting the time manually, just tap the box next to Set Time Zone, and then choose the time zone you're flying into. The time will be adjusted automatically. Just don't forget to switch it back when you get home.

Digitizer

Noticing a little "drift" in your stylus taps? You tap someplace, but it doesn't quite register, or it registers in the *wrong* place? It might be time to reset your screen's digitizer. You should do so the moment you notice a problem; the worse the drift gets, the harder it could be to get to this screen. All you do is select Digitizer from the menu and follow the instructions.

 Digitizer drift does occur over time, but if it becomes a frequent occurrence, it could point to a hardware problem. If your Clié is still under warranty, contact customer service to see if a replacement is warranted. In the meantime, there are software utilities designed to compensate for digitizer drift. See "How to Cure Mad Digitizer Syndrome" in the Appendix for more information.

Formats

Few users need to spend much time in the Formats screen, where you can change the way dates, times, and numbers are displayed. You can also specify whether you want the calendar week to start on Sunday (the default) or Monday.

General

Probably the most frequently visited of the Preferences screens, *General* contains the following settings:

- ■ **Auto-off After**   To help preserve battery life, your handheld will turn itself off after a designated period of inactivity. Here you can set the interval, from 30 seconds to 3 minutes. The lower you set it, the better your battery life will be.

- ■ **Stay On In Cradle**   When this box is checked, your handheld will remain while it's in the HotSync cradle. This can be handy if you spend a lot of time at your desk and frequently need to consult your handheld for addresses, schedules, and so forth, or if you want to use the PhotoStand application (see Chapter 16) to turn your Clié into a digital picture frame. (Note: Only rechargeable Cliés have this setting.)

- ■ **System Sound**   Adjust the volume for various system sounds (like beeps, HotSync tones, and so forth). If you want your handheld to be silent, set this to Off.

- ■ **Alarm Sound**   Adjust the volume for alarms.

- ■ **Alarm LED**   On some models, the power button doubles as an LED, which can be set to flash when an alarm goes off.

- ■ **Game Sound**   Adjust the volume for games.

- ■ **Beam Receive**   If this is off, you won't be able to receive programs and data beamed from other handhelds. However, keeping it off until you need it can help conserve power. Just *remember* that it's off, so you don't pull your hair out trying to figure out why you can't receive a beam.

HiRes

The *HiRes* option appears only on certain Clié models and pertains to how the device handles low-resolution software on its high-resolution screen. You see, although the vast majority of Palm OS programs were originally designed to run on lower-resolution screens (many of them have been updated now), the Clié gives them a coat of "high-resolution paint," meaning it enables them to take advantage of the extra screen pixels, so they look sharper. This is accomplished via High Resolution Assist, which, by default, is enabled in this screen.

However, some applications—most notably games—might have difficulty working properly when "assisted" by High Resolution Assist. If you start a program and see a lot of garbage on the screen, or your Clié crashes, find the program in the HiRes list, and then tap the checkbox next to it. That will make it run in its normal low-resolution mode, which should work.

NOTE   *You can't enable or disable High Resolution Assist for applications stored on a Memory Stick, but a freeware utility called SwitchDash can.*

Jog

The Jog screen enables you to tweak a few settings for the Jog Dial and Back button. We think the default settings are ideal for most users, so you probably won't need to fiddle with them too much. However, here's a rundown of what does what:

NOTE   *Newer Clié models, like the NX70V and TG50, don't have a Jog option in Preferences. We're not sure why.*

2

- **Power On With BACK button**   When checked, the Back button will turn on your Clié.

- **Use JogAssist**   *JogAssist* enables the Jog Dial to function in applications that don't innately support it. If you come across a third-party program that exhibits problems when the Jog Dial is used, you can disable JogAssist for that program. Just tap the Select Applications button, and then check the program in the list that appears.

- **Additional Menu**   As noted earlier in this chapter, most applications have drop-down menus, just like on a computer. To make one-handed Clié operation even more practical, you can add extra functions (up to three of them) to the menus found in every program. Tap the Select Additional Menu button to see what options are available.

- **Extended Push Of BACK button**   You have two choices for what can happen when you hold the Back button for two seconds. Either it can turn off your Clié (that's the Power Off option) or it can give you a Jog Dial-accessible cursor for accessing buttons and menus. We highly recommend using the latter option, which is selected by default.

Network

The slightly misnamed *Network* screen is where you enter the relevant information about your Internet service provider (ISP), if you're using a modem to dial into it. A handful of major ISPs are already listed in the Service menu, but you still need to provide your account username and password, plus the phone number for the ISP. The *Details...* button takes you to a screen with some advanced Internet settings, while *Connect* tells the modem to go ahead and dial in.

Owner

In the tragic event that you lose your Clié, you'd probably be grateful to have it returned. The Owner screen is where you can put your name and contact information (address, phone number, e-mail address—whatever you're comfortable with). Then, if you use the Palm Operating System's security features (which we detail in Chapter 9) to "lock" the device every time you turn it off, the information on the Owner screen is displayed when the unit is turned on again. Thus, if someone happens to find your handheld, they know how to return it to you, but won't have access to all your data. Smart!

TIP *Here's an even better way to retrieve a lost Clié: slap on a StuffBak sticker. Whoever finds your handheld simply needs to call a toll-free number or visit a web site to arrange for its return. Get more information on this great service at **www.stuffbak.com**.*

ShortCuts

Next, we come to *ShortCuts,* a tool designed to expedite the entry of often-used words and phrases. Let's say you're a Starfleet engineer, and you use your Clié to keep track of your repair duties. The phrase "holodeck emitters" comes up quite a bit—but do you really have to write it out every time? What if you could just write "h-e" instead, and have the words magically appear? That's the beauty of shortcuts.

NOTE   *Get the full scoop on creating and using ShortCuts in Chapter 4.*

Introduction to Palm Desktop

So far, we've talked mostly about the Clié itself: the hardware, the operating system, the basic setup procedures and considerations. There's one area left to cover before you venture into real-world Clié use: the Palm Desktop.

What Is Palm Desktop?

Wondrous as a Clié is in its own right, what makes it even more special is its capability to synchronize with your computer. This means all the data entered into your Clié is copied to your PC, and vice versa. The software that fields all this data on the computer side is *Palm Desktop*. (If you use Microsoft Outlook or another contact manager, you needn't use Palm Desktop at all. More on that in the next section.)

Viewed in a vacuum, Palm Desktop resembles traditional personal information manager (PIM) or contact-management software. It effectively replicates all the core functionality of the Palm OS, providing you with a phone list, appointment calendar, to-do list, and memo pad. If you've never used such software before, you'll no doubt find Palm Desktop an invaluable addition, as it helps keep you organized at home or in the office (whereas a Clié keeps you organized while traveling).

A Word About Synchronization

What happens when you synchronize your Clié with your PC? In a nutshell, three things:

- Any new entries made on your Clié are added to Palm Desktop.
- Any new entries made in Palm Desktop are added to your Clié.
- Any existing records modified in one place (the Clié, for example) are modified in the other (the desktop, same example), the newest changes taking precedent.

Therefore, synchronizing regularly assures your information is kept current, both in your Clié and in Palm Desktop.

Already entrenched in Microsoft Outlook? All Cliés come with software—a special version of Puma Technologies' IntelliSync—that allows direct synchronization with Outlook (bypassing Palm Desktop). If you have a different contact manager (such as Lotus Organizer) that you want to synchronize with, you might need to upgrade to the full version of Puma's IntelliSync.

Synchronizing with a Macintosh

Sorry, Mac owners. Unlike Palm and Handspring handhelds, Sony's models don't come with the software you need to synchronize. Fortunately, there's a third-party solution: The Missing Sync from Mark/Space. This $29.95 package provides everything you need to sync a Clié with a Macintosh.

Where to Find It

Web Site	Address	What's There
Puma Technologies	www.pumatech.com	Contact-manager synchronization utility IntelliSync
Mark/Space	www.markspace.com	The Missing Sync

Chapter 3

Introducing Your Clié to the PC

How to...

- Charge Your Clié
- Install the Palm Desktop software
- Configure the HotSync cradle
- Troubleshoot USB connection problems
- Set up the HotSync Manager
- Perform your first HotSync
- Interpret the HotSync log
- Keep your data synchronized just the way you like

A famous poet—it might have been Paul Simon, or perhaps John Donne—once said that no man is an island. Likewise, your Clié isn't an island, either—it's designed to interact with your desktop computer to synchronize important data.

That's pretty neat, because it means you don't have to waste your time duplicating information on your PDA that already exists on your home computer. And if you should ever lose your data because the Clié crashes or does something catastrophic—like falls off the roof of a building or into a lake—you can restore every last bit and byte of data as easily as pressing the HotSync button on your desktop's cradle.

NOTE *Not every Clié model comes with a cradle—if yours comes with only a HotSync cable, don't worry. When we talk about placing your Clié into its cradle, you can also take that to mean "plug in the cable." As for pressing the HotSync button (a cradle-only option), take that to mean "tap the HotSync icon in the middle of the Clié screen after starting the HotSync application."*

Now that you've had a chance to explore your Clié in Chapter 2, it's time to learn about how the device works with your home computer. The Clié comes with a slew of tools designed for the desktop, including a synchronization application for making sure it has the same data as the desktop. Let's get started.

Charging Your Clié

Virtually all Cliés come with integrated rechargeable batteries. We know that you're anxious to start playing, but be sure to fully charge your Clié (the first time usually takes about four hours) before you turn it on or start experimenting with it. To charge your PDA, place it in the HotSync cradle and plug the cradle into the AC adapter. Don't plug the cradle into your computer's USB port, though—that's a step you'll perform after the Palm Desktop software is installed.

If you don't fully charge your Clié before you start using it, you could limit its capability to charge and thereby cut down on its total battery life for as long as you own it.

3

NOTE *Don't plug the cradle into your PC until you're told to. Connecting it too soon can complicate the setup procedure.*

After you're up and running, remember that your Clié will charge whenever it's sitting idly in its cradle. Just make sure the cradle is, indeed, plugged into the wall outlet via its AC adapter. If the cradle isn't plugged into the wall, it can't charge your PDA. You can tell your Clié is being recharged because a power light on the PDA itself will light up. If you don't see the light, check to see if the AC adapter has come loose from the wall or the HotSync cradle.

Installing the Desktop Software

Before you can synchronize your Clié and desktop PC, you first need to install the Palm Desktop software suite on your computer. Palm Desktop is sort of like a personal information manager (PIM). It duplicates all the core applications from your Clié and serves as the headquarters from which you can use synchronized information from your Clié. While you definitely need to install Palm Desktop, you don't necessarily need to use it. If you already rely on Microsoft Outlook or another PIM, you can synchronize your Clié to that program instead and avoid the Palm Desktop entirely. But you have to install the Palm Desktop, because it includes important "conduits" that let your Clié talk to the PC.

The CD-ROM that accompanies your Clié includes everything you need to connect the handheld to your desktop, including your choice of synchronization to Palm Desktop or Outlook. Installation is very straightforward. Follow the installation instructions that appear after you insert the CD-ROM.

Installing Palm Desktop

The Palm Desktop CD-ROM includes a step-by-step installer that gets you up and running within minutes of taking your Clié out of the box. Specifically, Sony divides the install process into a number of sections. Start by installing the Clié Desktop, which is really the Palm Desktop. You might

Palm Desktop and Clié Desktop Are the Same Thing!

The Palm Desktop is so named because it was designed for the first Palm OS PDAs. It continues to work with all Palm OS devices like the Clié, though. So don't be thrown off by the name—the Palm Desktop is designed for Cliés just as well as Palms, Treos, and all the other Palm-powered devices out there. You might notice that on the install disk, Sony calls it the Clié Desktop, but your Start menu calls it Palm Desktop for Clié. By the time you actually run the program, it's called just the Palm Desktop. We hope that's not too confusing.

also want to install some of the Clié Add-ons—you might have the option to install stuff like an enhanced calculator from PowerOne, the SilkLauncher (you should definitely install this—on Cliés with virtual Graffiti areas, it gives you additional Graffiti writing areas, like a tappable onscreen keyboard), and some other odds and ends.

After installing the Desktop and any Add-ons, you need to perform your first HotSync before you install other programs, like the Clié Image, Audio, or Utilities.

As you install the Palm Desktop, you have one very important decision to make: do you want to synchronize your PDA with the Palm Desktop itself, or with Microsoft Outlook? If you have a copy of Outlook installed on your PC, the installer detects it and gives you the option of synchronizing your data to it, if you so desire. What data are we talking about? Stuff like contacts from the Address Book and appointments from the Calendar, as well as notes and tasks. If you're a regular Outlook user, you should certainly choose to synchronize your Clié with Outlook. Palm Desktop, on the other hand, is a serviceable PIM, though it's not as comprehensive as Outlook. If you use a PIM like Outlook, the software will install a copy of Intellisync Lite to manage the flow of data between your Clié and Outlook. If you sync with Palm Desktop, you don't need— and won't install—Intellisync.

If you ever switch from a third-party PIM to Palm Desktop or vice versa, just reinstall the Palm Desktop software and change your answer to this question to properly configure your computer's software.

Finally, at some point in the install process, the installer will ask you to assign a unique HotSync name to your Clié. You can use your own name or give your handheld a unique descriptor—anything from **Dave's Clié** to **Clié-33A** to just plain **Mike** is acceptable. Is the name important? Yup. If you have more than one Clié, each one absolutely must have a different name. If you give two or more Cliés the same name, you can end up seriously messing up your data. If you ever forget your HotSync name and need to find it again, just tap the HotSync app on your Clié.

 If you purchase Clié software, it will probably be registered to a specific device name. So if you upgrade to a new Clié, your old software will only work if you use the same name as the old device.

Installing the HotSync Cradle or Cable

Once the software is installed, it's time to connect the HotSync cradle or cable to your computer. Your HotSync cradle's appearance could differ from the ones we picture in this book, but its appearance doesn't matter—it performs the same function: transferring information between the PC and PDA. Plug the cradle or cable into an empty USB port on the computer or a USB hub. You don't even have to turn the computer off first. Many new PCs have USB 2.0 ports, which are much

Did you know?

HotSync Doesn't Have Anything to Do with Dating

HotSync, a term coined by Palm, Inc., refers to the act of synchronizing the data stored on your handheld and desktop computers. These days, all PDA companies use a special term that means more or less the same thing—for instance, Microsoft's Pocket PCs use the term *ActiveSync* instead.

more robust and have far greater bandwidth than older USB 1.1 ports. Nonetheless, USB 2.0 ports work like older USB 1.1 ports unless USB 2.0–compatible devices are plugged in. Right now, all Cliés are plain old USB 1.1 devices.

As we mentioned earlier, make sure you've installed Palm Desktop before you connect the cradle or cable. If you don't, you could wind up with some serious setup headaches that go beyond the capability of this book to help you solve.

You don't absolutely have to plug the AC adapter into the HotSync cradle to transfer data between the PC and Clié. If you don't use the AC adapter, though, the batteries in the Clié won't recharge and, eventually, its batteries die and cost you your data.

Configuring Intellisync

If you opted to synchronize your Clié with some third-party PIM program like Outlook or Lotus Notes, you'll need to configure Intellisync before your first HotSync. If you're going to sync with Palm Desktop, skip to the next section "Your First HotSync." No peeking . . . go already. Can't you see we have work to do?

After the installation program puts Intellisync on your desktop, you'll need to configure the program to your specific software. You'll see a dialog box that looks like this:

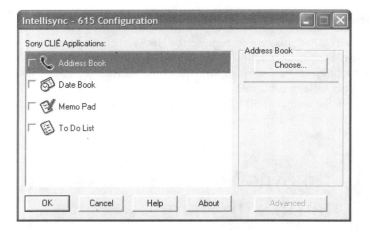

You can sync or ignore each of the four main Clié applications but, by default, nothing syncs at all. Odds are that you'll want to synchronize all your Clié data with the desktop, so click each of the four check boxes. For instance, when you check the box for Address Book, you'll see a list of programs you can sync with. Select the program you actually use, and then click OK. Repeat this process for each of the four programs on your Clié.

Also note that there's a button for advanced settings. For each of the four programs, you can click Advanced at the bottom of the dialog box and tell Intellisync how to handle conflicting data. If you change the same entry on both the desktop PIM and the Clié, for instance, you can choose from among these options:

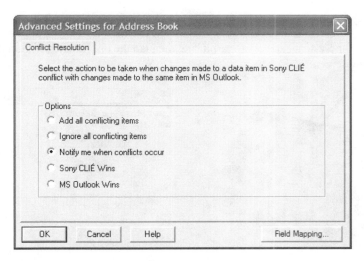

You can change these options at any time by running the Intellisync Configure application in your Start menu.

Your First HotSync

After you load the software onto your computer, install your cradle, and have a nice, relaxing break watching television (Dave recommends *Andromeda,* though Rick prefers "Britney Spears in Concert"), it's time to perform your first HotSync.

HotSyncing—especially if you already use a PIM like Outlook—is pretty cool because it transfers all your desktop-based data (like appointments, contacts, and to-dos) to your Clié, so you don't have to enter any new data to get started with your new PDA. If you're starting from scratch with Palm Desktop, though, you'll have to enter your contacts and appointments because they aren't already on the computer. Here's what you need to do to make sure you're ready:

- Make sure your HotSync cradle is connected to the PC.
- Place the Clié in the cradle.
- Make sure the HotSync Manager software is running. You should see the HotSync icon in the System Tray. If you don't see it, start it now. Choose Start | Programs | Sony Handheld | HotSync Manager.

> **TIP** *The System Tray is the region at the bottom of the Windows Desktop that's found to the right of the taskbar. It contains the clock and icons for special programs like the HotSync Manager. If you use Windows XP, the icon could be "hidden"—click the little arrow to reveal all hidden icons and you should see the one for HotSync Manager.*

Pressing the HotSync Button

Press the button on the HotSync cradle. Of course, a few Clié models don't have a cradle or a HotSync button—if that sounds like yours, you'll need to find the HotSync application on the Clié (it's usually in the System category), start it, and then tap the big HotSync button that appears in the middle of the screen.

The Best Films of All Time

Taking that TV break before the HotSync got us just a tad distracted. Truth be told, we took the opportunity to go watch some movies. And that led to the inevitable arguments . . . what are the best movies of all time?

Dave: There's no way a rational person could disagree . . . *Aliens* is the best movie of all time. Space Marines fighting xenomorphs with 23rd century machine guns! Woo hoo! What could possibly be cooler than that? And it has some of the best movie lines ever. This, mind you, is the film in which Bill Paxton made the words, "Game over, man," a part of my daily lexicon. After *Aliens,* my list gets a bit more introspective. *The Matrix, Memento, The Sixth Sense, Almost Famous,* and *O Brother, Where Art Thou?* have to be several of the most amazing films ever made. Now let's see what lame movies Rick thinks are cool. My prediction: His favorite films include *Tron, Dirty Dancing,* and *Weekend at Bernie's 2.*

Rick: I've had just about enough of your *Weekend at Bernie's 2* bashing, mister. Don't make me tell everyone about your strange fondness for Will Smith. Anyway, in no particular order, my Top Five Movies are as follows: *Life is Beautiful, City Lights, The Shawshank Redemption, Toy Story 2,* and *Star Trek II: The Wrath of Khan.* Yes, I know only one of those movies has things blowing up, which means you won't care for the other four. The age of *Ah*-nold has passed, leatherneck. Grow up already.

After you press the HotSync button, here's what should happen:

1. Your Clié turns itself on (if it wasn't on already).
2. You hear a series of tones indicating the HotSync has begun.
3. A message box appears on the Windows desktop, which informs you of the HotSync status.
4. You hear another set of tones when the HotSync is complete.
5. The Clié displays a message indicating the HotSync is complete.

Exploring the HotSync Manager

The HotSync Manager software does exactly what it sounds like—it manages the connection between your Clié and your computer, enabling you to HotSync. It contains all the options and configurations needed to keep the two devices talking to each other. To HotSync, you needn't mess with anything on the Clié at all. You only need to tweak the HotSync Manager.

To get to the HotSync Manager's options in Windows, you need to visit the HotSync menu. Click the HotSync Manager icon in the System Tray and a context menu appears.

TIP *You can click the HotSync Manager icon with either the right or left mouse button; the result is the same.*

These are the first options you encounter in the HotSync menu:

- Local USB
- Local Serial
- Modem
- Network
- Infrared (you'll only see this one on a laptop with an infrared port installed)

For now, the only one that must be checked is Local USB. This means you can perform a HotSync using the USB-powered cradle you've already installed.

Configuring HotSync Setup

Click the Setup option on the HotSync menu. You should now see the Setup dialog box. This is the place where you get to configure how the HotSync manager behaves. Four tabs are on the Setup dialog box.

The General Tab   The *General tab* lets you specify how often the HotSync Manager "listens" to the USB or serial port for a HotSync request. It has three options, as you can see in Figure 3-1.

- **Always Available**   This is the default setting. As soon as you press the HotSync button on the cradle, you synchronize your data. It's fast and convenient, and is probably the way most people use their PDAs.

- **Available Only When The Palm Desktop Is Running**   This solution dates back to when PDAs connected via the serial port; these days, it's not that useful.

- **Manual**   Just like it sounds, the HotSync Manager doesn't run at all unless you choose it from the Start menu (Start | Programs | Sony Handheld | HotSync Manager). This is the least convenient of all the options, but you might want to choose it if you HotSync only on rare occasions. Even so, we suggest sticking with the default, which is to always leave the HotSync manager running and available.

The Local Tab   The *Local tab* is for those poor suckers still using the computer's serial port instead of USB—don't worry about it.

The Modem and Network Tabs   Both of these tabs are used to specify settings for more advanced HotSync techniques. After you've seen all the tabs in the Setup dialog box, click OK to save changes or click Cancel to leave the dialog box without changing anything.

What's a Conduit?

Conduit is the term your Clié uses to describe the software that connects data on your PDA with similar data on your computer. The *Calendar conduit,* for instance, makes sure the Clié's Date Book and the computer's calendar stay completely in sync. Every application on your Clié that has a corresponding program on the PC is connected with its own conduit, and the Custom menu option is where you turn to adjust these conduits.

Customizing the HotSync Operation

To customize the HotSync Operation, right click the HotSync Manager icon in the Sywstem Tray and then choose Custom.

This is arguably the most important dialog box in the HotSync software because it enables you to specify with great detail exactly what data will get transferred. Before we look at this dialog box, however, we should describe a few conduit states the Clié uses to perform data synchronizations. If you make the wrong choice, you could delete data you need.

■ **Synchronize The Files**   Suppose you added new files to both the PC and the Clié since the last HotSync. The new data from the Clié is copied to the PC, and the new data from the PC is copied to the Clié. Both devices will have a copy of everything. *This is the best setting to use most of the time. In fact, it's the default for most conduits.*

FIGURE 3-1   The General tab determines when the HotSync Manager runs and how easy it is to perform a HotSync.

■ **Desktop Overwrites Handheld** This option supposes the desktop data is correct at the expense of anything that might be on the handheld. If you add new files to both the PC and the handheld, for instance, and then perform this kind of synch, the new files on the Clié will be lost. The desktop data overwrites whatever was on the PDA.

■ **Handheld Overwrites Desktop** This is exactly the opposite of the previous case. Assuming the handheld data is more correct for some reason (we assume you have your reasons), any files that are different or new on the desktop PC are lost after the synchronization. Both systems will have the Clié data.

■ **Do Nothing** With this option selected, no changes are made to either device during the HotSync.

Remember: each conduit can be adjusted independently. This means you can, say, set the Clié's Date Book to overwrite the PC's, while the e-mail conduit is set to Do Nothing and the Notes conduit synchronizes.

> **TIP** *If you're ever in doubt about the state of your conduits, be sure to check the action before you press the HotSync button by right-clicking the HotSync icon and choosing Custom. If you ever accidentally configure the HotSync Manager to Handheld Overwrites Desktop, for instance, you'll lose changes you made to the Palm Desktop or Outlook when you HotSync.*

With those options in mind, let's look at the Custom dialog box. As you can see in Figure 3-2, the top of the box displays the name of the Clié. Managing more than one Palm-powered device from each PC is possible, so you select the proper unit from the list menu before continuing. If you have only a single Clié, don't worry about this option.

FIGURE 3-2 The Custom dialog box enables you to specify how each conduit behaves when you HotSync.

The Custom dialog box in Figure 3-2 displays a list of conduits and their actions. As you can see from the list, there's a unique conduit for each kind of application on your Clié. Your Clié might include some or all of these conduits right out of the box:

- **Mail**   If you installed the Clié Mail conduit, e-mail messages are synchronized between your desktop mail application and the Clié—see Chapter 11 for details.
- **Date Book**   Shares data between the Clié and desktop calendar.
- **Address Book**   Shares data between the Clié and desktop Address Book.
- **To Do List**   Shares data between the Clié and desktop to-do list.
- **Memo Pad**   Shares data between the Clié and desktop memo pad.
- **Install**   Transfers Palm OS applications or data from your PC's hard disk to the Clié's system memory.
- **Install to Card**   Transfers data or applications to the Clié's memory card.
- **System**   Transfers other files created by your Clié to the PC.

NOTE   *If you install additional software, you might end up with more conduits. Many programs come with their own conduits to control the flow of information between your Palm and desktop applications.*

To configure a conduit, either double-click an entry or click it once, and then click the Change button. Depending on which conduit you open, you'll find you have all four synchronization options, or perhaps fewer.

When you configure a conduit, whatever selection you make applies only to the very next time you HotSync unless you check the box marked Set As Default.

Reading the HotSync Log

Did your HotSync session go as planned? Did all your data get transferred properly and did files get copied the way you expected? Usually, it's pretty obvious if everything went well, but sometimes it's nice if your computer can tell you what actually happened—especially if the HotSync dialog box reports some sort of error.

During each HotSync, the HotSync Manager makes a record of everything that happened. This log is easy to read and can answer that nagging question, "Why didn't the calendar update after I added an entry for the Sandra Bullock Fan Club?" If the HotSync Manager noticed something went wrong during a HotSync, it'll even tell you. Figure 3-3, for instance, shows the result of a HotSync that generated an error. The log reveals what happened.

To see the log at any time, click the HotSync icon in the System Tray and choose View Log.

 You can't perform a HotSync when the log is open.

The log displays a list of the actions that occurred for each of your last ten HotSync sessions. The top of the log is the most recent, and older sessions are listed as you scroll down the page. Each session is separated by a text message that indicates when it started and ended.

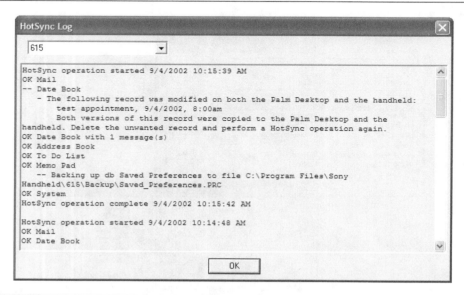

FIGURE 3-3   The HotSync log records the details of the last ten HotSyncs, as well as any errors that occurred along the way.

3

What kind of information does a log reveal? Each conduit reports its status, and these are the messages you're most likely to see:

- **OK** This is good news; the conduit's action succeeded with no errors.
- **Sync Configured to Do Nothing** If something didn't happen, this could be the cause—the conduit was intentionally, or mistakenly, set to Do Nothing.
- **Truncated** This means a file stored on the PC (such as an e-mail or address book entry) was so long, all of it wouldn't fit on the Clié.
- **Records Were Modified in Both Handheld and PC** You made changes to the same file on both the PC and the Clié. Because the HotSync Manager doesn't know which change is correct, it duplicated both files on both systems. You now have a chance to update the file and delete the one you don't want.
- **Synchronization Failed** There can be any number of reasons for this—see Appendix A for troubleshooting information.

NOTE   *The HotSync log is also available on the Clié itself, albeit only for the most recent HotSync session. To reach it, tap the HotSync application, and then tap the Log button.*

HotSync as a Way of Life

After your first HotSync, you might begin to see how convenient it is to have a duplicate of your desktop data on your Clié. But how often should you HotSync? The short answer is this: as frequently

How to ... **HotSync**

To HotSync, do the following:

1. Plug the cradle into your PC.
2. Set the Clié in the cradle or connect its HotSync cable.
3. Make sure the HotSync Manager software is running (by default, it should be already).
4. Verify the conduits are set properly to transfer and synchronize data just the way you want (by default, they should be already).
5. Press the HotSync button on the cradle.
6. Wait until you hear the "HotSync complete" tones before removing the Clié from the cradle.

Changing Conduits On-the-Fly

Often, you could find yourself changing all the conduits in your HotSync Manager, save one or two. For instance, you might want to disable everything except the Install conduit to quickly get a new program onto your Clié, or set everything except AvantGo to Do Nothing so you can get your news onto the PDA as you're running out the door to lunch.

Whatever the reason, you'll soon find there's no easy way to disable several conduits at once. Successively changing five conduits to Do Nothing is almost as time-consuming as performing the whole darned HotSync to begin with.

There's an easier way. Download the tremendously useful program called Ultrasoft NotSync from **PalmGear.com**. This program lets you quickly and easily change your conduits in seconds. The change applies only to the very next HotSync, so it never affects your default settings.

as you like. Most people HotSync daily, while others—whose data changes much less frequently—update their Clié only once a week or even less. Use the following guide as a rule of thumb:

- HotSync any time you leave the office with your PDA.
- HotSync when you return from a trip to update your PC with new info stored on the Clié.
- Many AvantGo Web channels (see Chapter 11) are updated daily. A HotSync each day keeps you current with the newest content.
- HotSync to install new applications on your Clié (discussed in Chapter 4).

3

What HotSync Does to Files

After your first HotSync, you have a set of data on both your Clié and desktop. The goal of the HotSync process is to make sure the data stays the same on both systems. So what happens when you change data on one or both of the computers? This table, which assumes the conduits are set to synchronize the files, should help you understand the subtleties of the HotSync:

Before the HotSync	After the HotSync
You add a file to the Clié (or the PC).	That file is added to the PC (or the Clié).
You delete a file from the Clié (or PC).	The file is also deleted from the PC (or Clié).
You change a file on the Clié.	The file is changed on the PC.
You changed the same file on both the Clié and PC—they're now different.	Both versions of the file are added to the Clié and PC. You need to modify the file and delete the one you don't want to keep.

With this in mind, you might not always want to use the Synchronize The Files option for all your conduits. Why not? Any number of reasons. Here are a few situations:

■ You might rely on your Clié to take notes you have no interest in copying to your PC. In other words, you want to keep one set of notes on the PC, which is relevant to what you do at your desk, and another set of notes for when you're on the road. In such a case, Do Nothing is probably the best option for your needs.

■ You might take notes you don't need to keep after a trip is over. In such an instance, you can use Desktop Overwrites Handheld for that conduit. After your trip, the handheld notes will be erased during the HotSync and replaced by the desktop notes.

■ Your computer has fallen victim to some kind of disaster, and now your Clié holds all your precious contact data. After you reinstall Windows, Palm Desktop, and so on you should set everything to Handheld Overwrites Desktop to make sure the data is restored to the PC. After that, you can return to synchronizing the files.

Don't forget, you can configure each conduit individually, so the Address Book might be set to Synchronize the files, while the Date Book is set to Desktop Overwrites Handheld.

Where to Find It

Web Site	Address	What's There
Sony	www.sonystyle.com	Software updates, news, and accessories
AvantGo	www.avantgo.com	Web page–like news and information channels you can carry on your Clié
PalmGear	www.palmgear.com	A great resource for Clié software

Part II

Everyday Stuff With Your Clié

Chapter 4

Get Information In and Out of Your Clié

How to...

- Determine if your handheld has Graffiti 1 or Graffiti 2
- Understand the differences between Graffiti 1 and Graffiti 2
- Use Graffiti to enter data into your Clié
- Type using the onscreen Clié keyboard
- Work with built-in keyboards
- Enter data using Palm Desktop
- Use alternative gestures to write in Graffiti more effectively
- Display Graffiti help
- Beam items to another Clié
- Beam your business card to another Clié
- Install new software on your Clié
- Install software on memory cards
- Delete unwanted applications

A handheld computer is only as good as the information you store inside it. Or, perhaps more to the point, it's only as good as the methods you have for getting information into it. After all, if storing your appointments or adding new contacts is too difficult, you won't bother doing it—and then all you have is an expensive paperweight.

Case in point: the Rex, a credit card–sized PDA that debuted a few years ago to generally favorable reviews. This little guy was so small it could actually fit into a wallet, yet it carried contacts and appointments like a champ. The problem? You couldn't add to it or make changes when away from your PC—you could only view whatever data was already loaded. For some people, this wasn't a big deal, but public reaction was underwhelming. Palm OS handhelds sell like hotcakes (the good ones, with the bananas in them) in part because they can be updated on the go, and quite easily as well.

You already know about some of the tools at your disposal for getting data in and out of your Clié. We talked in detail about how to HotSync (some would say too much detail, but we ignore those people) in Chapter 3, and you know you can enter data directly in the device using Graffiti, an almost-ordinary method of handwriting. In this chapter, you learn everything you'll ever need to know about Graffiti. We also cover other data entry methods, including the onscreen keyboard and beaming data between Cliés using the built-in IR port.

The Three Ways to Enter Data

One of the first things you'll want to do with your new handheld is enter data—phone numbers, e-mail addresses, memos, to-dos, and so on—into your various applications. Hey, don't look so surprised. The core programs, like Date Book, Address Book, Memo Pad, and To Do List rely on you to fill them with interesting things you can later reference.

You can enter data into a Palm OS device in three primary ways:

- Write it in using Graffiti, the built-in handwriting recognition software.
- "Tap type" using the onscreen keyboard (or use the built-in keyboard if your device has one).
- Enter data into Palm Desktop (or Outlook) on your PC, and then HotSync the data to your handheld. This is the preferred method for people who are just starting out with a PDA, as it's the path of least resistance. If you have an old-fashioned paper address book, for instance, and you want to copy all the names to your handheld, it's much easier to enter them into your PC than into the device itself. Similarly, if you have an electronic address book from another program or PDA, you can probably import the data into Palm Desktop or Outlook, then HotSync it all to your new PDA.

> **TIP**
>
> *You can also connect a full-size keyboard to your Clié and type directly into the device—no PC required. For information on PDA-compatible keyboards, see Chapter 23. Yet another way to get data into your handheld is by beaming, which we discuss in the section "Beaming Data Between PDAs."*

If you're on the go, you definitely need to use either Graffiti or the keyboard to enter data. If you're at your desk, though, you might find entering data into the Palm Desktop, and then HotSyncing, easier because your desktop computer sports a full-sized keyboard.

All About Graffiti

Graffiti is a specialized handwriting recognition system that enables you to enter text into a Clié handheld virtually error-free. Before we go any further, however, we have to talk about the two versions of Graffiti that now exist. In the early months of 2003, PalmSource (the operating-system division of Palm, Inc.) announced plans to abandon the original Graffiti and adopt new handwriting-recognition software, which it dubbed Graffiti 2. We won't bore you with the details as to why (hint: lawsuits were involved—aren't there always?), but suffice it to say, our job here just got a lot harder.

That's because the vast majority of existing Palm OS handhelds have "Graffiti 1," but the latest models use Graffiti 2. PalmSource was also expected to offer an optional software patch that would endow older handhelds with the new Graffiti, though at press time that wasn't yet available. To further complicate matters, some Cliés—most notably the TG50—don't even have Graffiti areas. Instead, they have little keyboards (which some people find easier for data entry than the handwriting software—either version).

> **NOTE**
>
> *As you'll learn in the section "Using the Onscreen Keyboard," it's still possible to use Graffiti with keyboard-equipped models.*

In the face of all these data-entry differences, what's a pair of dedicated book authors to do? Much as we'd like to throw up our hands and say, "Ahh, go read the manual," we don't quit that easily. (Actually, Dave does—he's a quitter from *way* back—but Rick dragged him kicking and screaming

Determine Which Version of Graffiti You Have

As you now know, there's the original Graffiti (let's call it Graffiti 1 just for clarity) and there's Graffiti 2. How can you tell which version is installed on your handheld? It's fairly important that you find out, so you know which of the following sections to read. Fortunately, it's not hard. All handhelds equipped with Palm OS 4.1 or earlier have Graffiti 1. If your handheld has Palm OS 5 or later, it *might* have Graffiti 2. (Not sure which version of the Palm OS in on your handheld? Sheesh—do we have to teach you *everything*? Oh, right, the book title.... Anyway, tap the Home button to return to the main screen, and then tap Menu | App | Info. Then tap Version to see which version of the OS is installed.)

At press time, only the Clié NX73V and NX80V had Graffiti 2. By the time you read this, there will undoubtedly be more models equipped with the new software. The absolute easiest way to tell for sure is to check for a Graffiti 2 icon on the Home screen (it will be in the System category). If you've got one, you've got Graffiti 2, natch.

back to this chapter.) In the pages to come, we show you everything you need to know about entering data on your PDA. It could get a little bumpy along the way, but we think you'll come through better for the experience.

A Drive-By Introduction to Graffiti 1

Unlike other handwriting recognition systems, Graffiti 1 neither interprets your ordinary handwriting nor learns or adapts to the way you write. Instead, you need to slightly modify the way you write and make specific kinds of keystrokes that represent the letters, numbers, and punctuation you're trying to write. Don't worry, though, this isn't hard to do. You can learn the basics of Graffiti inside of a day—heck, you can probably master most of the characters in an hour or less.

When entering text into your Clié, you can't write directly on the part of the screen the Clié uses to display data. Instead, you write inside the small rectangle at the bottom of the display—the one that sits between the four icons. We call this the *Graffiti area*. (Some models have a "virtual" Graffiti area—see the sidebar "The Virtual Graffiti Area" for more info.)

TIP *There's a Palm OS utility, called a Hack, that enables you to write above the Graffiti area, right on the main screen. Some people find this way of entering text more intuitive because the characters appear directly under where they're writing. See Chapter 13 for more information on this tool.*

The rectangle is divided roughly in half: the left side is used to enter letters, while the right side is used to enter numbers. Unlike writing with pen and paper, with Graffiti you don't write from left to right; instead, you input one character on top of another. This can seem a bit awkward at first, as it's wholly unnatural compared to the way we're all used to writing. But like mastering the Graffiti characters themselves, it just takes a little practice.

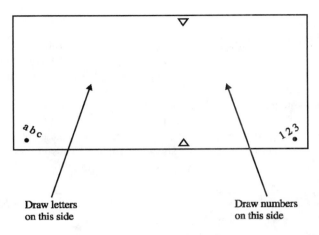

**Draw letters
on this side**

**Draw numbers
on this side**

4

TIP *If you aren't getting the results you expect from Graffiti, make sure you're writing on the correct side of the rectangle. The right side is for numbers, the left side is for letters, and either side works for punctuation.*

Your Clié came with a Graffiti "cheat sheet," either as a laminated card or a sticker. Take a look at this guide and you'll see that most characters are single-stroke shapes (called *gestures* in Graffiti-ese). The characters must be drawn in the direction indicated on the Graffiti guide: the heavy dot indicates the starting position. To write a character, mimic the Graffiti guide by drawing the shape starting with the dot and—in most cases—finish the character in a single stroke without lifting the stylus.

For more details on writing in Graffiti, see the section "Getting to Know Graffiti."

A Drive-By Introduction to Graffiti 2

Graffiti 2 is a lot like its predecessor, to the extent that you should read the previous section if you haven't already. However, whereas Graffiti 1 forced you to learn a simple, but somewhat unusual, set of characters, Graffiti 2 lets you write more naturally. You can't write in cursive or anything like that, but you can make a "*k*" just like you normally would—with two strokes. Indeed, that's the primary difference between Graffiti 1 and Graffiti 2—the latter supports two-stroke characters.

The Virtual Graffiti Area

Some Clié handhelds, like NR/NX/NZ series, employ what's called a virtual Graffiti area—a Graffiti area that's part of the software instead of part of the hardware. (We first talked about this in Chapter 2. You *did* read Chapter 2, right?) It looks just like a regular Graffiti area, except it can disappear when you don't need it, thereby giving you some extra screen estate for icons, text, and so on. Think of it as "Graffiti on demand."

To open and close the Graffiti area on these PDAs, tap the arrow at the bottom of the screen. In many cases, the current application should shrink or enlarge to accommodate it. Here's an example of what a Clié looks like with the Graffiti area open and closed:

One of the coolest aspects of virtual Graffiti is this: you can see your pen strokes as you make them in the Graffiti area, just as you can when writing on paper. (Of course, on a PDA the "virtual ink" disappears the moment you lift your stylus. Let's see a piece of paper do that!) Many people find that seeing their input helps them improve their Graffiti accuracy.

There are a few exceptions. You can't make a capital "A" with two strokes, though you can draw a lowercase cursive "a"—something you couldn't do with Graffiti 1. Thus, while Graffiti 2 is a bit more accommodating than Graffiti 1, there's still a learning curve.

For more details on writing in Graffiti 2, see the section "Getting to Know Graffiti."

Using the Onscreen Keyboard

Even after you get comfortable writing with Graffiti, at times you'll need or want to input specific characters without using pen strokes. After all, remembering how to make some rarely used characters in the middle of taking real-time notes can be hard, and having access to a keyboard can be a real lifesaver.

When you have to enter a password, for instance, tapping it out on the keyboard is easier than writing it with Graffiti. Using the keyboard, you can be sure you're entering the right characters, error-free.

Introduction to Decuma

Sony just loves to keep us on our toes. The Clié NX73V and NX80V, which were introduced just as we were wrapping up this book, come with yet another handwriting-recognition alternative. No, not Graffiti 3—it's called *Decuma*. This interesting option replaces the standard Graffiti area with a special box in which you write a few words at a time, left to right, just like you would on paper. If you're interested in trying Decuma, you'll have to install it from the software CD that came with your Clié. Once that's done, tap the Silk Plug-In icon (it's located in the bottom-of-the-screen toolbar, just to the right of the Find icon), and then select the Decuma Input option and tap OK. Notice that the virtual Graffiti area disappears, having been replaced with the "Decuma area." (To switch back, tap the Silk Plug-In icon again, and then choose Standard Input.)

To experiment with Decuma, load Memo Pad and start a new memo. Then just start writing in the Decuma area. You'll see almost immediately how the software works: after you write a letter and lift your stylus, Decuma immediately recognizes it. If it gets it wrong, just tap the back arrow to erase, and then try again. As with so many aspects of the Clié, experimentation is the best way to learn.

Because Decuma is currently included with just two Clié models, we're not going to cover it in any greater detail. You can visit the Decuma web site (**www.decuma.com**) to find a detailed manual (the Clié doesn't come with one, for some reason). For the record, Dave found its accuracy to be mediocre at best, while Rick found it to be nearly perfect after a few minutes' practice. However, Rick also thinks that where writing on a PDA is concerned, it's actually more comfortable to write one letter on top of another (as with Graffiti), rather than going left to right. Our collective advice: tinker with both and see which you prefer!

All it takes to use the onscreen keyboard is a tap. At the bottom of the Graffiti area, you see the letters *ABC* on the left and the numbers 123 on the right. Tap either spot to call up the appropriate keyboard (alpha or numeric).

NOTE *The keyboard appears only in situations where it's appropriate—specifically, when a cursor is in a data field. If no application is open into which you can insert text, you simply hear a beep when you tap the keyboard dots.*

Once the keyboard is open, note that you can switch between letters and numbers by tapping the selector at the bottom of the screen. A set of international characters is available as well.

Remember the following tips about the onscreen keyboard:

- In handhelds that use versions of the Palm OS prior to 4.0, you can't use Graffiti at the same time you have the keyboard open. Drawing on the Graffiti area has no effect. Fortunately, most Cliés have OS 4.0 or later.

- Use the SHIFT key on the keyboard in the same way you'd use a real keyboard; tap it to create an uppercase letter.

- The CAP key is actually a CAPS LOCK key, which makes all subsequent letters uppercase until you tap it again.

- If you're typing with the CAPS LOCK on and you want to make a single character lowercase, tap the SHIFT key.

- The numeric keyboard provides access to special symbols and punctuation.

Using Built-In Keyboards

There's a growing trend among handheld PCs: a real keyboard in place of handwriting recognition. Okay, maybe "real" isn't the right word—let's say "tiny" instead. Models like the NR70V and NZ90 have built-in keyboards in addition to their virtual Graffiti areas, while the Clié TG50 (as well as selected handhelds from Palm and Handspring) don't have Graffiti areas at all—they have little keyboards instead (see Figure 4-1).

These keyboards are fairly self-explanatory, but allow us to offer a few tips and guidelines for using them:

- On the NR/NX/NZ models, you can alternate between the keyboard and Graffiti at any time. In other words, you don't have to access any special mode to use one or the other. They're both "live" at all times.

- The keyboards' number keys are "doubled up," meaning they share space with the top row of keys. To get a number, hold down the FN key (or the "gray bar" key on the TG50), and then press the desired key.

Using Graffiti on Models with Built-In Keyboards

Just because your TG50 lacks a Graffiti area doesn't mean you can't use Graffiti. There might be times when it's quicker, easier, or just plain preferable to write instead of type. Fortunately, the TG50 has a Graffiti option: a pop-up Graffiti area that pops up on the screen when you press the round button to the right of the Memo Pad button. Unfortunately, it obscures more than half the screen, but at least the option is there if you want it.

FIGURE 4-1 The Clié TG50 has a keyboard instead of a Graffiti area—though this particular model also lets you input data with Graffiti.

Using Palm Desktop

Graffiti and the keyboard(s) are great when you're on the go, but what about getting data into your Clié when you're sitting comfortably at your desk? The better bet: use the keyboard on your desktop PC to type into the Clié much more quickly and efficiently.

How? By using Palm Desktop or another program with a HotSync conduit. In other words, suppose you need to enter a long note into your Clié. Instead of writing it slowly using Graffiti, create a note in Palm Desktop or Outlook, depending on which program you use, and then HotSync.

Let's add a note to the Clié's Memo Pad using Palm Desktop. Do this:

NOTE *If you configured your Clié to synchronize with Microsoft Outlook or another PIM, use that program's memo or note pad for this exercise.*

1. Start Palm Desktop in Windows by choosing Start | Programs | Palm Desktop | Palm Desktop.

2. In Windows, switch to the Memo Pad view by clicking the Memo button on the left side of the screen.

3. Click the Memo Pad and type a note.

4. When you finish typing your note, click anywhere in the Memo list. The note is automatically saved and the memo's subject line shows as much of the note as would fit on the line in the list.

5. When you finish entering data, place the Clié in its HotSync cradle and press the HotSync button. (For details on how to HotSync, see Chapter 3.)

Getting to Know Graffiti (1 and 2)

Earlier in the chapter, we took a quick look at using Graffiti to enter data into your Clié. Graffiti deserves a lot of attention, though, because it's your principal way of interfacing with your PDA. We're willing to bet that more than 90 percent of the time you need to add a note, contact, or To Do, you end up whipping out the Clié stylus and entering your info with good old Graffiti. Knowing Graffiti like the back of your hand is essential to using your Clié effectively.

NOTE *In this section, we mostly refer to Graffiti in a generic sense, meaning the information applies to original Graffiti (aka Graffiti 1) and Graffiti 2. We jump in where necessary to note any important differences.*

TIP *If you just upgraded to a newer Clié that has Graffiti 2, but you're fluent with Graffiti 1 and miss it horribly, all is not lost. TealPoint Software's TealScript, which is discussed in detail in Chapter 12, effectively restores Graffiti 1. Now wipe those tears away....*

As we pointed out earlier in this chapter, Graffiti doesn't interpret whatever chicken-like scrawl you happen to draw into the Clié's Graffiti area. While it might be nice if the Clié could interpret unmodified handwriting, we've all seen what happened to that technology.

Specifically, Apple's Newton MessagePad—the first PDA—tried hard to understand free-form handwriting. And while it did a darned good job, first-time users faced an uphill battle getting it to understand them. Not until you had a chance to use the Newton for a few hours did it start behaving like it comprehended English. To make matters worse, Apple insisted on putting MessagePads in stores with big signs inviting people to saunter over and try them. The result? People would scratch out a sentence in sloppy handwriting and the Newton would convert the result into total gibberish, kind of like what you think Lou Reed might be muttering in a Velvet Underground song. The public never got any confidence that Apple had a workable handwriting recognition engine, and while the Newton was a great little PDA, it failed largely because of public perception. (For the record, Rick thinks it failed because it was an overpriced brick.)

Palm didn't make the same mistake in designing the Palm OS. Its handwriting recognition engine is designed to recognize particular gestures as specific characters, thus reducing the possibility of error. In fact, if you routinely draw the characters according to the template, you should get just about 100 percent accuracy. Graffiti doesn't have to understand 50 different ways of making the letter *T,* so it's both fast and accurate.

TIP *There's a Graffiti cheat sheet built into the Clié. By default, you can see it by drawing a line from the Graffiti area up to the top of the LCD screen.*

General Tips and Tricks for Graffiti

Before we get started with the nuts and bolts of writing with Graffiti, it might help to remember a few things. Despite Graffiti's simplicity, a few tips and tricks can make writing on a Clié a lot easier.

- Draw your characters as large as possible, especially if you're having trouble with Graffiti misinterpreting what you're writing. Use all the Graffiti area (top to bottom), if necessary.

- Don't cross the line between the letter and number portion of the Graffiti area. Make sure you make your gestures on the correct side of the fence to get the characters you want.

- Don't write at a slant. Some handwriting recognition engines can account for characters being drawn at an angle to the baseline, but Graffiti can't. Vertical lines should be perpendicular to the Graffiti area baseline.

- Don't write too fast. Graffiti doesn't care about your speed; but if you write too fast, you won't have sufficient control over the shape of your gestures and you can make mistakes.

- If you have a hard time making certain gestures consistently, try the character a different way. Specifically, refer to Table 4-1 (which is specific to Graffiti 1) for a list of primary and secondary gestures for each character. Use the ones that work best for you.

Graffiti 2 Numbers and Letters

Graffiti 2 is very similar to Graffiti 1, though there are a few exceptions. In the following screenshot, captured directly from Graffiti 2's built-in help screens (draw a stylus stroke from the Graffiti area to the top of the screen to view them yourself), you can see the basic strokes. What this cheat-sheet doesn't illustrate is that you can also draw lowercase characters for many letters. Open a blank memo and try it for yourself. Whichever version of Graffiti you have, practice and experimentation is the hands-down best way to learn.

Writing Letters and Numbers

The easiest way to learn Graffiti is simply to practice writing the alphabet a few times. Use the Graffiti reference card that came with your Clié, or refer to Table 4-1 for a guide on how to draw each character. The advantage of using this book, of course, is that we show you a few alternative gestures that might make certain characters easier to draw consistently. Give them a shot.

In Graffiti 1, you might notice some letters and numbers have identical gestures. The letter *L* and the number 4, for instance, are both made in the same way (see Figure 4-2). How does Graffiti tell the difference? That's an easy one—don't forget, the Graffiti area is divided into a number side and a letter side.

Gesture	Character	
L	L	4
I	I	1
3	B	3

FIGURE 4-2   The letter *L* and the number 4 are made exactly the same. So is the letter *I* and the number 1.

Letter	Gestures
A	∧
B	ℬ β 3
C	C ≺
D	D D △
E	ε ξ
F	Γ Γ
G	G G
H	h H
I		
J	J J
K	∝
L	L ∠
M	m m
N	N ∞
O	O O
P	P P
Q	ʊ ʊ
R	R R

Letter	Gestures
S	S S
T	⌐ ⌐
U	U ✓
V	V V
W	w w
X	X ∞
Y	y γ
Z	Z 2
0	O O U
1		∧
2	2 ⩔
3	3
4	L ≺
5	5 5
6	6 ∞
7	7 ⊃ ⟩
8	8 8 ⅄
9	9 ε

TABLE 4-1 Graffiti 1 Numbers and Letters

TIP *If you're really having trouble mastering Graffiti 1, there's a great tutorial program called PenJammer (**www.penjammer.com**). It's not for Windows or Macintosh—it works right on your handheld, teaching you every Graffiti character via animated helpers. Very cool, very helpful, and very inexpensive (it's just $7.95).*

Capital Letters

You've probably noticed there's no distinction in the Graffiti gestures for lowercase and uppercase characters. That's a good thing, actually—you don't have to learn 50+ gestures because uppercase

The Hardest Characters

Everyone seems to have trouble with some Graffiti character. Even if you can never get your Clié to recognize your letter *B,* that doesn't make you a failure—it just means you should learn an alternate stroke for that letter or put extra care into drawing it carefully and slowly. Even we have trouble with some letters....

Dave: It's unfortunate my last name is "Johnson," because I can't get Graffiti to take my letter *J* to save my life. Half the time, it's my own fault. As many times as I've made the *J,* I can't remember it starts at the top and curves down. I always try to start at the bottom and hook up—which gives me a letter *U* every time. But, even when I remember how to do it, I end up with a *V* or a new paragraph. Of course, now that I'm drawing it for this chapter, I can't seem to do it wrong—ten perfect *J*'s out of ten. I think the letter just hates me. And I know I'm not crazy, by the way, despite what my dog keeps telling me.

Rick: If you'd ever seen Dave's chicken-scratch excuse for handwriting, you'd understand why he sometimes has trouble with Graffiti. To be fair, though, a few characters seem tougher to make than others. It's the *V* that drives me up the wall—I always forget to put the little tail on the end of the upstroke. But I know a secret: if you write the letter backward, it comes out perfectly every time—and you don't need to draw the tail!

and lowercase letters are drawn the same way. Here's how to tell Graffiti you want to make an uppercase letter:

TIP *If you have Graffiti 2, you can ignore most of this advice. To make a capital letter, just write it across the invisible line separating the letter and number sides—that is, the middle of the Graffiti area.*

- ■ **One capital letter**   To make the next character uppercase, first draw an uppercase gesture: a vertical line from the bottom of the Graffiti area to the top. This works only on the left side of the screen; it won't work in the number area. You see a symbol like this one, which indicates you're now in Uppercase mode:

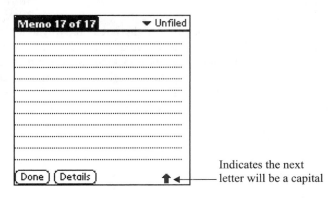

Indicates the next letter will be a capital

■ **All capital letters** To switch to All Caps (or Caps Lock) mode and write all capital letters, draw the vertical gesture twice. You see this symbol to indicate All Caps mode:

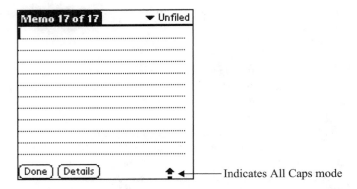

Indicates All Caps mode

■ **Lowercase letters** If you're already in All Caps mode, you can exit and write in lowercase again by making one more vertical gesture. The All Caps symbol should disappear to show that you changed modes.

 Uppercase mode doesn't affect numbers, so it doesn't matter which mode you're in when writing numbers. This means you needn't drop out of Uppercase mode just to write numbers amid a bunch of capital letters.

 One of our all-time favorite Hacks (see Chapter 13) is called MiddleCaps, *which saves you having to write the upstroke before each capital letter. Just write the letter across the imaginary line separating the letter and number sides of the Graffiti area. Absolutely indispensable, and it's a freebie! Find it at PalmGear (**www.palmgear.com**). Of course, Graffiti 2 has this capability built right in.*

Spaces, Backspaces, and Deleting Text

Words are arguably more useful when you can put a space between them, thus enabling the casual reader to discern whereeachoneendsandthenextonebegins. In Graffiti, it's easy to insert spaces. So easy, in fact, you might be able to figure it out on your own (but we'll tell you anyway). Draw a line that starts on the left and goes to the right (not all the way to the right—it's just a little dash, really), and you'll see the cursor skips ahead a space. You can use this gesture to insert spaces between words or to perform any other space-making task you might need. And, yes, you can insert multiple spaces simply by performing this gesture as many times as needed.

The backspace, not surprisingly, is exactly the opposite. Draw a gesture from right to left and the cursor backs up, deleting any text it encounters along the way.

 Space and backspace gestures work fine in both the letter and number sides of the Graffiti area.

Using the backspace gesture is great if you want to delete one or two characters, but what if you want to delete a whole sentence? That backspace swipe can get tiring if you have a lot of text to kill or replace all at once. Fortunately, there's an easy solution: select the text you want to delete. The next thing you write replaces the selected text. Here's how to do it:

1. On the PDA, find a region of text you want to replace.

2. Tap and hold the stylus down at the start of the text you want to select, and then drag the stylus across the text and pick it up when you've selected all the text in question. This is not unlike selecting text in your favorite word processor, but the stylus takes the place of the mouse.

3. In the Graffiti area, write some new text. The old text is immediately erased and replaced with the new text. If you simply want to delete the text, use the backspace gesture instead.

Adding Punctuation

To add punctuation to your prose, you need to (surprise, surprise) enter Graffiti's special Punctuation mode (punctuation in Graffiti 2 is a bit different—see Figure 4-3). All it takes is a tap in the Graffiti area. You see a dot appear, which indicates you can now enter punctuation. Table 4-2 displays the punctuation gestures you commonly need. Note, this refers solely to Graffiti 1.

The most common punctuation mark is a period; and, because it's simply a dot, you can add a period to the end of a sentence by performing a quick double-tap (a single tap in Graffiti 2). Some other symbols are trickier, though, and could take some practice. The comma, parenthesis bracket, and apostrophe are so similar, for instance, it's not unusual to get one when you're trying for another.

 If you have a lot of trouble with specific symbols, you can always use the onscreen keyboard along with Graffiti to write your text.

If you enter the Punctuation mode by tapping on one side of the Graffiti area, you need to complete the punctuation gesture on the same side. Tapping once on the number side and again on the letter side has no effect, for instance.

FIGURE 4-3   Most punctuation in Graffiti 2 approximates normal writing. You make a period just by tapping (once, not twice like in Graffiti 1), an exclamation point with a line and a dot, and so on. There's no special punctuation mode that precedes your strokes—but there are some special strokes to learn.

Using ShortCuts

Everyone loves shortcuts. In desktop applications like Microsoft Office, many folks eschew the mouse for keyboard shortcuts that speed tasks like text formatting and saving files. The Clié also has the capability to save you time and effort using shortcuts. Even better, Clié *ShortCuts* are user-definable, so you can create your own library of them and you needn't be satisfied with whatever came in the box.

So what are ShortCuts, exactly? If you have a word or phrase you frequently write over and over (such as "Dave throws like a girl"), you can assign an abbreviation to it and let Graffiti do the hard work of writing the phrase in its entirety. To see how easy using shortcuts is, try this, using one of the shortcuts that come built into your Clié:

1. Open the Memo Pad and tap the New button to open a new memo page.

2. Draw the ShortCut gesture (shown at left). The *shortcut gesture* tells Graffiti that the next thing you write is going to be an abbreviation, which should be expanded in accordance with the shortcut library.

3. Write **br**, which is the shortcut for "breakfast." As soon as you finish writing the *R,* the text should expand into the word "breakfast."

That's all there is to it. We hope you can see the value of creating ShortCuts that are relevant to what you frequently write.

4

Punctuation	Gestures
Period	•
Comma	/ (draw low)
Question mark	? ⌐
Exclamation point	!
Colon	V
Semicolon	⩘
Open parenthesis	(
Close parenthesis	)
Tab	⌐
Apostrophe	' (draw high)
Quotes	N
Slash	/
Backslash	\
At Symbol	O
Asterisk	⋋
Number sign	ᴎ h
Greater than	<
Less than	>
Percent	ᘁᘁ 𝓍
Equal sign	Z
Plus sign	⋌
Dollar sign	S

TABLE 4-2   The Most Common Graffiti Punctuation Gestures

Storing Your Own ShortCuts

Your Clié comes with roughly half a dozen ShortCuts and you can easily create new ones whenever you want. To create a ShortCut, do this:

1. Display Preferences by tapping the Prefs icon.

2. Choose ShortCuts from the list of Preferences in the upper-right corner of the screen.

3. Tap the New button to display the ShortCut Entry window.

4. Give your shortcut a name. This is the abbreviation you write to summon the entire shortcut text. If you want to create a shortcut that reads "Dear Sir," for instance, you might want to use "ds."

5. Enter the complete shortcut text. Remember, you're limited to a maximum length of 45 characters. If you reach that limit, you hear a beep when you try to write additional text.

6. Tap the OK button to save your ShortCut.

Once you create a ShortCut, you can use it anywhere in your Clié that you can write with Graffiti. And they work in Graffiti 2, too.

Don't go overboard with ShortCuts right away. They become a lot less cool if you have so many of them that you can't remember what the abbreviation is to summon the entire text. Start with two or three, and, once you know them like the back of your hand, add a few more.

Another Kind of Shortcut: Menu Commands

If you're a big fan of hitting CTRL-S in Microsoft Word to save your work, then you should love this. The Clié has its own menu shortcuts you can access with Graffiti. To do that, though, you must be prepared by remembering two important items:

- How to draw the Graffiti Command stroke
- What the shortcut character is for the menu command you want to invoke

The Command stroke is easy. To put your Clié in Command mode, draw the gesture on the left. After you draw the gesture, your Clié displays the Command bar. You simply need to write the proper character to invoke the menu item—say, *C* for Copy or *F* for Font.

As you can see in the following screenshot, the Command bar also displays icons that allow quick access to certain commonly used functions, like beam, copy, and delete. These icons appear in a context-sensitive fashion, so don't be surprised if you don't always see the same ones. If you haven't selected any text, for instance, there's nothing to copy, so you won't see the copy icon.

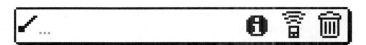

Most menu items have no corresponding icon in the Command bar, however, so you have to learn what the shortcuts are for each item. To do so, display the menu (tap the Menu button and you'll see something similar to Figure 4-4). As you can see, many menu items have associated shortcuts.

The Command mode only lasts for a few seconds, after which the bar disappears. If you don't write the shortcut character (or tap an icon) quickly enough, you'll need to perform the command stoke again.

Beaming Data Between PDAs

On *Star Trek,* transporters are used to beam people and equipment from one location to another. While we're a long way from being able to beam physical things around, the Palm OS makes it possible to beam almost any kind of data between handheld PC users.

All Clié models have an infrared, or IR, port. On most models, you can find it on the front edge of the case. If you haven't located your Clié device's IR port yet, find it now. It's a small, black,

FIGURE 4-4   Many menu items have Graffiti shortcuts associated with them.

The Command Bar

So, you tried entering a command, but you're curious about the Command bar. What are all those little symbols and what do they do?

Actually, the Command bar is a clever tool you can use to access common features of your Clié rapidly. It's context-sensitive, which means the bar will look different—it'll have different icons—depending on when you make the Command stroke.

Try this: make the Command stroke when you're viewing the Home screen. The three icons on the right side of the Command bar represent Info, Beam, and Delete (just as if you tapped the Menu button and selected Info, Beam, or Delete from the App menu).

Now open the Date Book and select an appointment by dragging the stylus across some text. Make the Command stroke again. Voila! You now have different choices, like cut, copy, and paste. You can experiment with the Command bar in various locales around your Clié to see what kinds of shortcuts you can effect.

translucent strip of plastic. Using this IR port, you can beam information in a surprising number of ways. You can do the following:

- Use your handheld as a TV and stereo remote control (as explained in Chapter 19).
- Send data between your Clié and a cell phone or pager.
- Print Clié data on an IR-equipped printer (using software detailed in Chapter 12).
- Beam data to other Clié users.
- Play two-player games "head-to-head."

These things are pretty cool, but mostly you'll probably use beaming for exchanging mundane business data. All the core applications (Address Book, Memo Pad, and so on) support beaming, so you can beam the following:

- Contact listings
- Your own "business card" from the address book
- Appointments and meetings
- Memos
- Tasks

In addition, you can beam entire applications to other Palm OS handheld users. If you download a freeware program from the Internet and want to share it with friends or coworkers, go ahead: it's a snap to transmit the item wirelessly.

How to Beam

No matter what you're planning to beam—or receive—the process is essentially the same. Actually seeing the process demonstrated is faster than reading about it, but because neither Dave nor Rick is handy to stop by your office today, here's the process in a nutshell:

1. Orient the two handhelds so their IR ports face each other, and are between a few inches and 3–4 feet apart. If you're any closer than three inches, the PDAs could have a hard time locking onto each other. Too far away, the signal won't be strong enough to reach.
2. As the sender, you should choose the item you want to beam—a contact, memo, or whatever.
3. Choose the Beam command from the menu.

TIP   *If you beam often, you might want to use the beam shortcut—a Command slash gesture followed by the letter B. Or, you can configure your Clié so a stroke from the bottom of the Graffiti area to the top of the screen can start a beam of any given item. To do that, tap the Prefs icon, and then select the Buttons item in the list at the top-right corner of the screen. Tap the Pen button and choose Beam Data.*

4. A dialog box appears to indicate the beam is in progress. First, you see a message that your Clié is searching for the other handheld. That message then goes away and the data is transmitted.

5. After the beam, your Clié goes back to business as usual—you won't get a message indicating the beam was successful. The receiving PDA, on the other hand, gets a dialog box that asks permission to accept the beamed data. As the receiver, you need to decide what category to file the information into (if it's something that can be categorized) and tap either Yes or No, depending on whether you want to keep the item. If you tap Yes, the data is integrated into your Clié in the category you specified. (There's no category decision to make if you're receiving an application or some other non-core-app data.)

TIP

As the receiver, a good idea is to specify a category in which to file the data you just received. If you let stuff like Address Book entries accumulate in the Unfiled category, it can later become difficult to find what you're looking for.

To Accept or Not to Accept

By default, your Clié is set to automatically receive beamed items. However, you might want to disable autoreceive for beaming for two reasons:

■ Because the IR port is constantly on and searching for transmissions from other handhelds, your Clié uses slightly more battery power. Is this a big deal? We don't think so. The extra power consumption is marginal.

■ With all the concerns about viruses and other malicious programs that exist for PCs today, some folks are nervous about leaving their Clié in a state that receives data all the time. Our call: viruses for the Palm OS aren't a threat (yet), and you have to manually accept a beamed program after reception anyway. Don't worry about it.

So, while we obviously don't think autoreceiving beamed items is a big deal, here's how to disable that feature if you want to:

1. Open the Clié's Preferences by tapping the Prefs icon.

2. Choose the General category from the list at the top right of the screen.

3. Change Beam Receive from On to Off.

After changing your preferences to disable beaming, other Cliés can't send you data unless you reenable beaming from Preferences.

Selecting Items for Beaming

So, now that you know the rudiments of beaming, you're no doubt eager to start. While we're usually a pretty down-to-earth couple of guys, we have to admit a certain coolness factor is involved in beaming things in the middle of a meeting or on the show floor at a trade show. It's definitely better than writing notes by hand or trading easily scrunched business cards.

Beaming Appointments

If you work with other Clié users, you can make sure everyone is on the same schedule by beaming entries from the Date Book. To do that, select an appointment, and then choose Menu | Record | Beam Event.

TIP

Speaking of keeping everyone on the same schedule, Palm DualDate 1.0 *(a freeware utility available from* **PalmGear.com***) lets you display two calendars side by side on your PDA—ideal if you want to keep track of, say, a spouse's or coworker's schedule. It's basically an enhanced replacement for the stock Date Book application. Check it out!*

Best Games for Beaming

Some very generous Palm OS programmers have created some very good freeware games. They're not only fun to play, they're fun to share with others as well. Because they're freeware, you can beam them with a clear conscience. Two of our favorite freebies are Vexed, a maddeningly addictive puzzle game, and Patience, a collection of 21 Solitaire games. You can find them both at **Freewarepalm.com** and **PalmGear.com**.

Beaming Contacts

If you're like most people, the Address Book is the most well-exercised part of your Clié. And, instead of exchanging paper-based business cards, now you can beam the information between Cliés, which can later be HotSynced back to Palm Desktop (or Outlook). In recognition of just how important the Address Book is, you have not one, not two, but three options for sending data from this application:

- **Beam the current entry**   To send an Address Book entry to another user, find the name you want in the address list, tap it, and then choose Menu | Record | Beam Address.

- **Beam a whole bunch of entries**   You can send any number of contacts—even every name in your Clié, in fact—using Beam Category. To do that, first choose the category you want to beam by picking the category from the list at the top-right corner of the screen. Then tap Menu and choose Beam Category. (On some models, the option might be called Send Category.) To beam all the entries in your entire address book, you should set the category to All—but if you do that, the recipient loses the categories, and everything ends up on the destination Clié as "Unfiled."

CAUTION   *Be careful before you beam or try to receive a whole category's worth of contacts—make sure it's something you really need to do. This operation could include hundreds of entries, which could take more time than either of you are willing to spend pointing your PDAs at each other.*

- **Beam your own entry**   What's more common than handing your business card to someone? You can configure your own Address Book entry as your personal business card and beam it to other handhelds. For details on configuring an entry as your business card, see Chapter 6. Once configured, however, you can send it by opening the Address Book, tapping Menu, and choosing Beam Business Card.

TIP   *There's a faster way to beam your business card to someone: hold down the Address Book button for two seconds. This automatically tells the Clié to beam your business card.*

Beaming Memos and Tasks

Memos are handy to pass off to other Clié users. You can give them notes, action items, short documents, and even meeting minutes in this way. Likewise, if you want to delegate a task to someone else in your office, tell that person to "visit my cubicle—and don't forget to bring your Clié." You can beam memos and to-do items in two ways:

- ■ **Beam a Memo or a To Do**   To beam a single item, select it, tap Menu, and then choose Beam Memo (for a Memo) or Beam Item (for a To Do).
- ■ **Beam a bunch of stuff at once**   As with Address Book, you can select a category in Memo Pad or To Do List, and then choose Beam Category from the menu. To beam all your memos or tasks at once, remember to set the category to All.

Beaming Applications

Now for the best part. You can use the Clié's beaming prowess to transfer entire applications from one Clié to another. If you meet someone who shows you a cool new game or utility, for instance, you can ask him to beam the program to your handheld.

NOTE   *Not all applications are free, so don't use your Clié's beaming capability for piracy. Actually, many commercial programs are "locked" to prevent beaming, and shareware applications often require an unlock code to access all the features in the registered version. You can beam trial versions around, but don't share registration codes—that's piracy.*

Not all programs can be beamed. The core applications that come with your Clié are "locked," making them nonbeamable. Many commercial programs are also locked, and some programs have a resistance to beaming—like Hacks (discussed in Chapter 13). In addition, if you have a program that requires supporting database files, the files won't be beamable. This means you must go home and install the program the old-fashioned way, using your PC.

Now that we've told you what you can't do, let's talk about what you can do. Beaming an application isn't much different than beaming data from one of the Clié's programs. Do this:

1. Tap the Home button on your Clié to return to applications.

2. Tap Menu, and then choose Beam. You see a dialog box with a list of all the applications on your Clié, as in Figure 4-5. Some applications have little locks; these aren't beamable.

3. Select an application and tap the Beam button. If the desired program is stored on a memory card, tap the arrow next to Beam From and choose the card instead of Handheld. You'll then see a list of the programs stored on the card. This designates only where programs are beamed from—programs you receive from others are always stored in main memory (though you can easily offload them to a memory card later on).

TIP   *If you want to beam more stuff, get a program called FileZ. This freeware file manager makes it possible to beam certain kinds of apps (like Hacks and databases) that the Palm OS can't do on its own.*

FIGURE 4-5   Choose a program from the list to beam it to another Clié. If it has a lock, however, it can't be beamed.

Installing New Software on Your Clié

Did you know you can install tons of additional programs on your Clié? Thousands of free and commercial applications are out there, just waiting to be installed. They include enhancements to the core applications, utilities, games, and more. In fact, one of the best reasons for choosing a Palm OS device (instead of a Pocket PC device or some other kind of organizer) is because there's such a wealth of software.

But you might wonder: how the heck do I get all this cool stuff onto my Clié?

The answer is that Palm Desktop includes a handy Install Tool for loading Clié apps. (If you sync with Outlook, don't fret—*Install Tool* works independent of your desktop contact manager. While you can run it directly from within Palm Desktop, you can also access it directly as a standalone program.)

Prepping Applications for Installation

Throughout this book, we make reference to our favorite applications and recommend that you try them. Perhaps the single best resource for Palm OS software is a web site called **PalmGear.com**.

Most of the time, downloaded applications aren't immediately ready for installation. If you download an application from the Internet, it usually arrives in the form of a SIT file (if you're a Mac user) or a ZIP file (if you use Windows). You need to expand these SIT and ZIP files to get to the actual program files before they can be installed on your Clié. We recommend these tools for managing compressed files:

- **Windows**   Use WinZip to uncompress ZIP files.
- **Macintosh**   Use Aladdin StuffIt Expander to manage SIT files.

Install New Applications

4

1. Run the Install Tool by choosing Start | Programs | Sony Handheld | Install Tool.

2. Click the Add button. You see the Open dialog box for selecting Clié applications.

3. Locate the program you want to install (you'll have to navigate to the correct folder on your hard drive) and select it. Click the Open button.

> **TIP** *You can select multiple applications at once by holding down the CTRL key as you click programs in the file list.*

4. With your application displayed in the Install Tool dialog box, click Done.

5. The next time you HotSync your Clié, the selected application is installed.

> **TIP** *You can skip most of these steps by simply opening the Windows folder containing the program you want to install, and then double-clicking the program's icon. That will launch the Install Tool and add the program to the queue. Click Done, HotSync, and you're finished!*

Install to a Memory Card

If your have a memory card, you can install applications directly to it. That's handy, especially if you want to install a huge application or data file that simply wouldn't fit if copied to the Clié's more limited internal memory.

After you've used Install Tool to select a program for installation, click the Change Destination button. You'll see the Change Destination dialog box. Then just click the program you want to install directly to the memory card, and then click the arrow to move it to the right side of the screen, which represents the PDA's memory card. (Note: the Change Destination option appears only if you're using a handheld that runs Palm OS 4.0 or later.)

When you've configured your to-be-installed applications to your liking, click OK, close the Install Tool (by clicking Done), and then HotSync.

Of course, if you already happily expand compressed files with another program, keep up the good work; these are just our favorites.

■ Once expanded, most Clié files have the file extension ".prc." In a ZIP or SIT with lots of little files, you can generally grab just the PRC file and install that. Of course, if in doubt, read whatever documentation accompanied the application. Very often you'll need to install more than one file, and the manual (or "readme" file) will tell you which ones.

Deleting Applications

You won't want every application you install on your Clié forever. Some programs you won't like, others will outlive their usefulness. And, sometimes, you'll need to remove some software to make room for more, because the Clié has limited storage space (unless you have a memory card, that is—see Chapter 22 for more details).

Deleting programs is easy. Tap the Home button, and then tap Menu | Delete. You see a list of all the applications currently stored on the handheld. At the top of the screen, you also see a bar that shows how much memory remains on your Clié.

If your handheld has an expansion slot, you can tap the arrow next to Delete From, and then choose the memory card from the list. That lets you delete applications stored on the card.

To delete an application, select it and tap the Delete button. This is similar to the Beam interface—in fact, it's so similar, you should be careful you don't accidentally delete an app you're trying to beam to a friend.

When you delete an application, you also delete all the data it generated. If you have a document reader, for instance, deleting the app also trashes any Doc files it might contain. To preserve these files, HotSync before deleting anything—that way you can later restore the files from the Backup folder on your hard disk if you need to.

Chapter 5

The Date Book

How to...

- Use the Day, Week, Month, and Agenda Views
- Customize the Date Book's appearance
- Add appointments to the Date Book
- Beam an appointment to someone else
- Create an appointment using the Address Book
- Create repeating events
- Add a note to an appointment
- Make an appointment private
- Edit appointments in the Date Book
- Delete events in the Date Book
- Set an alarm for an appointment
- Use the Clié with Outlook or Palm Desktop

Are you busy on Tuesday at 3 P.M.? If you have your Clié handy, you'd probably already know the answer to that question. In an informal survey conducted in Dave's living room, we found that Date Book is the single most popular core application on the Clié. In the old days—before Sony packed Cliés full of multimedia tools—people would buy a PDA just for the scheduling software.

Indeed, the Date Book is a modern miracle. It can show you your schedule by day, week, or month. The Date Book handles recurring appointments and can notify you about upcoming events. It synchronizes precisely with your desktop calendar. And the Date Book fits in the palm of your hand. It's better, Rick might tell you, than *Star Trek*. Dave, on the other hand, would be inclined to say it's better than *Babylon 5*.

Viewing Your Appointments

When you switch to the Date Book, by default, it starts by showing you any appointments you have for today. Start the Date Book by pressing the Date Book button on your Clié or tapping the Date Book icon in the Main or All category of the Application screen.

Navigating the Day View

When you start the Date Book, the first thing you see is the Day View. You can see it shows the currently selected date in the tab at the top of the screen. Next to that are seven icons, one for each day of the week.

5

 TIP   *Tap and hold the date tab to see the current time. If you let go too quickly, the Record menu will drop instead.*

As you can see in the previous illustration, you can shrink the virtual Graffiti area on Clié models with the large HiRes+ screen to see more of your schedule onscreen at once.

In the middle of the screen, you see the current day's calendar. You can enter new events on the blank lines. If you have any appointments already entered, note that long appointments (those lasting for more than 30 minutes) have duration brackets. *Duration brackets* appear to the immediate left of the appointment time and show you what time an appointment is scheduled to end.

Other icons also appear near appointments. In fact, you should get used to seeing these three icons:

- ■ **Alarms**   This icon indicates you'll get notified by the alarm sound that the appointment is due to start.

- ■ **Notes**   If you attach a note to your appointment (perhaps with directions to the location or agenda details, for instance) you see this icon.

- ■ **Repeating meetings**   If the meeting is configured to happen more than once, this icon appears.

Did you know?

Operating System Oddities

Although most Cliés work more or less the same way, they don't all use exactly the same operating system (OS). Likewise, the Palm Desktop software on your PC could vary a bit, depending on which model you own. We wrote this book with version 5 of the Palm OS in mind, though your Clié might differ slightly. Nevertheless, the basic functionality of applications like the Date Book remains the same, so don't worry if you have a different OS.

If you tap any of these icons, seen in Figure 5-1, you see the Event Details dialog box, which we discuss in detail in the section "Making Your Appointments Repeat."

Finally, the bottom of the screen has several important controls. Icons exist to change the current view, as well as to create a new appointment, to view the Event Details dialog box, and to go to a specific day.

Changing View Options

By default, the Day View compresses your calendar by not showing blank times of the day. This way, you can have appointments that span from 6 A.M. to 11 P.M. and have them all appear onscreen without needing to scroll at all. Whenever it can, the Day View includes blank events between existing events for better readability.

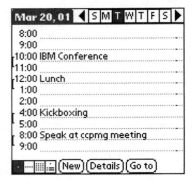

What happens if you have such a busy day that all your appointments won't fit onscreen at once? You need to tap the scroll button at the bottom of the screen. It only appears when needed.

FIGURE 5-1   These icons tell you valuable information about your appointment. Tap on them to edit the details.

NOTE   *Lots of users try pressing the Scroll button or rolling the scroll wheel to see more appointments in the same day. Of course, that simply changes the view to the next day.*

Not everyone likes the Day View compression. If you frequently add events to your schedule during the day, for instance, you might want to have blank lines available for all the hours of the day. If this sounds like you, here's how to turn off compression:

1. Choose Options | Display Options from the menu.

2. Uncheck the Compress Day View option.

3. Tap the OK button.

Now when you use the Day View, you see all the blank lines for your day. On the other hand, using this setting virtually guarantees you need to use the Scroll button to surf around your daily schedule.

When you configure your Day View, you also have to decide what kind of person you are. Are you

- Neat and orderly—and opt for less clutter whenever possible?
- Impatient—and want everything at your fingertips all the time?
- Apathetic—and don't want to bother changing the default settings?

You can change the display of the Date Book to accommodate the way you want your Clié to look. If you're the neat and orderly sort, for instance, you might want the Date Book to be a blank screen, unless it actually has appointments already scheduled for that day. If this is the case, choose Options | Preferences and set the Start Time and End Time to be the same thing—like 7:00 A.M. After configuring your Clié in this way, you should find days without appointments are essentially a blank screen with a single blank line—the time you set in Preferences.

More of an impatient sort? Then choose Options | Preferences and configure your Start Time and End Time to span the full range of hours you plan to use. If you ever add events to the evening, for instance, set the End Time for 10 P.M. or later. This way, you have a blank line available immediately for writing a new entry.

If all this sounds extremely pointless to you, leave the Preferences alone. The default settings cover most of the hours you routinely need.

Getting Around the Days of the Week

As you might expect, there are several ways to change the view to a different day. You can figure out most of them on your own, but we bet you can't find 'em all. Here's how you can do it—use the method that's easiest for you:

■ Switch to a specific day by tapping the appropriate day icon at the top of the screen:

■ To move ahead one week at a time, use the forward button to the right of the week icons. If you're currently on Tuesday, for instance, tapping the arrow takes you one week ahead to the following Tuesday. Obviously, you can go back a week at a time by tapping the Back arrow instead.

■ To move forward or backward one day at a time, press the Scroll button or turn the jog wheel on your Clié (depending on which model you have).

■ If you want to find a specific day quickly, tap the Go To button and enter the date directly in the Go to Date dialog box. When you use Go To, remember to choose the year and month first, because you go to the selected date as soon as you tap a date.

■ To get back to "today" from somewhere else in the calendar, tap Go To, and then tap Today on the Go to Date calendar dialog box.

Navigating the Week View

Now that you're used to the Day View, we'll let you in on a little secret: there's more where that came from. That's where the icons at the bottom of the screen come in. Tap the second one to change to the Week View.

> **TIP** *The Date Book button also serves as a view changer. Every time you press the button, the view cycles from Day View to Week View to Month View to Agenda View, and then back to Day View again. If your Clié has a scroll wheel, press it in to do the same. It's convenient to jab with your thumb as you view your various schedule screens.*

5

This screen uses a grid to display your appointments. The top of the grid is labeled by day and date, while the left side contains time blocks throughout the day. The gray blocks represent scheduled events. Obviously, this view isn't ideal for determining your daily schedule in detail, but it's handy for getting your week's availability at a glance. Use it to pick a free day or to clear an afternoon, for instance, when you're in a meeting and trying to choose a good time to get together with an equally busy person. As you can see in the following, the full-screen mode on Cliés that can minimize the virtual Graffiti area works well on busy schedules.

Tap to change weeks

Event with no scheduled time

Tap to display discription

Busy day—scroll to see more

Tap blank to create new event

> **TIP** *If you have an appointment you need to move to another time anywhere in the week, tap the event, hold the stylus down, and then drag it to another place on the schedule. As you move the block around, you can see the exact time to which the event is being moved. To abort this process without changing anything, move it back to its original location without lifting the stylus.*

If you enable the right features in Preferences, you can see untimed and multiday events in the monthly calendar.

Navigating the Month View

If you press the Date Book button again or tap the third icon at the bottom of the screen, you're transported to the Month View. It displays an entire month at a time (see Figure 5-2).

How to ... Add Some Holidays

One thing the Date Book doesn't come with is a database of holidays. When's Christmas? That one is easy—but if you want to know when we celebrate President's Day, Veteran's Day, or Arbor Day, then it helps to have a calendar with holidays already nailed down for you.

Thankfully, a number of holiday databases are online, many of them free or extremely inexpensive, and all of them easy to install on your Palm. After loading the appropriate files, your Date Book will know exactly when all the major holidays are and display them in all the various views.

Try either one of these—if you prefer, search online and you'll find many others as well:

■ **TinyDates**   For a mere $4, you get a huge database of holidays that synchronizes with the Date Book, includes free updates in future years, and has a detailed description of the background of all the holidays.

■ **MegaHolidays**   This holiday database costs $13 and comes in its own application that resides outside of the Date Book.

Both of these programs are available on **www.Palmgear.com**.

Blocks of busy time are now replaced by little hash marks. You can't tap on these marks to see the appointment details because they don't actually represent individual events. Instead, the three possible marks represent events in the morning, afternoon, and evening, as seen in Figure 5-2. In addition, this view shows untimed events as plus signs (+) and multiday events as a series of dots that span several days. If you tap any day in this view, you're automatically taken to the Day View for that day.

NOTE *By default, both of these special display features are disabled on your Clié. To turn them on, choose Options | Display Options from the Day View screen. Then, in the Month View section of the Display Options dialog box, enable Show Untimed Events and Show Daily Repeating Events.*

5

Managing Your Day from the Agenda View

The last of the Date Book views—the Agenda View—is a favorite for many people. Why is the Agenda View so cool? Because, like some desktop day planners, the *Agenda View* combines your appointments and to-do tasks into a single screen. You can see at a single glance all your responsibilities for the day without switching screens or pressing buttons.

Take a look at the Agenda View:

You can see that the top of the screen shows you any appointments and untimed events that might be scheduled for the day. After a horizontal line, your Clié lists your To Dos.

You can change the current day by tapping the arrows at the top of the screen to change a day at a time. If you want to hop directly to another day, tap the date between the arrows. This displays the Go To Date dialog box, just as if you'd tapped the Go To button at the bottom of the screen.

To jump to the current date, tap the Go To button, and then tap the Today button at the bottom of the Go to Date dialog box.

Filtering Your To Dos

You might not always want to see all the To Do tasks stored in your Clié. If you're at work, for instance, you might not want to see any To Dos filed in a personal category.

To fine-tune the To Do List, tap the down arrow for the category list and choose the category you want to see displayed. You can choose any category you like, including All, as shown next.

The Agenda Zoom

The Agenda View is great for viewing your day's schedule, but it's also a cool way to make changes to your daily itinerary. Just tap on a calendar item to switch to the Day View so you can make schedule changes. Or tap directly on a To Do item to go to the To Do List for editing.

It would be great if you could automatically start your Clié in Agenda View all the time. Alas, you can't quite do that. But, if you set your Clié to the Agenda View, and then visit another application, the Agenda View automatically returns the next time you start the Date Book. If you're in a hurry, remember, you can always press the Date Book button several times to cycle through the Date Book's various screens to arrive at the Agenda View.

Creating New Appointments

Now that you've mastered the fine art of viewing your schedule from every conceivable angle, you probably want to know how to add new events to the schedule. You can add appointments to your Clié in two ways: via the PC—which we discuss later in the section "Using Outlook," and right from the Clié itself. The only place you can enter data about a meeting is from the Day View.

The Coolest PDA Innovation Ever

Dave: Sony has been a company of busy beavers, adding all kinds of enhancements and refinements to the basic Palm-Powered PDA, now known as the Clié. But of all the additions Sony has made—a second memory slot, a jog wheel, a larger screen, a built-in camera—which is the best? If you could only have one thing that Sony has added to the various Clié models, which would it be? For me, I think I'd have to vote for the larger, half-VGA screen with the collapsible Graffiti area. I love all the extra screen space, and I've grown dependent on having all those extra pixels. And you can't beat having the capability to change the look for the Graffiti area—after all, it's virtual, so why not apply different "skins" from time to time?

Rick: Much as it pains me, I have to agree: the HiRes+ screen is the primary reason I've chosen the Clié (first the NR70V, and then the NX70V) over other PDAs. I especially like it because I read a lot of e-books, and the extra space means more text fits onscreen. In that same vein, my other favorite innovation is the jog wheel (see Chapter 2), which enables me to scroll book pages easily, and with just one hand. Together, these two seemingly minor goodies make the Clié NR/NX/NZ models the best e-book readers on the planet.

Add Events

Most of the time, your schedule will be full of meetings that take place at a specific time of day, such as:

```
Meet with Susan from accounting
3-5 P.M. in Conference Room A.
```

This is what the Clié refers to as an *event*—but most people call it an appointment. No matter what *you* call it, here are three ways to add an event to your Clié:

■ **Use the New button**   Tap the New button on the Day View. Then, within the Set Time dialog box, select a Start Time and an End Time, and tap OK. Now, enter the meeting information on the blank line provided for you.

Make a Date

If you're setting up an appointment with someone in particular, you can have a lot of fun with your Clié. Okay, it's not better than listening to Pink Floyd with the lights out, but it's pretty cool, nonetheless. Suppose you need to meet with someone who's already in your Address Book. Switch to the Day View and tap on a blank line at the time you want to start your meeting. Then choose Options | Phone Lookup. You see the Phone Number Lookup dialog box, which displays all the names in your Address Book. Find the name of the person you're meeting with and tap it. Tap Add. What do you get? The person's name and phone number positioned at the start time of the meeting.

Now it gets even better. Does your associate have a Clié or some other Palm OS device? If so, make sure the appointment is still selected and choose Record | Beam Event. You've just given your associate a copy of your meeting in her PDA. She now has no excuse if she's late.

■ **Start writing** Tap on a blank line that corresponds to the meeting start time and write the details of the meeting on the line.

■ **Pick a time from the Week View** If you're looking for a free space to place a meeting, the Week View is a good place to look because it gives you the "big picture" of your schedule. When you find a spot you like, tap it and the Day View should open to the desired start time. Then write the meeting info.

SHORTCUT *A fast way to create a new event at a specific time is to write the start time in the Graffiti area. A Set Time dialog box appears and you can proceed from there. For example, writing a **4** automatically launches the Set Time dialog box for 4 P.M.*

A Closer Look at the Set Time Dialog Box

To set a time in this dialog box, tap an hour (in the selector on the left) and a minute (on the right) for both the Start Time and End Time. You can change your mind as often as you like, but the time must be in increments no smaller than five minutes. You can't set a Start Time of 11:33, for instance.

You can also use Graffiti to set the time, a real convenience for folks who are faster at writing than tapping. 335 is interpreted as 3:35. To change between A.M. and P.M., write an *A* or a *P* in the letter side of the Graffiti area.

If you need to back up and start over, use the Backspace gesture. When you want to move between the Start Time and the End Time box, use the Next Field gesture. Finally, when you've finished entering times, use the Return gesture to simulate tapping OK. Now you're back at the Day View, ready to write in your meeting name.

> **TIP** *You can also create activities that don't have a specific time associated with them; they appear at the top of the Day View and attach themselves to the entire day.*

Making Your Appointments Repeat

Some schedule events just don't go away. Weekly meetings, semiannual employee reviews, and the monthly dog-grooming sessions are all examples of events you might want the Clié to automate. After all, you don't have the time or energy to write the same weekly event into your Clié 52 times to get it entered for a whole year. An easier way exists. To create a recurring event, do the following:

1. Select the entry you want to turn into a recurring event and tap the Details button at the bottom of the Day View screen.

2. In the Event Details dialog box, the Repeat box is currently set to None. Tap it. The Change Repeat dialog box should appear.

3. Now you need to tap a repeat interval. Will the event repeat daily, weekly, monthly, or annually? In other words, if the event takes place only once a year, or once every five years, tap Year. If you have a meeting that takes place once a month, or every other month, tap Month. For meetings that occur every week or every five weeks, use the Week button. Finally, if you need to schedule meetings daily, every other day, or every ten days, tap Day.

4. You now have more options, depending on which interval you choose. A common interval is Week, which would enable you to set up a weekly meeting. Tell the Change Repeat dialog box how often the meeting will occur, such as Every 1 Week or Every 3 Weeks.

5. If you selected a monthly interval, you can also choose whether the meeting will repeat by day (such as the first Monday of every month) or by date (as in the 11th of every month).

6. If the event will repeat more or less forever (or at least as long as you can imagine going to work every day), then leave the End On setting at the default, which is No End Date. If you're creating an event with a clear conclusion, tap End On to set the End Date for this repeating event.

7. Your selection is turned into a plain English description. If you agree the repeat settings are what you want, tap OK.

If you're attending a multiday event, such as a trade show, you can display this in your Clié by creating an untimed event and setting it to repeat daily (Every 1 Day). Don't forget to set an End Date.

Making an Appointment Private

You might not want all your appointments to be available to the public. While we generally believe honesty is the best policy, you can flag certain appointments as private—and they'll be hidden from everyone except you. If you want to hide an appointment, do this:

1. On the Day View screen, select an appointment.

2. Tap the Details button.

3. On the Event Details dialog box, tap the Private box to add a check mark. Once you select this option, the current record is flagged for privacy. Tap the OK button, and you see this dialog box:

4. Tap OK to close the dialog box.

You might notice the event probably isn't hidden yet. To make it go away, you need to enable the Private Records feature in the Security application. For details on how to do this, see Chapter 9. Using this feature, you can hide and show private data whenever you want.

> **TIP** *You can display more than one calendar on your Clié at once. If you collaborate with coworkers or a spouse and want to see their calendars side by side with yours, try DualDate at* **www.palm.com/support/dualdate***.*

Editing Recurring Meetings

With most appointments or events, you can alter them just by tapping and entering the needed change with a little Graffiti. Changes to repeating meetings require a little more care. In general, when you change some aspect of a meeting that repeats, the Clié asks you whether you want to change only this one meeting or every meeting in the series.

If you need to move a specific meeting—like the one in November—to a different time, but all the other meetings are held at the traditional time, select Current. The event is unlinked from the series and any changes you make to the rest of the repeating event don't affect the one you changed. On the other hand, if the meeting is moving to a new day permanently, choose All:

There's an exception to this rule: if you change any text in the name of the appointment, then the Clié makes the change to the entire series without asking. If you want to change the text of one instance of the event without changing the rest, you need to unlink it from the series. To do that, follow these steps:

1. Change something else about the event, like its time.

2. You're asked if you want to change the current event or all of the events. Choose Current. The event is now unlinked from the series.

3. Change the name of the unlinked event.

4. If you need to, fix whatever you changed in step 2.

Working with Alarms

If you need a reminder about upcoming events, then you should use the Clié's built-in alarm feature. Any event you enter can be set to beep shortly before the event, giving you enough time

How to ... **Pick Your Own Alarm Sound**

If, like us, you're easily bored, you might be interested in changing your Clié's default alarm sound. It's easy to do—just visit **PalmGear.com** and search for alarm sounds. You'll find tons of downloads that give your Clié alternative sounds. Remember, if your Clié has "enhanced sound," many of the ordinary alarm replacements won't work. You'll need a special program, like Clié Sounds (which you can find at **www.PalmGear.com**). Alarm replacement programs can give you special effects like science fiction or animal sounds, while others deliver complete songs, TV themes, and movie scores. If you've ever wanted your Clié to sound like a *Star Trek* communicator, here's your chance.

Of course, it's not all fun and games—a distinctive alarm sound can make your Clié easier to hear in noisy environments.

to jump in your car, pick up the phone, or start saving for the big day. You can assign an alarm setting to your events as you create them, or at any time afterward.

NOTE   *Timed events play an audible sound. Untimed events don't play a sound but, instead, show a screen advising you the event is pending.*

Setting Alarms for Specific Events

To enable the alarm for a particular appointment, do the following:

1. In the Day View, select an appointment.

2. Tap Details.

3. In the Event Details dialog box, tap the Alarm check box. You should see a new control appear that enables you to set the advance warning for the event.

4. Select how much advanced warning you want. You can choose no warning (enter a zero) or set a time of up to 99 days in the future. The default is five minutes.

5. Tap OK.

Setting Alarms for Everything

By default, the Clié doesn't turn the alarm on for your appointments. Instead, you need to turn the alarm on for every event individually. If you find you like using the alarm, though, you can tell the Clié to turn the alarm on automatically for all your appointments. Then it's up to you to turn the alarm off on a case-by-case basis when you don't want to be notified of any events.

To enable the default alarm setting, do the following:

1. In the Day View, choose Options | Preferences.

2. Tap the check box for the Alarm Preset. Set your alarm preference; configure the alarm time, the kind of alarm sound, and how many times the alarm will sound before giving up.

You can try out each of the alarm sounds by selecting them from the list. After you choose a sound, it plays so you can hear what it sounds like.

3. Tap OK.

Importing Alarm Settings

Much of the time, you probably get appointments into your Clié via your PC—you HotSync them in from Palm Desktop or Outlook. In that case, the rules are different. The Clié keeps whatever alarm settings were assigned on the PC and doesn't use the Preference settings on the Clié. If you want a specific alarm setting, you need to change the alarm setting on the desktop application before HotSyncing, or change the alarm on the Clié after you HotSync.

Some folks would like to have two separate sets of alarms for their appointments: one for the Clié and another for their desktop calendar program. If you have a PC and Microsoft Outlook, try Desktop to Go. This alternative conduit enables you to configure the Clié to use a completely independent set of alarms from Outlook.

Controlling Your Alarm

If you use an alarm clock, you know the only thing better than having an alarm is being able to turn it off.

Remember, the Clié isn't all that loud. If you need to hear your Clié, don't bury it in a backpack or briefcase where the sound will be hopelessly muffled. However, what if you're in a quiet meeting room with a CEO who turns into Darth Vader every time a cell phone rings? In that case, temporarily silence it (before he silences you). To do so, open Preferences and choose the General view, where there's an option for Alarm Sound. Choose Off from the Alarm Sound list.

Working with Palm Desktop

If you use Palm Desktop as the calendar on your desktop PC, you benefit because it looks similar to the version on your Clié. Granted, Palm Desktop is a lot bigger than your Clié screen and it's in color. But aside from that, you find the modules share a common appearance and the overall philosophy of the program is similar.

Using the Day View

The Day View looks similar to the Clié display. Look at Figure 5-3 for an overview of the major elements in this display.

The easiest way to double-book a time slot is to click the Time box. A new blank appears to the right of the existing appointment.

You might recall that on the Clié, you can create an appointment by using the Phone Lookup feature—this grabs a name and phone number from the Address Book, and places it in a time slot in the Date Book. You can do the same thing in Palm Desktop. Under the calendar, you can see the To Do List and Address Book minilists. Choose which you want to see by clicking Address or To Do. Then drag a name (or even a To Do) into a time slot.

Editing Appointments

You can make lots of changes with the mouse. To change the duration of an event, drag the arrow-shaped duration handle up or down; to move an appointment, drag it by its event handle on the right edge; and to see the Edit Event dialog box, which lets you edit the text and includes alarm and privacy controls, double-click anywhere in the event.

You can move an appointment to another day by dragging it via the event handle to the calendar and dropping it on the desired day.

Using the Week and Month Views

Both of these views are quite similar to their Clié counterparts. In the Week View (seen in Figure 5-4), though, the event blocks work a little differently than you might expect. The following is a general rundown:

■   To move an event to a different time, drag it by the event handle.

■   To display the Edit Event dialog box and change options like text, time, repeat settings, or the alarm, double-click the event.

■   To change the duration of the event, drag its duration handle up or down.

The Month View is a bit more helpful than the one in your Clié. The Month View shows you what events are scheduled, not just that you have a mysterious "something" scheduled. You can't edit the events in this view, though. Instead, you can double-click the appropriate day to get to the Day View or add a new event to a specific day by right-clicking the day and choosing New Event from the menu.

5

FIGURE 5-3   The Day View combines appointments with either To Dos or Addresses, depending on how you configure the screen.

FIGURE 5-4   The Week View enables you to add and edit appointments.

Using Alarms on the Desktop

Want to be notified about upcoming events while working at your desk? You need to use Palm Desktop's Alarm Manager—a new feature in Palm Desktop 4.1, which you can download from Sony's web site if you have an older Clié. While Alarm Manager is linked to Palm Desktop, it's technically not a part of it. What we mean is that it runs outside of the program and hangs out in the Windows System Tray, just like HotSync Manager.

To activate the Alarm Manager, choose Tools | Options, and then click the Alarm tab. You'll see three choices in the Options dialog box:

- **Always Available**   When you choose this option, Alarm Manager loads when you start Windows, even if Palm Desktop itself isn't running. It ensures that you hear all of your alarms. Most folks, we think, want this option.

- **Available Only When The Palm Desktop Is Running**   This is pretty self-explanatory—but we can't think of a lot of reasons why you'd use this option.

- **Disabled**   Alarms won't ring at all—which makes sense if you don't need to worry about event alarms or you use another PIM, like Outlook.

Once you set up the Alarm Manager to your liking, you can configure alarms in the Clié Desktop when you create new events. At the bottom of the New Event or Edit Event window, you'll find the alarm options (which work just like they do on the Clié itself).

Using Outlook

Of course, Microsoft Outlook synchronizes with the Clié just fine, and many people use it instead of Palm Desktop. The Outlook Calendar View is a handy tool for seeing your current and upcoming events. By default, you see today's appointments. To switch to a specific day, click the date you want in the minicalendar (see Figure 5-5). You can also see several days at a time. To do this, click and drag a range of days in the minicalendar.

5

FIGURE 5-5   Many users synchronize with Outlook instead of Palm Desktop.

The toolbar includes buttons for viewing the work week, an entire week, and a month at a glance. To switch back to a single view of today, you need to click both Day (to switch to a single day view), and then Go To Today (to view the current day).

Adding Appointments

You can add an appointment to Outlook in several ways. Pick the method that's easiest for the kind of event you want to add.

- Create a simple 30-minute meeting: simply click a time slot and start typing. Press the ENTER key when you finish.

- Create a simple meeting that lasts for 60 minutes or more: Click a time slot and drag the mouse down to extend the length of the appointment for an hour or more. When a block of time is selected, type the subject of the meeting and press ENTER.

- Create a meeting that repeats or has detailed notes: Find the start time of the meeting and double-click the block. An untitled Appointment window should appear. Fill in the meeting details as needed.

If you use the Location line of the Outlook appointment box, this information appears in parentheses after the subject text on your Clié.

Tweaking Alarms for the Clié

By default, every Outlook appointment comes with an alarm that sounds 15 minutes before the event. If you create most of your appointments within Outlook, you might end up with alarms you don't want on the Clié after a HotSync. To change the length of the default alarm—or to disable alarms entirely—choose Tools | Options from the Outlook menu and click the Preferences tab. In the Calendar section, edit the Default Reminder option to suit your needs. If you remove the check mark, the alarm is then disabled for new appointments.

5

Better Date Books

Looking for an alternative to the Date Book? You have quite a few choices. The Date Book hasn't changed much since Palm originally created it in the mid '90s. You can't categorize appointments the way you can in Microsoft Outlook, for instance, and you can't synchronize with Microsoft Exchange Public Folders. Another annoyance: you can't "link" appointments with items elsewhere in your Palm, like the contact information for people attending your meeting. Don't worry, though, because numerous alternatives are available.

Some of the best replacements for the Date Book include the following:

- **DateBk5**   www.pimlico.com
- **Agendus**   www.iambic.com
- **Beyond Contacts**   www.dataviz.com
- **KeySuite**   www.chapura.com

These programs offer a wealth of features and capabilities you won't find in the integrated Date Book. DateBk5 and Agendus, for instance, let you attach colorful icons to appointments, making it easy to tell them apart at a glance in any calendar view. The other programs integrate with Outlook more coherently, utilizing categories, more data fields, and other important features.

Chapter 6 The Address Book

How to...

- View Address Book entries
- Customize the Address List display
- Search for an entry by name
- Search for an entry by keyword
- Create new Address Book entries
- Add pictures to your Address Book
- Display a specific phone number in the Address List
- Use the custom fields
- Assign a category to an entry
- Delete Address Book entries
- Use the Windows Address book
- Use your Clié with Outlook

What's the big deal? It's only an address book. Yes, but as one of the four big "core" applications—the main programs that ship with your Clié—you'll use the Address Book a lot. And the Address Book is an elegant program, designed to get the information you need quickly, perhaps more quickly than any other contact manager on the market.

We're sure you'll get a lot of mileage from the Address Book. You can store thousands of entries and not run out of memory. Despite how many names you add to the list, your Clié doesn't really slow down in any meaningful way. In addition, the Address Book isn't really a stand-alone application (though it can be if you want). The Address Book synchronizes with desktop applications like Palm Desktop and Microsoft Outlook. This means you only need to create a contact list once, and then it's maintained on both your PC and your Clié.

Viewing Your Addresses

When you switch to the Address Book, the program displays all the entries in your list onscreen. As you might expect, you can start the Address Book by pressing the Address List button on your Clié or tapping the onscreen Address icon in the Clié's applications.

As you can see in Figure 6-1, the Clié lists your contacts alphabetically in a view called the Address List. On a standard 360×360-pixel screen, there's room for 11 entries onscreen at one time. If you have a HiRes+ model like the NX80 pictured in Figure 6-1, there's room for 16 entries. In either case, the rest appear above or below the screen, depending on where you are within the Address List. To get around in the Address List, just use the Scroll buttons. Each time you scroll, the Clié moves the list by one complete page of entries.

You can also get around with categories. If your contacts are divided into more than one category, every time you press the Address button, you switch categories. You can cycle through the first page of names in each category by repeatedly pressing the Address Book button.

FIGURE 6-1   The Address List is a database with all your contact information.

Viewing by Company Name

For most folks, the default Address List is great. This list displays the entries by name (last, first) and a phone number. If you prefer to work with your contacts according to the company they work with, you can change the Address List.

To change the View mode of the Address List, do this:

1. Display the Address List View.

2. Choose Options | Preferences from the menu.

3. Choose Company, Last Name from the List By list.

4. Tap OK to save your changes.

Notice that after making the change, you can see the company name in the list. If no company is associated with a particular entry, then you only see the individual's name, as you did before. You can switch back to the default view at any time.

Finding a Specific Name

If you're looking for a specific entry in the Address List, you can simply scroll down until you find it. If you only have a few dozen contacts, that's not so hard. But what if you're like us and your Address List is brimming with over a thousand contacts? Scrolling might take a while, especially if the guy you're looking for is named Nigel Walthers or Earnest Zanthers. That's when you use the Look Up function.

To search for a specific name, start writing the person's last name in the Look Up field at the bottom of the screen. The Address Book adjusts the display as you write; so if you enter the letter **J**, it displays all the names that begin with the letter *J*. If you write **JO**, it narrows the search and shows names that begin with those letters.

If you're using the List By: Company, Last Name option in the Address List View, it's a little more complicated. If the entry has a company name, you need to search for that entry by company name. If the entry doesn't have a company name, though, you must find it by the last name.

Once you start searching, you can keep writing letters until the Clié displays exactly the name you want, or you can write one or two letters, and then use the Scroll button to find the name you need. If you want to clear the Look Up field to write in a new name, just tap one of the Scroll buttons.

Conducting a Detailed Search

You might have noticed that the Look Up field only searches by last name. What happens if you want to find someone, but you can only remember that person's first name or the company where he works? The Look Up field won't do you any good.

In this case, use the Find tool. Tap the Find button, enter the word you want to search for, and then tap OK. You get a list of every entry in the Clié with that word—even items from the other applications—as shown in Figure 6-2. The current application is searched first, so make sure you're in the Address Book before you start using the Find tool.

Viewing a Name

Once you locate the name you were looking for, tap on it. You'll see the Address View, which displays the contact's name, address, and phone numbers, as shown in Figure 6-3.

Creating New Entries

To create a new Address List entry on the Clié, tap the New button at the bottom of the screen. From there, start filling in the blanks. Start by writing the last name of the person you're adding.

FIGURE 6-2   The Find tool is a powerful way to locate an entry even if you don't remember the person's exact name.

When you're ready to move on to the first name, you need to change fields. You can do this two ways:

- Tap the next field with the stylus, and then write in the Graffiti area.
- Use the Next Field gesture to move to the next field.

TIP   *The Next Field gesture takes a little practice because it's easy to get the letter* U *by mistake. Although the gesture template shows a curve in the first part of the stroke, you get the best results by going straight down, and then straight up again.*

Even though you only see a single line for text in each field, the Address List secretly supports multiple lines of text in each field. If you're entering the company name, for instance, you can use two or more lines to enter all the information you need about the company, department, and so on, for the individual. To write multiple lines of text in a field, use the Return gesture to create a new line. You won't see the multiple lines in the Address List, but you can see them when you select the entry and view the Address View.

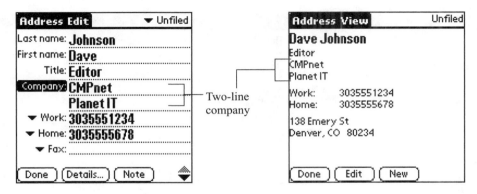

When you finish adding information about this new person, tap the Done button.

FIGURE 6-3 The Address Book shows you all the details about the selected individual.

TIP

What if you're Canadian, French, or living in some other non-American location? The Clié defaults to address details like city, state, and ZIP code—which might not be appropriate for your locale. The solution is to start the Prefs application and select Formats from the menu. Then, set the Preset To: menu to whatever country you desire.

Using Multiple Phone Numbers

The Address List gives you a few options when you enter contact information. Specifically, you can set what kinds of phone numbers your Clié has for each contact. Conveniently, this needn't be the same for everyone. For one person, you might list a home phone and a pager, for instance, while another entry might have a work number and an e-mail address. The Clié keeps track of everything for you.

To control these numbers, tap on the phone number list and choose the desired label. Then, write the number or e-mail address in the field next to the label. You can specify up to five entries for each person in your Address List.

If you're on the ball, you might wonder which of those numbers shows up in the Address List View. Remember, the list shows the name and a phone number for each contact—this means you might not have to open an entry simply to dial a phone number because it's right there in the List View. The answer, though, is that the first phone number you enter into the Edit View is the one that appears in the List View—no matter where it appears in the list of phone numbers.

 If you later decide you want a different number to appear in the List View, tap the Details button, and then select the number label you want from the Show In List menu.

Using Extra Fields

The Address List has plenty of preconfigured fields (like name, company, and phone numbers) for most users, but it's flexible enough also to accommodate the special needs of everyone else. You might want to track birthdays, web pages, spouse names, or other personal information. If so, you're in luck—four custom fields are at the bottom of the Address Edit View, which you can rename as you like.

To label these four bonus fields into something more useful, do the following:

1. Choose the Address Book. Any view will do.

2. Choose Options | Rename Custom Fields from the menu.

3. Select the text on the first line (which should say Custom 1) and write a name for the field. Name the other fields—or as many as you need—in the same way.

4. Tap OK when finished.

Once you create labels for these fields, you can find them at the bottom of the list of contact info in the Address Edit view.

 The custom fields are global. This means you can't have different custom fields for each entry or even for each category. Once named, the custom fields apply to all entries in the Address List. You needn't fill them out for every entry, though.

Adding Pictures to the Address Book

Most Clié models come with a very cool feature in the Address Book—the capability to attach photos to your contacts. This is great because it lets you associate names and personal information with the individual's actual picture. If you have a lot of acquaintances you don't know very well in your Clié, this can be a wonderful feature for jogging your memory before a meeting.

Does *your* Clié support pictures? There's an easy way to find out:

1. Start the Address Book and tap on an entry.

2. Tap the Edit button at the bottom of the screen.

Do you see the words "No Image" in the upper-right corner of the screen? If so, you can add pictures to your Clié. The spot that says No Image is where the picture appears.

You can get pictures into the Address Book in two ways: the easy way and the not-quite-so-easy way. That translates to using a Clié digital camera or an external digital camera. If you import digital images from some source other than the Clié camera, you'll have to transfer them to the Clié through your PC. Let's look at both methods.

 Once you associate a picture with an entry in the Address Book, you don't have to keep the original around just for the Address Book's sake. Instead, the Clié makes a small copy of the image and keeps it in the Address Book database.

Using Your Clié Camera

To use your Clié camera, do the following:

1. Activate your Clié's camera. It doesn't matter whether you have a built-in camera, like the one in the NX80V, or you're using a Memory Stick camera you've attached to your PDA.

2. Take a picture of someone.

3. Start the Address Book and open the entry for the person you just photographed.

4. Tap the Edit button to get to the Address Edit page.

5. Tap the No Image text in the upper-right corner of the screen. You should see thumbnail images for all the pictures stored on your Clié.

6. Tap the picture you want to display for this entry.

That's all there is to it! Remember: you can always change pictures later. You can even remove a picture. To do that, enter the Address Edit page, tap the image, and choose No Images from the bottom of the screen.

Using Images from Your PC or Digital Camera

If you have images on your digital camera or PC's hard disk, you can use those in the Address Book as well. If you have a desktop Memory Stick card reader, it's easy: just insert the Memory Stick in your reader, find the folder in which the Clié stores digital images (it's called DCIM), and drag-and-drop your pictures there. Done! Put the Memory Stick back into your Clié, and you should be able to link those pictures to your contacts.

What if you don't have a Memory Stick card reader connected to your computer? Then you'll have to accomplish an extra step or two. Here's what you should do:

1. Start by running PictureGear on your desktop PC. You should have received PictureGear with your Clié or your Clié digital camera. You might not have installed it, however. If you didn't, dig out the original CD-ROM and install it now.

2. Find the picture—or pictures—you want to use by browsing your computer's hard disk drives.

3. When you find the images, select them. You can hold down the CTRL key while clicking images to select more than one.

4. Choose File | Output Services | Install The Image During The Next HotSync.

5. When you see the Install dialog box appear, click the Still Settings button.

6. Change the size of the image to Small because that's all you'll need for the Address Book. Click OK twice to close both dialog boxes.

7. Perform a HotSync. Afterward, the images will appear on your Clié and you can use them in your Address Book.

NOTE
There's a big downside to attaching pictures to your Address Book entries: memory. Be selective about how many images you use and monitor the free space remaining on your Clié.

Our Favorite Books

Dave: Rick, it occurs to me that we often argue about movies, but rarely talk about our favorite books. I realize that's because you only recently got your equivalency diploma and reading still gives you a headache, but I was wondering if you were ready to weigh in with a few titles. Personally, I think that Orson Scott Card's *Ender's Game* is perhaps one of the very finest, but most under-appreciated novels in American literature—it's probably dismissed by academics because it's a genre title. After Ender, though, I'd count Joseph Heller's *Catch 22*, C. S. Lewis's *Perelandra,* and T. H. White's *The Once and Future King* among my very favorites. In a nutshell, I seem to have a thing for authors with three names.

Rick: I'm really surprised you didn't mention your collection of Little Lulu comic books or fondness for *Go, Dog, Go*. Well, I enjoyed *Ender's Game,* but certainly wouldn't call it great literature. For that I'd point to modern gems like *The Corrections* and *The Amazing Adventures of Kavalier & Clay*. I would also count *Angela's Ashes, The Good Earth,* and *Microserfs* among my favorite novels. Oh, by the way, there are only two names in "Joseph Heller." Didn't *Go, Dog, Go* teach you anything?

Assigning Categories

Your new contact can easily get lost within a sea of names and addresses if you aren't careful. With only a few names to manage, this isn't a big deal. But what if you have 500 or 1,000 contacts in your Address List? This is when categories could come in handy.

Choosing a Category

As you might remember from Chapter 2, categories are simply a way of organizing your Clié data more logically into groups you frequently use. To assign a contact to a specific category, do the following:

1. From the Address Edit screen, tap Details. The Address Entry Details dialog box should appear.

2. Tap the Category List and choose the category name you want to assign to this contact.

3. Tap OK to close the dialog box.

Of course, you needn't assign a category if you don't want to do so. By default, new contacts are placed in the Unfiled category.

TIP   *The Clié's Address Book doesn't support as many categories as Microsoft Outlook. If you have dozens of categories assigned in Outlook, you might want to look at an alternative Clié Address Book, like KeySuite or Beyond Contacts.*

Editing and Deleting Addresses

In this fast-paced world, a contact once entered in an address book isn't likely to stay that way for long. You might need to update an address, phone number, or e-mail address, or to delete the entry entirely.

To edit an entry, all you do is find the entry in the Address List and tap it. You're taken to the Address View where you can see the existing information. Then, tap the screen and the display changes to the Address Edit screen, which you can change to suit your needs.

If you have a contact you simply don't need anymore, you can delete it from the Clié to save memory and reduce data clutter. To delete a contact, do the following:

1. Choose the entry from the Address List. The Address View should appear.

2. Choose Record | Delete Address from the menu.

 If you check the box marked Save Archive Copy on PC, then a copy of this entry is preserved in Palm Desktop in archive form. In general, you probably needn't archive your data, but it lets you restore deleted data in a crisis.

Creating and Beaming Your Business Card

One of the coolest things about taking your Clié to meetings and trade shows is the capability to beam your personal information into other peoples' PDAs. This is a lot easier and more convenient than exchanging a business card. Heck, a paper business card? That's so . . . '80s! Use your Clié instead.

Before you can beam your personal information around, though, you need to create a business card. That's not hard to do. Find your own personal information in the Address List (or, if you haven't done this yet, create an entry for yourself). After you select your card and can see your personal information on the Address View screen, choose Record | Select Business Card from the menu.

From here on, you can beam your card to others either by choosing Record | Beam Business Card from the Address List menu or, more simply, by holding the Address List button

Create an Address Book Entry

In summary, here's how you can create entries in the Address Book:

1. Press the Address Book button on your Clié to switch to that application.
2. Tap the New button on the bottom of the Address List view.
3. Enter all the information to create an entry for the person in question.
4. Tap the Details button and assign the entry to a category, and then tap OK.

down for two seconds. When you beam, you'll have to choose whether to send the address with—or without—the picture, if you have one attached. You can choose With Image if you're beaming to another Clié, but the beam will fail if you try sending the picture to any other kind of PDA.

> **TIP** *Is your Address List entry selected as your business card? If so, on the Address View screen you should see an icon representing a Rolodex page at the top, just to the right of the title.*

Working with Palm Desktop

Palm Desktop obviously has its own counterpart to the Address Book found in the Clié. Using Palm Desktop, you can not only create, edit, and refer to entries on your PC, but you can also put them to use in ways unavailable on the Clié itself. Next, we look at Palm Desktop.

Using the Address Book in Palm Desktop is a radically different experience than using the Clié. In most respects, it's better because the larger desktop screen, keyboard, and mouse enable you to enter and use the data in a more flexible way. After you start Palm Desktop, you can switch to the Address Book by clicking the Address icon on the right side of the screen or by choosing View | Address Book (see Figure 6-4).

The Address Book interface enables you to see both the Address List and Address View simultaneously. To see a specific record's contents, click it in the list and the information then appears in the column on the right.

FIGURE 6-4   The Address Book looks sparse, but it has more features than the Clié itself.

TIP

You can print a detailed Address Book based on your Clié contacts by choosing File | Print. The Address Book is nicely formatted.

Creating and Editing Entries

Some of the most dramatic differences in the Address Book appear when you create and use the Address Book. Remember these notes:

- To create a new entry, click the New button at the bottom of the screen or double-click a blank spot in the Address List.

- The Edit and New dialog boxes let you enter the same information as on the Clié. The dialog box also has a list box for specifying the category and a check box to make the entry private.

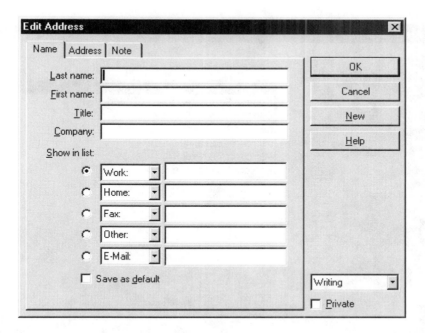

■ To specify which phone number will appear in the Address List, click the radio button to the left of the appropriate phone number.

■ To edit an existing entry, either double-click the entry in the Address List or its equivalent in the Address View on the right.

■ You can also change the custom fields in Palm Desktop. To do so, choose Tools | Options and click the Address tab.

Importing Contacts Into Palm Desktop

If you have a history with another contact manager, you could have dozens or even hundreds of names and addresses that should be copied over to Palm Desktop to be synchronized with the Clié. Thankfully, Palm Desktop makes importing all those contacts possible with a minimum of fuss. All you need is a contact manager capable of saving its data in either a comma-separated (CSV) or a tab-separated (TSV) format. To import your data from another program, do the following:

1. In your old contact manager, find the menu option to export your data in either CSV or TSV format. If the program gives you an option to remap your data as it's saved, don't worry. We'll map it properly as it's imported into Palm Desktop. Save the exported data to a file on your hard disk. (Make a note of where you save this file because you need to find it again in about two steps.)

2. In Palm Desktop, choose File | Import. The Import dialog box should appear.

3. Select the file you just created with the old contact manager. You might have to choose the proper file extension (like CSV or TSV) from the Type of File list box to see the file you created. Choose Open.

4. Now you see a Specify Import Fields dialog box, as shown in Figure 6-5. This is the hardest part of the process and the one step that isn't terribly automated. Here's the deal: the data in a typical contact entry includes items like name, phone numbers, and address. But those fields won't be in the same order in any two contact management programs, so you need to help Palm Desktop put the old data in the right fields as it imports. To map the fields properly, drag each field on the left (which is Palm Desktop) until it's lined up with the proper field on the right (which represents the old program). Line up last name with last name, for instance, and match phone numbers, e-mail addresses, and any other important fields. If you don't want to import a certain field, deselect its check box.

TIP   *You can use the arrows to cycle forward through the database and make sure you assigned the fields properly.*

5. When you finish lining up the fields, click the OK button.

FIGURE 6-5   Carefully rearrange the fields in the Specify Import Fields dialog box, so your old data is imported properly into Palm Desktop.

If you did everything right, you should see your contacts in Palm Desktop. Any newly imported entries are highlighted. If you messed something up, all isn't lost. Simply delete all your records, and then try to import your contacts file again.

Using Outlook

As we mentioned in Chapter 5, Outlook is a perfectly good alternative to Palm Desktop. To see your contacts in Outlook, start by clicking the Contacts icon in the Outlook Shortcut bar. Outlook should switch to the Contacts view, where you'll see a complete list of your names and addresses.

You can view your contacts in many ways. That's good, because if you're anything like us, you have hundreds of entries—and sorting through them can be like finding a virtual needle in a digital haystack. To see your options, click the Organize button in the Outlook toolbar. The Organize pane should open. Click Using Views and you can experiment with arranging your contacts by category, by company, or nearly any other way imaginable.

To find a contact quickly from any view in Outlook, type the person's name in the Find A Contact field on the Outlook toolbar and press ENTER. Outlook displays a list of names that matches your criteria or, if only one name appears, displays its entry.

Address Book Alternatives and Enhancements

Don't think you have to stick with the Address Book just because it came with your trusty old Palm. Personally, we prefer the Clié's Address Book to most of the alternatives, but here are a few you might want to look into if you feel like expanding your contact management horizons:

- **Agendus** This Address Book replacement combines the To Do List, Date Book, and Address Book to deliver a single, integrated interface for tracking, alarming, and viewing your daily itinerary. This program has lots of die-hard fans because of its many powerful features for managing contacts. You can try it out at **www.iambic.com**.

- **KeySuite** This program from Chapura could well be the answer to every power user's dreams. While the ordinary Address Book doesn't synchronize many of Outlook's fields, *KeySuite* is a replacement that transfers absolutely everything—including all those extra fields in the other Outlook Contact tabs and all the categories as well. Visit **www.chapura.com**.

- **Contacts 4** This Address Book alternative provides all sorts of cool features, like advanced search functions, "skins" that let you customize the program's appearance, phone dialing via Bluetooth and infrared, and more. Find it at the web site **www.pdaperformance.com**.

- **PopUp Names** This Hack (see Chapter 14 for details on Hacks) pops the Address Book onto the screen with a simple stroke of the stylus, and puts it away when you're done. This lets you keep the application you were using open, so you don't lose your place or have to hunt around to get back to what you were doing. You can find it at **www.benc.hr**.

Chapter 7

The To Do List

How to...

- View To Do List entries
- Create new To Dos
- Create a To Do based on an Address Book entry
- Prioritize your To Dos
- Add notes to your To Dos
- Edit To Dos from the List view
- Customize the To Do List view
- Beam To Dos to others
- Use Palm Desktop for Windows
- Export To Dos to Word and Excel
- Using Outlook with the Clié

The To Do List is admittedly one of the smallest of the core applications, but don't let that fool you. There's a lot of convenience under the hood. What good is this little program? Well, think of it this way: would you be more organized if you carried a list of things you needed to do—big and small—with you all the time? Finish a task and cross it off the list for a sense of immediate gratification. Or, think of something you need to do while you're away from the office and add it immediately to your Clié, knowing the entry will be added to your PC's master To Do List as soon as you HotSync. The To Do List is a way to take charge of all the little things that make up your daily agenda.

Viewing the To Do List

As with most of the core applications in your Clié, you can start the To Do List by pressing its button (it's the one that looks like three "checklist" lines) or by tapping its icon on the Application screen.

As you can see in Figure 7-1, the Clié lists your To Dos in a fairly straightforward list that you can use to see what tasks you have coming up or, in some cases that are past due (you might want to take care of those pretty soon, by the way). A standard Clié screen has room for 11 entries at one time (more, as in Figure 7-1, if you have a HiRes+ Clié); the rest appear "off the screen," and you can scroll to them. Getting around is easy. Simply scroll down to see more names, either with the onscreen scroll arrows or the Scroll buttons on the case.

FIGURE 7-1 The To Do List displays all your pending tasks.

Each time you scroll, the Clié moves the list by one complete page. This means if you scroll down, the bottom entry on the page becomes the top entry after scrolling.

Another way to get around is by using the categories. If your tasks are divided into more than one category, every time you press the To Do button, you switch categories. You can cycle through the first page of tasks in each category by repeatedly pressing this button. Our favorite way of getting around is by rolling the scroll wheel on the side of the Clié (if yours has one).

Creating a To Do

To add a To Do to your Clié, just start writing in the Graffiti area. The text appears automatically in a brand new To Do entry.

If you want to create a task with a specific priority, tap on a To Do entry that has the priority you want, and then tap New. The new To Do takes the priority of the previously selected task, saving you the trouble of choosing a priority later.

 The Agenda Shows To Do Items

You can view your To Do items in the Date Book. The Agenda view lets you see all of today's appointments and upcoming To Dos at a glance, all on the same screen. See Chapter 5.

Friends Are a Chore

It's true! Having friends and coworkers can be actual work. Suppose you need to meet with Ed Grimpley from accounting sometime this week to talk about why you've gone through 18 mouse pads in the space of a month. You don't have an appointment in your calendar; you'd rather pop in sometime when it's convenient. The To Do List is your answer. Create a new To Do and choose Options | Phone Lookup from the menu. Find Ed in the Phone Number Lookup dialog box and tap Add. What you get is Ed's name and phone number in the To Do entry. It's a handy way to remind yourself to call someone without setting up a rigid appointment in the Date Book.

While most tasks can be summarized in only one line of text, there's no reasonable limit to how long you can make a To Do entry. If you need more than one line of text to describe your task, you can use the Enter gesture to get the Clié to display a new blank line in the same To Do. Remember, though, creating multiline To Dos might make it hard for you to read your tasks later, as you can see here:

Instead of making long, multiline tasks, we recommend you add a note to your task instead, as discussed in the next section.

Adding Some Details

Once you finish entering the name of the task, tap elsewhere on the screen to save the entry. If you prefer, you can add additional information, like a priority, category, and due date. You don't have to enter any of these special settings, but using them enables you to track your tasks with greater accuracy. Here's what you need to do:

1. Select the task you want to edit by tapping the name of the To Do.
2. Tap the Details button.

3. Tap a number to represent the priority of your task. You can select any number from one to five (the lower the number, the higher the priority).

4. Choose a category from the Category list.

5. Choose a due date from the Due Date list. You can choose to make a task due today, tomorrow, or in a week, or you can choose a date directly from the Calendar dialog box.

6. Tap OK to save your changes to the task.

> **TIP** *While you can make a task almost any length, most people find it's better to keep the To Do short and add a note. To add a note to a To Do, select your To Do, tap the Details button, and then tap Note.*

Working with the List View

When you switch to the To Do List, all your existing tasks are arranged onscreen, usually in order of importance (as determined by the priority number assigned to each To Do). As you can see in Figure 7-2, six elements, which are discussed next, are associated with each task.

- **Check box** If you complete a task, you can indicate it's done by tapping the check box. That places a check mark in the task. Depending on how you configured the To Do Preferences, the entry either disappears or remains onscreen but, nevertheless, it's marked as done.

- **Priority** Not everything is the most important thing on your task list. If you want to arrange your tasks by importance or urgency, use the priority numbers—1 through 5. Tap the number to get a list of all the priority choices.

> **TIP** *We recommend you use priority numbers for your tasks—they help you sort through the clutter of your various To Dos and determine what's important from one day to the next.*

- **To Do description** You can edit the description of the task by tapping in this field and editing the existing text.

FIGURE 7-2   The To Do List lets you modify your tasks without tapping the Details button.

- **Note icon**   If you already created a note for the task, you can read the note or edit it by tapping the icon to the right of the To Do name field. If no note already exists, you can add one by selecting the task and choosing Record | Attach Note from the menu.

- **Due date**   You might have tasks that need to be accomplished by a specific date. If this is the case, use the final column. If a dash is in that slot, this means you haven't yet assigned a due date. Tap it and choose a date. You can also change the due date in the same way.

- **Category**   Change the category to which a task is assigned by tapping the category column and choosing the desired category from the list.

NOTE   *Some of these columns aren't displayed by default—to enable them, tap the Show button and choose the columns you want to appear in the To Do Preferences dialog box.*

Changing the View Options

If you're anything like us (and if you are, well, our condolences), you could be perfectly happy with the default look of the To Do List. It's easy to modify, though. Tap the Show button and you see the To Do Preferences dialog box. Here are your options:

To Do or Appointment?

We know what you're thinking—if you can assign due dates to items in the To Do List, why bother with appointments? Or, from the other perspective, why use To Dos if you have the Date Book? That's a good question. We use the To Do List whenever we have tasks that need doing by a certain date—but not at a certain time of day. If it requires a time slot, we put it in the Date Book. So, stuff like "buy lemons" or "finish Chapter 20" (hint, hint, Rick…) are To Dos. "Meet with Laura for lunch at 11:30" is a Date Book entry. There's also the matter of alarms: your Clié has an alarm for appointments, but not for To Dos. If that bothers you, consider trying an alternative like DateBk 5 (**www.datebk5.com**) or Agendus (**www.iambic.com**), two programs that let you alarm To Dos as well as appointments. Here, you can see DateBk5 with the split To Do and Calendar screen—and the top To Do is alarmed.

7

Sorting Options

The first item you encounter in the Preferences dialog box is a Sort By list. This determines the way the To Do List shows the tasks onscreen. The four options are shown next:

- **Priority, Due Date**   This groups all the Priority 1 tasks first, followed by Priority 2, and so on. Within each priority group, the earliest deadlines are listed first, while tasks with no deadlines are listed last. This option works best if you need to work on tasks with the highest priority and due dates aren't particularly important to you.

- **Due Date, Priority**   This selection arranges all the tasks by due date, with the soonest due dates listed first and those tasks with no due dates listed last. If several tasks have the same due date, they're listed by priority order. This is probably the best display option for most people. Tasks due soonest are listed at the top of the page and, within each group of due dates, top priorities are arranged first.

- **Category, Priority** Arranges your tasks by category, with categories arranged in alphabetical order. If you have more than one task in a given category, they're arranged by priority order within the category. Use this category if seeing tasks visually arranged into different categories—like work and personal—is more important to you than arranging them by due date or category.

- **Category, Due Date** This selection also arranges your tasks by category, where the categories are arranged in alphabetical order. If you have more than one task in a given category, they're arranged by due date within the category. Tasks with the nearest deadlines appear first, while those with no due date are listed last in each category.

Using Filters to Customize the Display

The next section in the To Do Preferences dialog box controls what kind of tasks are displayed onscreen. Actually, that's not true, but we're trying to apply some logic to the way Clié chooses to group the items on this screen. Here's what each of these three items does:

- **Show Completed Items** As you check off tasks you complete, slowly, but surely, they clutter up your screen unless you do something about them. If you uncheck this option, completed items are hidden. If you need to see items you've completed, simply check Show Completed Items and they reappear.

NOTE *If you hide completed tasks in this way, they're not deleted. They still take up memory on the Clié. To find out how to get rid of them for good, see the section "Deleting Old To Dos."*

- **Show Only Due Items** If you're only concerned about tasks due today, check this item. Any tasks with a due date after today disappear from the screen and only reappear on the day they're due.

CAUTION *Be careful with this option because it hides To Dos from the screen that aren't due today, regardless of priority. It's easy to get caught off guard by a major deadline this way.*

- **Record Completion Date** This interesting little feature changes the due date of a completed item to the date it was completed. If you didn't assign a due date to a task, the completion date becomes the due date. In this way, you can track what day you completed each of your tasks.

CAUTION *This option overwrites the due date with the completion date. You can't get the original due date back even if you uncheck the task or turn off the Record Completion Date option.*

Modifying the Task Columns

As you probably already saw, you can tweak the data the To Do List shows you for each task in the list. That tweaking occurs here, in the last three options of the To Do Preferences dialog box. Your To Do List can look sparse, highly decorated, or anything in between by changing the Show options, as shown in the following illustration.

- **Show Due Dates**   The due date format is day/month, which takes some getting used to. If you don't assign a due date to a task, you see a dash instead. On the To Do List, if you tap a due date, you see a list for changing the date.

- **Show Priorities**   This displays the priority to the left of the To Do name. The priority can be adjusted by tapping the number on the To Do List view.

- **Show Categories**   The category of the task appears on the right edge of the To Do List view if you use this option. You can assign a category to an unfiled To Do (or change the category of a previously filed entry) by tapping the category name on the To Do List view.

Deleting Old To Dos

For most people, To Dos are not like diamonds—they don't last forever. After you check off a task that says "pick up a loaf of bread," how long do you need a record of having accomplished that goal? That's why your Clié provides a method of removing tasks you no longer want. You can eliminate tasks in two ways:

- **Delete them one at a time**   If you need to delete only one To Do, tap the To Do to select it. Now choose Record | Delete Item from the menu and the To Do is gone forever.

- **Delete a whole bunch at once**   If you use the To Do List a lot and develop a back list of hundreds of completed tasks, axing them one at a time could become a full-time job. Instead, purge them. A *purge* deletes all completed tasks, so be sure you want to do this. To purge your To Do List, choose Record | Purge from the menu. The Purge dialog box appears, asking if you really want to delete your completed To Dos. Tap OK.

TIP   *If you want to preserve a copy of your completed tasks, check Save Archive Copy on PC, and then load the archive into Palm Desktop when you need to refer to the entries.*

What Sony Does Best

Dave: The optimist in me says that what Sony does best is release absolutely stunning hardware that pushes forward people's understanding of what a handheld can be and do. They constantly test the boundaries and create cool PDAs with clever features—like universal remote control software, digital cameras, music players, and super-hi-res screens. For me, looking at a new Clié is always like being in a hi-tech candy store. But the pessimist in me says that what Sony does best is tease us with a constant parade of new devices, each one just slightly better than the one before. These days, I'm scared to buy a new PDA—like the superb NX80V—to replace my NX70V because Sony might enhanced the NX80V with Bluetooth or a foot massager in two months and call it the NX85. Sony never lets me come up for air and simply be happy with what I have. They release too many PDAs, too soon, with too similar features. It's driving me nuts! Are they crazy, or just insane?

    Rick: Nuts, crazy, and insane—words that describe you to a tee, my friend. Yes, Sony has gotten a little out of control with the new-model-of-the-month approach, but it's nice to see so much innovation. You're just a victim of stuff-lust—you gotta have the latest and greatest everything all the time. Repeat after me: "I will be *happy* with what I have. I don't *need* more RAM. Bluetooth is *useless*!" Actually, as a self-respecting gadget freak, I do have to admit that Sony has fallen just shy of creating the perfect PDA. There's one model that's close, but it's too big and expensive. Cheaper models are missing just a few key features. But someday, my prince—er, PDA—will come.

Sharing Your To Dos

Delegation is the key to successful management. At least that's what we've been told. We don't actually supervise anyone, but it sounds like solid business advice, nonetheless. You can use your Clié as a solid delegation tool by beaming tasks to other people. Just like in other applications, you can beam a single item or all the items in a specific category. Here's the skinny:

- **Beam a single To Do** To beam one To Do to someone, choose a task by tapping inside the To Do name. Then choose Record | Beam Item from the menu.
- **Beam a whole bunch of items** You can beam an entire category's worth of To Dos at once. To do this, switch the current view to show the category you want to beam. You can choose a category from the list at the top right of the screen or press the hard To Do button several times until the category you want appears. Then choose Record | Beam Category from the menu.

Working with Palm Desktop

Who says the only place you can enter To Dos is on your Palm? Not us! Palm Desktop has a module dedicated to tracking your tasks. Using Palm Desktop, you can enter To Dos and have them appear on your Clié when you're away from your desk.

The Windows To Do List

The To Do List's interface is a bit more spacious than the one in your Clié. As a result, Palm Desktop pulls off a cool trick—it displays both the list itself and the contents of the Details dialog box onscreen simultaneously, as you can see in Figure 7-3. Click a To Do and the details on the right automatically update to show you more information about the particular task you selected.

Turn To Dos into Appointments

Your Clié understands there's a tight relationship between your calendar and your tasks. Switch to the Date Book in Palm Desktop shown in Figure 7-4, and you'll find the right side of the screen has a window for displaying either addresses or To Dos. Click the To Do box to show To Dos; click

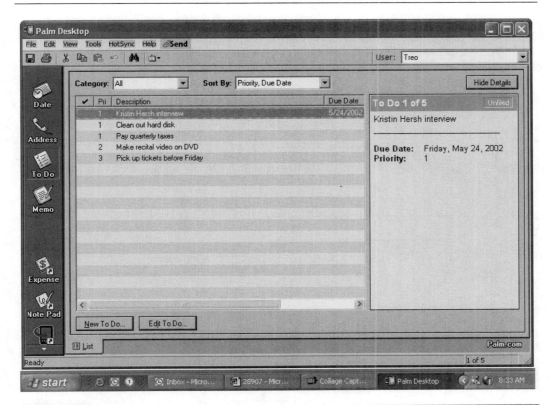

FIGURE 7-3   You can see the details on any To Do by clicking the appropriate description on the left side of the screen.

How to ...   Create Tasks on Your Handheld

We've talked a lot about To Dos, so here's a summary of how to create tasks on your Clié:

1. Press the To Do button on the Palm.

2. Start writing in the Graffiti area—this creates a new To Do.

3. Tap the Details button.

If you want to, assign a priority, category, and due date on the Details dialog box. Tap OK to close this dialog box.

Address to see your contacts. What good is it? Well, you can grab a To Do and drag-and-drop it into a calendar appointment. That lets you turn a task into a bona fide appointment. Unfortunately, you can't go the other way and turn an appointment into a task.

Creating and Editing To Dos

To create a new To Do, just click the New To Do button at the bottom of the screen. You'll see the New To Do dialog box, where you can enter text, assign priorities, and even set a due date for your task.

Using Outlook

If you're an Outlook user, you probably already know that Palm's To Do items become Tasks in Outlook. In fact, that's pretty much all you need to know to use Outlook with your Clié. To see your To Dos in Outlook, click the Tasks icon in the Outlook Shortcuts bar. The tasks are also displayed in the Taskbar section of the Calendar. But, remember, To Do categories and certain fields don't make the trip from Outlook to the Clié—stuff like % Complete, Status, and Owner aren't supported by the Palm OS.

> **TIP** *When you mark a task as completed in Outlook, it isn't deleted. To reduce clutter and save disk space, you might want to delete tasks occasionally. To do this, right-click a completed task and choose Delete from the menu.*

Understanding Task Priorities

The Clié and Outlook use two slightly different ways of assigning priority to tasks and To Dos. Thankfully, the two systems work together and are easy to figure out. Use this guide to correlate the Clié and Outlook systems:

Palm	Outlook
1	High
2	Normal
3	Normal
4	Normal
5	Low

7

Chapter 8 The Memo Pad

How to...

- View the Memo List
- Create new memos
- Cut, copy, and paste text in a memo
- Assign categories to memos
- Customize the appearance of memos in the Memo List
- Beam memos
- Make memos private
- Delete old memos
- Import text files into Windows memos
- Use memos in other Windows applications
- Use Outlook with the Clié

As you've already seen, applications like the Date Book, Address Book, and To Do List let you attach long notes to your entries. A note in the Address Book, for instance, enables you to list directions to the person's house, the names of all their kids, or ten reasons not to visit them for Thanksgiving. But there's also an application designed to do nothing but create notes. These memos can be memory joggers, information you need to take on a trip, or anything not explicitly connected to an address, an appointment, or a to-do. The Memo Pad is your chance, in a sense, to color outside the lines and leave yourself any kind of message you want.

Viewing the Memo Pad

The Memo Pad has two views—the *Memo List* (which is, not surprisingly, a list of all the memos you created) and the *Memo View*, which shows you the contents of whatever memo you select from the Memo List. When you start the Memo Pad, it always starts in the Memo List View. As you can see in Figure 8-1, the Clié displays each of your memos in a list, with the first line of the memo visible as a kind of title that lets you know what's inside. Getting around is easy—just scroll up or down to see more memos.

 Another way to get around the Memo List is by using the categories. If your memos are divided into more than one category, every time you tap the Memo Pad button, you switch categories. You can cycle through the first page of tasks in each category by repeatedly tapping this button.

Creating New Memos

You've probably noticed the New button at the bottom of the Memo List—but you don't need to use it to create new memos. Instead, start writing in the Graffiti area (or tapping on the keyboard) and the Clié automatically switches from the Memo List View to the Memo View.

Do Cool Things with the Memo Pad

Do you know what surprises us? Lots of things, actually. Dave is surprised Rick has no appreciation for the fine arts—specifically, bands like Pink Floyd, the Velvet Underground, Kristin Hersh, and the Throwing Muses.

More to the point, we're surprised at how many people can't seem to come up with good uses for the Memo Pad. They let it languish while they use the Address Book and Date Book all the time. To help you fully realize the potential of this cool little application, here are some helpful suggestions for how to use the Memo Pad:

- **A "Million Dollar Idea" memo**   Create a memo with a header that says **Million Dollar Ideas**. No matter when or where you come up with one of those incredibly amazing ideas to help you retire before you turn 50, pull out your Clié and jot it down.

- **Trade show category**   Got a lot of booths to visit at next month's lawn care trade show? Create a category and put all the memos for that event in the category. As you walk the show floor, you can reference your notes about the show in one easy-to-find set of memos.

- **Store passwords**   This one is dangerous, so make sure you keep it private. But, if you have a lot of passwords you routinely need—for your ISP, web sites, computer logons, and that kind of thing, you can store them all in one place in a memo for passwords. Note, we have to reiterate the danger in this—if your Clié is stolen, you could give all your passwords away if they're not protected properly. No IT department on Earth would sanction this particular tip, and we won't even admit to writing it down if questioned in court.

- **Meeting notes**   Take notes during a meeting and beam the memo to others when the meeting is over.

- **A "Phone Messages" memo**   Name a memo Phone Messages and when you check voice mail, jot down notes in your Clié using this memo. If you're diligent about it, you won't end up with a million yellow stickies all over your desk after each VM-checking session. Plus, names and phone numbers will be in your Clié where you need them, not splayed all over your desk.

- **Store your new words**   Dave makes up new words in an effort to evolve the English language at a grass roots level. If you, too, make up new words frequently (and that's a beautiquious thing to do), store them in a **New Words** memo so you don't accidentally forget them. Chizzy! (Rick is working on a way to delete that particular memo from Dave's Clié, perhaps by using a large hammer.)

8

FIGURE 8-1   The Memo List (on the left) displays all your memos. Tap on one to see the Memo View (on the right).

The memo can be as long as you want—up to 4,096 characters, or about 700 words. That's pretty long and it should suit your needs most of the time. You can include blank lines and divide your memo into paragraphs—anything you need to make it logical and readable.

TIP   *You can't name your memos in the sense that you can save files on the PC with a specific filename, but the first line of the memo is what appears in the Memo List. To keep things neat and organized, you can write a brief description of the memo on the top line, and then start the memo itself on the next line.*

Using Editing Tools

The familiar cut, copy, and paste tools are available in every Clié application, but nowhere are they more important than in the Memo Pad, where you're likely to be writing more than a sentence or two. Remember, you don't have to create text from scratch all the time. Using these edit tools, you can move text from other applications and rearrange it to suit your needs.

Suppose, for example, you previously had a Date Book appointment that read:

```
Meeting with Ted
```

Within that appointment, you might have created a note that looked like this:

```
Discuss performance review
Get feedback on budget for 2Q
Agree on approach for marketing plan
```

If you want to have a record of your meeting with Ted, take notes in a memo. Open the appointment note and select the three lines of text from the note. With the text selected, choose

Edit | Copy from the menu (or use the Command gesture and write *C*). Then switch to the Memo Pad, create a new memo, and paste the text into the memo using Edit | Paste (or COMMAND-P using the Graffiti shortcut).

After pasting the text into the memo, you can use it as your agenda items—and insert notes as needed, giving you a complete record of the meeting. When you HotSync your Clié, you can then paste that data into Word or some other application and generate a formal report.

Assigning Categories

After you accumulate a few memos, you might find the Memo List View getting a bit crowded. Clean it up with the Clié's ever-helpful category filing system. You can assign a category by doing the following:

1. Create a new memo.

2. Tap the Details button. The Memo Details dialog box appears.

3. Choose a category from the Category list.

4. Tap OK to close the Memo Details dialog box.

After your memos are arranged into categories, you can cycle through them easily by pressing the Memo Pad hard button on the Clié case.

Memo Pad Assistants

Many tools can enhance the experience of creating long notes in the Memo Pad. Here are a few examples you might want to try.

A pair of programs—*TextPlus* and *WordComplete*—can suggest common words as you write, even before a word is complete. By offering likely options for what you might be writing, either of these applications can significantly reduce the time you spend creating text in the Memo Pad. You can find both of these programs at **PalmGear.com**.

Peering Into Madness: Dave's and Rick's Memos

Dave: I have a Memo Pad category called Lists. In this category, I have a bunch of memos I refer to all the time. I have a list of movies—whenever I think of a film I want to rent, I add it to the list. Then, when I go to **Netflix.com**, I can add it to my queue. I also have a Songs memo where I can jot down the names of songs I hear on the radio that I might want to download from an MP3 service. I have a list called meals—things I'd like to eat—that I can refer to when I go grocery shopping and get the appropriate ingredients. Finally, I have a Top 10 list. When I think of a funny Top 10 topic—like "Restaurants you won't want to eat at" or "Reasons to own a Clié"—I jot it down, so I have something funny to start a speaking engagement.

   Rick: If Dave ever starts reading one of his "funny" Top 10 lists in your presence, turn and run the other way as fast as you can. Unless you're really good at polite laughter. Anyway, I compile similar lists of books I want to read, movies I want to rent, and wines my wife and I have tried and liked. I also use memos to jot down business ideas, and any other brainstorms I don't want to forget. Memos are also ideal for jotting down room measurements before you head off to Home Depot and realize you forgot to bring room measurements.

Arranging Memos in the Memo List

Computer users are, for the most part, fanatical organizers. We tend to spend hours straightening up the Desktop so icons appear in exactly the right place when the computer starts each morning. That said, we're sure you want to organize your memos. This isn't pointless busy work: if you need to open the same memo over and over, having the memo appear at the top of the list whenever you open the Memo List can help. At the very least, we're sure you'll want to understand how to take control of the way memos appear onscreen.

   When you add memos to the Memo List, by default, the newest ones always appear at the end of the list. The default order of Memo List entries is essentially chronological, with the oldest entries at the top and the newest ones at the bottom.

   It's a little more complicated than that, though. You can specify the sort order of memos by choosing Options | Preferences. You get two choices:

■ **Manual**   This is the default mode your Clié uses out of the box. New memos are added to the bottom of the list, but you can drag-and-drop memos to different positions in the list. Suppose you have a frequently used memo that you want to appear at the top of the screen. Tap and hold the stylus on the entry, and then drag the stylus up to the position where you want it to appear. You should see a line move with the stylus, indicating where the memo will land if you release the stylus.

■ **Alphabetic**   This option sorts all entries into alphabetical order. If you select this option, the drag-and-drop method of moving memos won't work unless you revert to the manual method.

Working with Your Memos

You have the same 4,096-character limit on writing memos as you have with notes in other parts of the Clié suite of applications. That's plenty of space to write, as long as you're not trying to draft

Use Blank Lines for Emphasis

Here's a trick you can try if you think the Memo List is too cluttered. If you use the manual ordering method and arrange your memos in a specific order in a near-fanatical way, you might be bothered by the fact that memo number 4 is "touching" memo number 5. Rick, for instance, is adamant about not eating his mashed potatoes if they come in contact with his peas. Maybe you suffer from the same kind of problem with your Clié.

Try this: Create a new memo with a blank first line. You have to enter at least one character on the second line, because the Clié doesn't let you create a completely blank memo. Close the memo and you'll see you've made a new memo with a blank header. Drag this memo between two memos you want separated and voilà—you've found a way to separate memos.

8

your autobiography (if you are trying to create an extremely long document, see Chapter 12 for details on applications that let you do that).

Beaming Memos

You can send a memo or a group of memos to another Clié owner just as easily as beaming any other kind of information. Here's how:

- ■ **Beam one memo** To beam a memo, you need to tap on the memo you want to beam—this displays the memo in the Memo View. Then choose Record | Beam from the menu. That's all there is to it.

- ■ **Beam a bunch of memos** To beam more than one memo, they all must be in the same category. Make sure you're in the Memo List View and switch to the category you want to beam. You can do this by choosing the category from the list at the top right of the screen or by pressing the Memo List hard button on the Clié case until you see the category you want. Then choose Record | Beam Category from the menu.

Making a Memo Private

If you have private information stored in a memo, you can easily hide specific memos from prying eyes. The procedure is essentially the same as with other Clié applications. To do this:

1. In the Memo List, select a memo by tapping it.

2. Tap the Details button. The To Memo Details dialog box appears.

3. Tap the Private box to add a check mark. Now the entry is marked as private. Tap OK and you see this dialog box:

4. Tap OK to close the dialog box.

If the memo isn't hidden yet, there's one more step you can take. To make it disappear entirely, you need to enable the Private Records feature in the Security application. For details on how to do this, see Chapter 9.

Create New Memos

Working with the Memo Pad is a snap. In summary, here's what you need to do to create memos:

1. Press the Memo Pad button on your Clié.
2. Start writing in the Graffiti area to create a new memo.
3. Tap the Details button and assign your new memo to a specific category.
4. Tap the Done button to close your new memo.
5. Drag the memo to put it in a specific place in the Memo List.

Deleting Memos

No matter how much you like your memos, eventually you might need to delete some. To delete a memo, tap the memo you want to delete. Then choose Record | Delete Memo from the menu. The memo is then deleted from your Clié. If you prefer, you can save a backup of this memo to Palm Desktop by choosing Save Archive Copy On PC.

Working in Palm Desktop

You can create and review your notes and memos on Palm Desktop. That's good, because many kinds of memos might come in handy on the desktop. For instance, if you took our earlier advice about creating a Phone Messages memo, you'll appreciate the capability to type directly into the PC when the phone rings.

The Windows Memo Pad

Because the Clié has pretty limited real estate on the small screen, you have to switch between the Memo List and Memo View. But, on Palm Desktop, you can see both at once. To see a memo, click the header on the left, and the memo's contents appear in the window on the right. It should look like Figure 8-2. Double-clicking a memo header has no effect.

Most of the Memo Pad's operation is obvious. The controls aren't identical, though. Here are some things to remember:

- You can't rearrange memos, but you can sort them alphabetically or by how they appear on the Clié. Use the Sort By drop-down menu at the top of the screen.

- You can display memos in a list or through icons (like Outlook's Notes) using the tabs at the bottom of the screen.

8

FIGURE 8-2 On the desktop, Palm Desktop memos look a lot like memos in Outlook—except that Palm Desktop adds a convenient text window on the right.

Importing and Exporting Memos

You needn't create memos from scratch. Heck, you don't even have to cut-and-paste to create a memo. Palm Desktop lets you import text files from elsewhere on the computer. To import a text file, do the following:

1. Choose File | Import. The Import dialog box appears.

2. Choose Text (*.txt) from the File Of Type list box.

3. Find the file you want to import. It has to be a plain text file in ASCII format—no Word or other specially formatted file types are allowed. Select the file and click the Open button. You then see the Specify Import Fields dialog box.

4. The text file should be ready to import, with the text lined up with the Memo field. If it isn't, drag the Memo field on the left until it lines up like the one shown here:

5. Click OK.

6. If your text file is too large to fit in a single memo, the Palm Desktop automatically divides it into multiple memos.

7. Click OK.

What about the other case, where you have a memo that you'd like to get into Microsoft Word? Piece of cake! Just right-click a memo and choose Send To | MS Word from the menu. The text will automatically appear in a new blank document in Word.

Using Outlook with the Clié

Outlook's *Notes View* is, like the Clié's Memo Pad, a place to store free-form notes of any kind. You can use it to record phone messages, jot down reminders, leave long-term documents (like things to bring on a trip), or remind yourself about web sites you want to visit. It doesn't matter what you put in these notes. By default, Outlook's notes look like little Post-It notes. You can change their appearance in two ways:

1. To change the color of a single note, right-click it and choose Color from the menu. You can choose from five colors to make certain notes stand out visually.

2. To change the default color and size of all notes, choose Tools | Options from the Outlook menu and click the Preferences tab. Click the Note Options button and set your preferences. Click OK to close the dialog boxes. All new notes you create appear with these settings.

Look Ma, No Scroll Bar!

Outlook's notes have an annoying glitch—lacking scroll bars, it's hard to read a long note that trails off the bottom of the sticky note window. Don't know what we're talking about? Copy a long Word document into a new note. Or create a really long Clié memo and HotSync. You'll find the text extends beyond the bottom of the note window in Outlook and there's no scroll bar to get at the rest of it.

The solution is deceptively simple: click in the note window to place the cursor in the note, and then use the down arrow key on the keyboard to scroll through the document.

Why do we mention this? Rick didn't realize there was any way to scroll through the document at all—he thought anything that didn't fit in the sticky note window was totally inaccessible—until Dave showed him the keyboard arrow trick. So, if you were ever perplexed by the missing memo text, now you're at least as smart as Rick (fill in your own jokes here).

Quirks Between Outlook and Clié

While the Outlook Notes View and Clié Memo Pad are perhaps the simplest of all the features in these two programs, you should know a few things to ensure everything works smoothly when you HotSync:

- The Clié Memo Pad has a size limit—but Notes in Outlook don't. This means you can create a very long note in Outlook that doesn't transfer properly to the Clié. If you create a huge note in Outlook, only the first 4,096 characters appear in the Clié Memo Pad. You'll also see a warning saying this occurred in the HotSync log.

- The Clié's categories aren't used by Outlook. This means your Clié memos, when they appear in Outlook as notes, are unfiled. The same is true in the other direction.

A Memo Pad Alternative

Is the Memo Pad not powerful enough for you? Then flip over to Chapter 12, where we introduce you to a few powerful word-processing alternatives to the Memo Pad, such as Documents To Go and WordSmith. Or, there's a program called *Memo PLUS* (a good substitute for Memo Pad), which enables you to attach drawings to your memos, use templates, and more. You can find Memo PLUS on the Web at **www.handshigh.com**.

Chapter 9

The Rest of the Palm OS Team

How to...

- Access security features
- Set records as private
- Hide or show private records
- Set a security password
- Password-protect your Clié
- Find third-party security measures for your Clié and data
- Use the Find feature
- Find third-party utilities that extend your search capabilities
- Use the calculator
- Find third-party calculators
- Get started with Clié Mail
- Identify the rest of the Clié's bundled software

Now that we've looked at the stars of the Palm OS—the Address Book, Date Book, Memo Pad, and To Do List—let's turn our attention to the supporting cast. We're talking about the Security program, which enables you to hide private records and "lock" your Clié; the Find feature, a search tool that helps you quickly sift through all your data; the calculator, which, big surprise, calculates; and the potentially mystifying Clié Mail program, which is used to send and receive e-mail—sort of.

NOTE   *We designed this chapter as a kind of catch-all, a place to cover programs that don't really fit into specific categories or require their own chapters. That said, there might be programs bundled with your Clié that aren't covered here—or anywhere else in the book. That's because Sony keeps changing its bundle, and it's impossible to cover everything. We do, however, cover the important extras that are common to all models—and Security is foremost on the list.*

Clié Security

At the risk of sounding like a spy novel, listen up, 007. If your data falls into the wrong hands, it could spell disaster for *M, Q,* and lots of other letters of the alphabet. Fortunately, we've outfitted your Clié with foolproof security measures. Only you will have the access codes. Only you can view Heather Graham's phone number. (Can we have it? Please? Please?)

In all seriousness, it's not unlikely that you'll be storing some sensitive information in your Clié, information that should be kept private. Important passwords, account numbers, meeting locations, contact data—these are among the items you'd be loathe to let a stranger see. Fortunately, the Palm OS offers two effective ways to protect your data: marking individual records as private, and locking your Clié every time you turn it off.

In both scenarios, you—or anyone who's trying to access your Clié—must supply a password to gain access. It's a bit of a hassle to have to enter it over and over again, but at least you have the comfort of knowing your Clié and your data are totally secure.

> **TIP** *While you might want to familiarize yourself with the Palm OS's built-in security capabilities, we prefer some of the third-party solutions you can download and install. See "Other Security Software" later in this chapter for the scoop on those appealing alternatives.*

Security 101

To get started with Clié security, find and tap the Security icon. You'll see the screen shown in Figure 9-1. The first step is choosing a password. Notice that the Password box currently says "Unassigned"—meaning simply that you haven't entered your password yet. Before you do, read a little further.

What You Should Know about Passwords

The password you choose can be any combination of letters, numbers, symbols, and spaces. You can make it "Spock" or "H4T*Q" or "The quick brown fox." Ideally, it should be something reasonably short, as you'll probably wind up writing it frequently. Don't make it too obvious, like "123," but you could use something as simple as the last four digits of your Social Security number or your spouse's initials. Of course, the best password you can choose is something totally random, something no one would be able to figure out.

> **NOTE** *Capitalization doesn't matter. Even if you make a point to capitalize "Spock" when you enter it as your new password, you can write "spock" to unlock your Clié and it'll work just fine.*

FIGURE 9-1   In Security, you select a password for use in hiding private records and locking your Clié.

Whatever password you decide on, it's vital that it be something you can easily remember. If you forget it, you could wind up unable to access certain records—or your entire Clié! Thus, if you have even the slightest concern that you might forget your password, write it down on a piece of paper and store it in a safe place. Better safe than sorry.

Working with Passwords

Okay, let's enter a new password on your Clié. Just tap the "-Unassigned-" box, and then use Graffiti or the onscreen keyboard to enter your desired password.

NOTE *At this time you're also asked to supply a hint. If you use, say, your mother's maiden name as your password, you should put "mother's maiden name" in the hint field. This hint appears when an incorrect password is entered.*

Note the warning that's included here: "If you assign a password, you must enter it to show private records." This sounds a little scary, but don't worry—none of your existing records will immediately be affected by your selection of a password. Only when you mark one as private, as we explain later, does your password enter into play.

After you tap OK, you'll be asked to verify the new password by entering it again. And you'll see another warning about what'll happen if your password is forgotten. The moral of the story is, *don't forget your password!*

Tap OK again, and notice that the Password box now reads "-Assigned-".

TIP *You can tap this box again at any time to change or delete your password, but you have to supply the original one first.*

Now, when you mark records as private, they become hidden from view, requiring your password to reveal them. Additionally, if you use the "Lock & Turn Off…" option (as detailed in the section "Password-Protecting Your Entire Handheld"), you'll need to supply your password the next time you turn on your Clié.

 If you tap the abc *button in the bottom-left corner of the Graffiti area, the onscreen keyboard will appear. You can use this to enter your password!*

The "Lost Password" Button

Oh, the perils of the forgotten password. For the last time, just don't forget yours, okay? If you do, there's a scary but effective way to reestablish access to those records you've marked as private. In Security, when you tap the "-Assigned-" button under Password, you're prompted to enter your password. You also see a "Lost Password" button. Tap it, and your password will be deleted—and all your marked-as-private records along with it. However, those deleted records will be restored on your Clié the next time you HotSync.

Danger, Will Robinson, Danger!

The Palm Operating System's built-in security features are far too weak for the corporate environment. Consider the password, for instance. There's no mandatory length or required combination of letters or numbers: users can create a password from a single character, sure to send any system administrator into heart failure.

Passwords are also easy to bypass. A free utility called No Security, for instance, can easily circumvent the Palm security application, erasing the Palm's password and exposing all of the private records on the device. It's billed as a way to recover data if you've lost your password, but the reality is that such programs make it all too easy for thieves to retrieve sensitive data on a lost, stolen, or unguarded PDA. There's no need even to HotSync the device to install the application; No Security can be beamed from another handheld.

The moral of the story? Be careful what kind of data you store on your handheld, and take extra measures to protect it if it's valuable. Read on to learn about the software and techniques you need.

Password-Protecting Your Entire Handheld

If you really want to secure what's stored in your Clié, you need to password-protect the entire thing, not just certain records. That's where "locking" comes into play. When activated, your Clié becomes "locked" the next time it's turned off. Translation: When the Clié is turned on again, a screen pops up requiring the password (see Figure 9-2). Without it, there's no getting past that screen.

You can modify the information that appears on this "locked" startup screen by going to Prefs | Owner (see Chapter 2 for a refresher). We recommend including your name and phone number, and maybe even a reward offer—so anyone who finds your lost Clié will have an easier time returning it (and an incentive to do so). What's a good reward? Considering how much a new Clié would cost you, we think no less than $20.

Auto Lock Handheld

Palm OS 4.0 and later (which is found in nearly every Clié model) includes several automated locking options, all of them accessible by tapping the Auto Lock Handheld button in the main Security screen. Here's a quick rundown:

- ■ **Never**   No automatic locking.
- ■ **On power off**   The moment you turn your handheld off (or it shuts off after a few minutes of inactivity), it locks.

FIGURE 9-2	When you "lock" your Clié, only the correct password will unlock it.

- **At a preset time**   Set the handheld to lock at an exact time. For example, if you use it a lot during the day but rarely at night, you might set it to lock at, say, 6 P.M. That way, you won't have to keep entering your password all day.

- **After a preset delay**   This is our favorite option. It locks the handheld after a period of inactivity—ten minutes, three hours, whatever you choose.

The "Current Privacy" Menu

We've saved the Current Privacy option till last because it relates to the upcoming section on hiding and masking individual records. Simply put, when the Hide option is selected, all records you've marked as private will disappear from view. When you select Mask, private records are hidden but still listed. When you select Show, which you need your password to do, private records are made visible.

Hiding and Masking Your Records

In the four main applications—Address Book, Date Book, Memo Pad, and To Do List—any record can be marked private, meaning it suddenly becomes masked or invisible and, therefore, inaccessible. Here's how:

1. Select a record (just by tapping it) in any of the aforementioned programs.

2. Tap the Details… button. (In Address Book, you have to tap Edit to get to the screen with the Details… button.) You'll see a window containing some options for that record—and a box labeled Private.

3.   Tap that box, noticing the check mark that appears. This indicates that the record will become private after you tap OK.

4.   Tap OK.

Keep in mind that just marking a record as private has no effect unless you've chosen one of the two privacy options in the Security program. If it's set to Mask Records, records you've marked as private will turn into solid gray bars. If you choose Hide Records, records will just plain disappear. (Don't freak out—they're still in memory, just not visible.)

The Difference Between Masking and Hiding

The Mask Records option provides a middle ground between the visibility of "shown" records and the total invisibility of "hidden" records (which appear to have been wiped from existence—great security, but awfully inconvenient). Masked records still appear in your phone list, memo pad, and so on, but appear as solid gray bars (see Figure 9-3). This remains a less-than-stellar solution, as there's still no way to know what lies beneath until you tap the record and enter your password.

The Hide Records option goes a major step further, removing marked-as-private records from view altogether. To make them visible again, you must return to Security and select Show Records. Naturally, you'll need to supply your password at this time.

Passwords on the Desktop

Security isn't limited to the Clié itself. It also extends to Palm Desktop, working in much the same ways. Thus, you can hide certain records or password-protect the entire program. The same password you've selected for your Clié will automatically be used in Palm Desktop.

 Only Palm Desktop is affected by masked and hidden records. If you synchronize with Microsoft Outlook or another third-party contact manager, records marked as private on your Clié will still be visible on your PC.

FIGURE 9-3   When you choose Mask Records, all records marked as private are hidden by gray bars.

Hidden Records

Whenever you HotSync, any records marked as private on your Clié will become hidden in Palm Desktop—and vice versa. To change whether private records are visible or not, click the View menu, and then select the desired option: Hide, Mask, or Show.

Safety First—Well, Maybe Second

Dave: Call me a lazy, careless person, but I just don't get into most of these security precautions. Certainly, it's *way* too much trouble for me to enter a password every time I turn on my Clié. That defeats the whole idea of a PDA's instant accessibility. Instead, I've compromised. I put all of my most sensitive information in a program from Chapura called Cloak; when I need a program password or a credit card number, I enter one master password to access this encrypted area of my PDA. But if I ever lose my Clié, I need to hope for the best, because there's nothing to stop someone from getting all my address, calendar, and personal info.

Rick: Sadly, I'm just as lazy and careless as you—but at least I haven't abandoned showers. I use a similar program—DataViz's Password Plus—to protect my passwords, card numbers, and so forth. But I don't bother to safeguard my entire device, which is just plain foolish. So here's my New Year's resolution (never mind that it's August): to install and use a program like OnlyMe, which even a lazy person like me can handle. The "unlock code" can be a simple series of button presses, and the lockout won't engage each time I turn off my handheld—only after a predetermined amount of time has elapsed.

Keep Others from Accessing Palm Desktop

Suppose you step away from your desk for lunch or a meeting. You don't want coworkers or corporate spies poking around through your records. Fortunately, there's an easy way to password-protect Palm Desktop for Windows (alas, the Macintosh version has no security features). Just choose Tools | Options, click the Security tab, and check the box marked "Require password to access the Palm Desktop data." Now, whenever someone starts Palm Desktop, they must input the correct password (which is the one you created on your handheld) to access their data.

Password-Protecting Palm Desktop

Just as you can lock your Clié, so can you lock Palm Desktop. When you do, and then exit the program, your password will be required the next time it's started—by you or anyone else. Here's how to activate this setting:

1. Make sure Palm Desktop is running, and then click Tools | Options.

2. In the tabbed dialog box that appears, click the Security tab.

3. Click the box labeled "Require password to access the Palm Desktop data."

4. Click OK, and then exit Palm Desktop.

NOTE   *This security setting applies only to* your *data. If multiple users are sharing Palm Desktop on a single PC, they'll need to implement password protection for their own user profiles.*

Other Security Software

While the Palm Operating System's built-in security features are fairly comprehensive, there's always room for improvement. Hence the availability of numerous third-party security programs, which generally offer greater versatility and/or convenience. We've spotlighted some of the more intriguing solutions in the next few subsections.

Passwords Plus

Your Palm can be a handy place to store account numbers, PIN numbers, passwords, and other secret codes, but stuffing them all into a memo isn't the most practical solution. DataViz's Passwords Plus, one of Rick's personal favorites, is designed expressly to organize and protect your important numbers and passwords. You need to remember only one password (different from the one used by Palm Security) to access all this neatly categorized information. Passwords Plus also has a Windows-based counterpart, so you can manage and access the information on your PC.

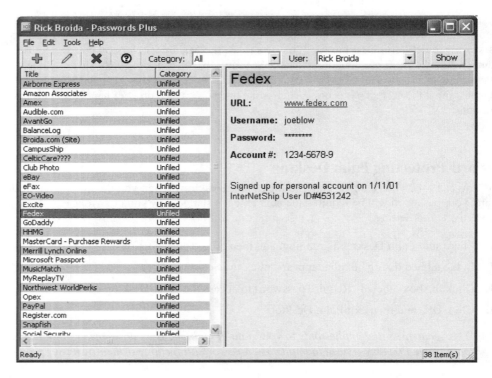

NOTE

*While Rick is a fan of Passwords Plus, Dave likes Chapura's Cloak—a similar product. It's worth checking out if you're interested in this kind of security. And these two are by no means the only choices. Visit **PalmGear.com** and search for security software to see some others.*

OnlyMe

Like Security on steroids, OnlyMe locks your Clié automatically whenever it's turned off. Your password is entered by tapping on a special six-button keypad, or by pressing the Clié's buttons in a particular sequence, or by entering certain letters or numbers in the Graffiti area. You can even create a password that's based on sliding your stylus over the special keypad.

Best of all, OnlyMe lets you set a "lock delay," so your Clié doesn't lock until after a designated period of time.

Sign-On

Passwords can be guessed or discovered, but it's a lot harder to duplicate your signature. Communication Intelligence Corp.'s Sign-On automatically locks your Clié when it's turned off, and then requires you to sign your name—right on the Clié's screen—to unlock it again. This is a great choice for those concerned about forgetting their password.

The Find Feature

The more you use your Clié, the more data you're likely to wind up storing. And the more data you have, the harder it can be to expediently find what you're looking for. Some examples:

- A couple days ago, you set up a meeting a few weeks in the future, and now you want to check the details of that meeting. Must you page through your calendar a day at a time to find the entry?

- You've got dozens of memos and need to find the ones containing the word "inventory." Must you open each memo individually?

- You have 1500 names in your address list and want to quickly find the record for that guy named Apu whose last name and company you can't remember. How will you locate him?

Using the Palm Operating System's built-in Find feature, you can unearth all this information in a snap. True to its name, Find sifts through your databases to ferret out exactly what you're looking for, be it a name, a number, a word, a phrase, or even just a few letters.

As we showed you in Chapter 2, Find can be found in the lower-right corner of the Graffiti area, represented by a little magnifying-glass icon. Using it couldn't be simpler: Tap it (at any time, no matter what program you're running), and then just write in what you want to search for (see Figure 9-4).

NOTE *Capitalization doesn't matter. Even if you're looking for a proper name like Caroline, you needn't capitalize the first letter.*

The search process should take no more than a few seconds, depending on how many records you've got on your Clié and the complexity of your search criteria.

TIP *If you use your stylus to highlight a word or chunk of text (done much the same way you select text using a mouse), that text will automatically appear in the Find field when you tap the Find icon.*

FIGURE 9-4   Looking for a specific word? Just write it in the Find box, and the Clié will find it for you.

How Find Works

When you execute a search, the Palm OS looks through all stored records (except those marked as private) for whatever text you've specified, starting with whatever program you were in when you tapped the Find icon. It looks not only in the main databases—those used by Address Book, Memo Pad, and so on—but also in the databases associated with any third-party software you might have installed.

> **TIP** *If you're looking for, say, a phone number, you can save a lot of time by loading the Address Book before tapping Find. That's because Find starts its search in whatever program is currently running.*

Keep in mind that Find searches only the beginnings of words. Thus, if you look up "book," it will find "bookcase," but not "handbook." There are third-party programs that can perform much more thorough searches—we talk about some of them in the section "Third-Party Search Programs."

> **TIP** *You can make your data a bit more "Find friendly" by using special modifiers. For instance, you might use the letters AP to preface any memo that has to do with Accounts Payable. Then, when you do a search for "AP," you'll quickly unearth all the relevant records.*

Running a Search

After you've written the desired search text in the Find box and tapped OK, the Clié will get to work. You'll see items appear in a categorized list as they're found. If you see what you're looking for, you can halt the search immediately by tapping the Stop button. Then, simply tap the item to bring up the corresponding record in the respective program.

If the Clié finds more instances of the desired item than can fit on the screen at once, it will stop the search until you tap the Find More button. This essentially tells it to look up another screen's worth of records. There's no way to return to the previous screen, so make sure you definitely need to keep searching before tapping Find More. (You can always run the search again, but that's a hassle.)

Third-Party Search Programs

Many users discover that Find isn't nearly as robust as it could be. If you want to maximize the search potential of your Clié, one of the following third-party programs might be in order. They're a little on the advanced side, meaning they require the program X-Master (which we talk about in Chapter 13). This doesn't mean you should shy away from them, just that they might prove a little more complicated to install and operate.

> **NOTE** *As you'll learn in Chapter 13, most Hacks don't work with Palm OS 5. Thus, if you have one of the newer Clié models, you'll have to live without Hacks.*

FindHack

The Rolls Royce of search programs, Florent Pillet's FindHack lets you specify whether to search all the installed applications, just the main applications, or only the current application. It also remembers the last six searches you ran, lets you preconfigure up to four "permanent" searches, and supports the use of wildcards. Best of all, it's faster than Find.

9

Find Ignore Hack

This simple Hack lets you select applications that should *not* be searched during the Find process. Why would you want to do this? E-books are a great example: if you have a few of them loaded on your Clié, they can slow a search considerably. With Find Ignore Hack, you could exclude your e-book viewer.

IntelligentFind

Quite possibly the most sophisticated Find replacement ever, IntelligentFind lets you ask questions in English ("What is Dave Johnson's phone number?") and displays the results ranked by the relevance to your questions. When in "simple" mode, IntelligentFind will search your handheld for multiple words and/or phrases at the same time, just like a web search engine. We'd have to call this the power-user's "find" tool.

The Calculator

What's an electronic organizer without a calculator? Not much, so let's take a quick peek at the Clié's. Activated by tapping the icon in the upper-right corner of the Graffiti area, Calculator operates like any other (see Figure 9-5). In fact, it's so self-explanatory that we're not going to insult your intelligence by explaining how to use it.

FIGURE 9-5   The Clié calculator functions like every other calculator you've ever used.

There are, of course, one or two features we feel obligated to point out. First, you can use the standard Palm OS copy option to paste the result of any calculation into another program. Second, you can review your last few calculations by tapping Menu | Options | Recent Calculations.

 Calc's buttons are large enough that you can tap them with a fingernail, so save time by leaving the stylus in its silo. Just keep in mind that oil and dirt from your fingers will grubby-up the screen.

Third-Party Calculators

Whether you're a student, realtor, banker, or NASA engineer, there's no debating the value of a good scientific and/or programmable calculator. Your Clié has ample processing power to fill this role—the proof is in the dozens of third-party calculators currently available. Let's take a look at some of the best and brightest.

LoanMax

Think the car salesman is sharking you? Need an amortization schedule to maximize your house payments? At times like these, a good loan calculator is worth its weight in gold. LoanMax makes it simple to calculate payments based on interest rate, loan term, down-payment amount, and so on. It can also generate on-the-spot amortization schedules (though, unfortunately, you can't save or print them). Not bad for a $10 piece of software.

The powerOne Series

Infinity Softworks offers a series of task-specific calculators: powerOne Finance, powerOne Graph, powerOne Scientific, and so on. They vary in price and capability, so visit the company's web site to see which one meets your needs.

The Clié Mail Program

An underrated member of the Clié's supporting cast of characters—er, programs—is Clié Mail. You'll learn more about it in Chapter 11, but a brief bit of explanation is in order now. Specifically, Clié Mail lets you read, compose, and send e-mail, but not in the traditional sense. That is, Clié Mail doesn't connect to your Internet service provider (ISP) (though it can do so, if you have a cell phone or modem connected—see Chapter 11). Rather, it synchronizes with your desktop e-mail program, such as Outlook or Outlook Express, absorbing copies of messages you've received and transferring outgoing messages you've written.

In practical terms, this means your Clié serves as a kind of portable e-mail viewer. Here's an example: In the morning, before heading off to work or the airport, you HotSync with your PC. All the e-mail messages you received the night before are transferred to your Clié. Throughout the day, you read through those messages and reply to those that require it. You can even compose new messages if the need arises. Later, when you return home, you HotSync once again. All the outgoing messages are transferred to your desktop e-mail program and then sent.

To get started with Clié Mail, you must first install the program from the software CD that came with your PDA, and then install the Clié Mail Conduit on your PC. See Chapter 11 for more details.

Picsel Viewer

Sony's latest Cliés, such as the NX80V and NZ90, come with a file-viewing application called Picsel Viewer. With it you can view Word, Excel, PowerPoint, PDF, and other popular file formats right on your Clié. Learn all about this nifty program in Chapter 12.

> **TIP** *If you like the sound of Picsel Viewer, but your Clié didn't come with it, try RepliGo (**www.repligo.com**). It offers similar functionality and works with all Palm OS devices. The viewer itself is a freebie, but you have to pay if you want to convert your own files for viewing on your PDA.*

All the Other Goodies That Came with Your Clié

While writing this book, Sony kept us on our toes by changing and expanding the roster of applications that come bundled with the various models. The model you have now might lack some of the programs listed in this section or it might have others that aren't listed here at all.

Fortunately, the documentation that Sony provided should have all the information you need to learn the basics. In the meantime, here's an overview of the most common bundled applications, and leads to where in the book you can learn more about them.

- **AudioPlayer** If your Clié supports audio playback (just look for a headphone jack if you're not sure), it will include *AudioPlayer,* a simple program for listening to your MP3 tunes. See Chapter 18 for details.

- **gMovie** With *gMovie,* you can view video clips right on your Clié. The Sony software CD includes a few samples, which you have to manually install (see Chapter 4) to view. Find out more about Clié movies in Chapter 16.

- **Movie Player** In place of gMovie, some Clié models have Sony's own Movie Player program, which we think is vastly superior. Again, see Chapter 16.

- **Memory Stick Autorun** Memory Sticks are a kind of removable storage media that can hold extra applications, data, and even a backup of your Clié. Normally, when you insert a Stick into the handheld, all that happens is you get access to its contents. However, it's possible to automatically run a program stored on the card, and that's where MS Autorun comes in. Tap the MS Autorun icon, and then choose which application (or database) you want to run the next time you insert the Stick.

- **Memory Stick Backup** As discussed in Chapter 2, you can create a backup of your entire Clié, storing all the applications and data on a Memory Stick card. With MS Backup, all it takes is a tap to start the process and to restore everything if the need arises. Find out more in Chapter 22.

- **Memory Stick Gate** The Palm OS lets you copy files to and from Memory Sticks, but it's a wimp compared to MS Gate. With this utility, you can not only copy files, but also move and delete them. Yep, you guessed it: see Chapter 22 for more details.

- **CLIÉ Files** Most newer models have CLIÉ Files, a much more versatile file-management utility, in place of MS Gate.

- **Memory Stick Import**   As you learned in Chapter 4, you can install applications and other files directly to a Memory Stick using the Palm OS Install Tool. However, when you have big stuff like photos and MP3 files, it would take forever to HotSync them. MS Import, when used in conjunction with MS Export (a Windows utility), turns your Clié into another drive that's accessible from within Windows. This makes it faster and easier to move, copy, delete, and organize Memory Stick data. Bop back to Chapter 4 for a refresher.

- **PictureGear Pocket**   This is an image viewer that lets you view photos transferred from your PC or a digital camera, or see those taken with a Clié's built-in camera or Sony's Memory Stick Camera. Some models have a program called CLIÉ Viewer instead. The full scoop on both can be found in Chapter 16.

- **PhotoStand**   If you're like us, your Clié probably spends a fair amount of time sitting on your desk in its cradle. Why not put the screen to good use? PhotoStand turns it into a kind of digital picture frame, running a constant slideshow of photos stored in memory. See Chapter 16 if you're intrigued.

Where to Find It

Web Site	Address	What's There
Chapura	www.chapura.com	Cloak
CIC	www.cic.com	Sign-On
DataViz	www.dataviz.com	Passwords Plus
Infinity Softworks	www.infinitysw.com	powerOne calculators
IntelligentFind	www.intelligentfind.com	IntelligentFind
PalmGear	www.palmgear.com	FindHack, Find Ignore Hack, and most other programs
Synergy Solutions	www.synsolutions.com	SynCalc
Tranzoa	www.tranzoa.com	OnlyMe
XiY Technologies	www.xiy.net	LoanMax

Chapter 10

Going on a Trip

How to...

- Organize your Clié's categories and data for travel
- Pack smartly so you're prepared for trouble
- Make sure your Clié doesn't run out of power during the trip
- Prepare for HotSync opportunities away from home
- Enhance the core apps for life on the road
- View your coworkers' Date Book entries on your own Clié
- Load your Clié with essential travel phone numbers
- Use the Clié as an alarm clock
- Use the Clié as a subway map
- Communicate in a foreign language with your Clié
- Use your Clié as a compass
- Get star charts on your Clié

Some people find their Clié so useful that—imagine this—they put it in their pocket and take it on trips away from the home and office! Daring, we know. But it's well-prepared for these kinds of "away missions." Its batteries mean you needn't plug it in and, because it synchronizes with your desktop PC, you can bring important information with you wherever you go. The Clié even has a built-in clock in case you forget your watch. What could be better?

Seriously, we know you already carry your Clié around town. But, if you plan to take it on an extended trip, you might want to read this chapter. We have all kinds of suggestions for how to prepare your Clié for a grueling business trip, as well as what kind of software you might need to make the trip a little smoother. And how about camping? Your Clié might not be the first accessory that springs to mind when you consider roughing it in the Rocky Mountains, but your trusty little handheld has a lot to offer in the wilderness, too.

Preparing Your Clié for the Road

When we go on a business trip, it's usually such absolute pandemonium—running around at the last minute, throwing power cords and HotSync cables in the travel bag—it's a wonder we ever make it to the airport in time. Because of our experiences with forgetting data, bringing dead batteries, and being unable to connect to the Internet in strange cites, we offer the following checklist to you for bringing your Clié on trips.

Set Up Your Data

Make sure your Clié is ready for the details of your upcoming trip. Specifically, consider the kinds of data you need to create while you're on the road and prepare your Clié ahead of time. Here's how you can make sure you're ready:

1. In the To Do List, create a trip checklist and enter everything you need to do before you leave, plus what you need to bring with you. If you have a comprehensive checklist, you're less likely to forget something important before you go.

TIP *You probably don't want to build your travel list from scratch each time. One solution is to create a comprehensive list of travel tasks and leave it in the Memo Pad. You can copy the entire memo and paste it into a new memo before a trip, and then erase individual lines as you complete them. The master list is still safely stored in a different memo entry.*

2. Create a new category in which you can store data related to your trip. If you're going to Chicago for a convention, for instance, create a category on the Address Book, the To Do List, and the Memo Pad called Chicago. (If you want to call it something else, that's okay too.) By using a special category on the road, you can find data related to your trip more quickly—both during the trip and after you return home. When you get back, you can recategorize the data any way you like.

3. Enter your itinerary in the Date Book. If you're flying, enter each flight's number, departure, and arrival time in your Clié, so it's available when you need it. An easy way to do this is to enter the flight number in the Date Book at the scheduled departure time, and note the arrival time there as well. That way, you can check your Clié in flight to see how much longer you have to grit your teeth and eat cashews (warning: may contain peanuts). You might even want to try a travel-specific alternative like TravelTracker—check it out in the section "Itinerary Tracking." In the following illustration, you can see an itinerary in DateBk5, complete with icons to identify the kind of activities.

10

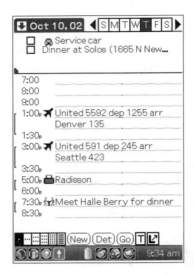

You can block out the dates of your trip on the Clié using an untimed event. The trip appears at the top of the Date Book and still lets you schedule actual appointments during those days.

Have a Backup Plan

Call us Luddites, but we don't like to rely 100 percent on a fragile piece of electronic gizmotry (and, yes, that's a word. Who are you, Daniel Webster?). What if you drop your Clié in the airport and it shatters on the nice marble floor? You'd better have a Plan B.

Dave: For me, the most important document to have access to on a trip is my flight itinerary. I always buy e-tickets—so I have no written record of my flight—and then I enter the flight information in my Clié. But, to be on the safe side, I also print a copy of my flight info and stick it in the back of my bag somewhere. That way, if my batteries die before I finish the trip or my Clié falls out of a five-story window, I can always refer to the piece of paper and get myself home.

Rick: For once I have to agree with Dave (despite the physical pain involved). I also recommend buying yourself a Memory Stick. With just a few stylus taps, you can back up the complete contents of your handheld's memory. Then, in the event that some catastrophe leaves you with a wiped handheld (it's been known to happen), you can restore everything in a matter of minutes. Well worth the money you'll spend for a memory card. See Chapters 13 and 22 for details on making backups on Memory Sticks and information on where and what to buy.

Get the Hardware Ready

When you leave on a trip, you should make sure your Clié is fully prepared to go the distance. There's nothing like being a thousand miles from home and remembering you forgot to bring some data from your desktop PC, or discovering you forgot an important cable.

To save yourself from calamity, remember these tips:

- ■ *Always bring a stylus with a reset pin.* Every Clié we've used includes a reset pin in the stylus—just unscrew the tail end to get to it. If you don't have one, bring a paperclip or a thin pin instead. And test the pin before you go! Rick once traveled with a paperclip too thick to fit in the hole. D'oh! Bottom line: there's nothing worse than having your Clié crash when you're away from home and discovering you have nothing small enough to fit in the reset hole.

- ■ *Perform a HotSync right before you leave.* This way, you're sure to have the latest info on your Clié, and you also have a current backup in case something unfortunate happens to your trusty handheld while you're away.

- ■ *Do you plan to do a lot of typing?* If so, pack a keyboard for the Clié. You have several options to choose from, from Sony's own fold-up Clié Compact Keyboard (also known as the Stowaway when sold by Fellowes) to the totally wireless Pocketop keyboard. See Chapter 23 for more details.

- ■ *Be prepared to restore.* Call us paranoid, but…hey, wait a minute, did you just call us paranoid? Sheesh, the nerve…. Anyway, if your Clié should lose all its data for some reason, you might want to have the capability to restore it while you're on the go. The easiest solution? Get a Memory Stick and use the MS Backup program that's found on most Cliés. Back up right before you walk out the door, and then continue to back up daily while you're on the road so you won't lose much if the unthinkable happens. (If you don't have MS Backup, try Botzam Backup, which we talk about in Chapter 13.)

10

Real-Life Tragedy

Last year, Dave spent a week in sunny Florida in the dead of winter to see a photography trade show and do a bit of scuba diving. At the time, he was still using a Visor Prism that, like the Clié, also uses the Palm OS. While there, his trusty Visor Prism held all his data—contact info, schedules, even flight information for the return trip. Thanks to quirky hardware, two days into the trip, the PDA performed a hard reset, erasing all the data on the device.

"I had thrown caution to the wind," Dave reports. "I thought I could trust my Prism, and I had no backup of any kind—no laptop, no backup module, not even a printout of my schedule."

In fact, Dave had to call home repeatedly to be updated on his daily schedule and to know what time to show up to the airport at the end of the trip. He reports that he plans to follow his own advice in the future.

Stay Powered

A dead Clié is no good to anyone. Take these steps to keep working when you're away:

- *Recharge right before you leave.* Or, if you have one of those few remaining Cliés that takes replaceable batteries, change them before you go out of town, especially if you'll be away for a week or more. If you generally leave a spare set of batteries in your travel case, score ten points for preparedness. If you use a battery tester before each trip to make sure your backup batteries are still in good shape, that's a bonus five points. Good job—you're close to winning a set of golf clubs.

- *Take a charger.* Because your Clié probably uses rechargeable batteries, it pays to bring some sort of charging solution with you—especially if you'll be away for more than just a day or two. You can bring the Clié's cradle and AC adapter, or check out something like Electric Fuel's Instant Power system (available for some Clié models). Or, there's Sony's Battery Adapter (which charges the PDA via a set of AA batteries). Sony also sells AC adapters and car chargers. There's no excuse to run out of power, even if you're traveling for a week or two. See Chapter 23 for more travel-charging accessories.

- *Bring batteries for any accessories you use.* This includes your modem, keyboard, cell phone, GPS receiver, and other gadgets.

Road Tips

We've done our share of traveling, and we've amassed a few handy tips for making the best use of your Clié on the road. Not all of these suggestions will appeal to you, but you're sure to find a few things to make your next trip a little more enjoyable.

- If you're in a different time zone, reset the time on your Clié. Otherwise, all your appointments will alarm at the wrong time and you'll show up late everywhere you need to be. To change the time, tap the Prefs app and choose the Time & Date page. Tap the Set Time Zone box and set it to your new location. The time will automatically update for you.

■ Your Clié could set off the metal detector at the airport. To save yourself time and hassle, go ahead and pop it into one of those little trays, along with all your loose change, *Sliders*-style alternate universe teleporter remote controls, roll of aluminum foil, and other personal items right at the outset when you go through a metal detector.

■ The Clié is considered a portable electronic device and you shouldn't use it at the beginning or the end of a flight. You probably already knew that, but your Clié can get you in trouble anyway if you're not careful. Specifically, don't enable any alarms for the start or end of the flight, or your Clié will come to life and start beeping during verboten moments.

■ You might need to print something stored on your Clié while you're on your trip. There are several ways to print. The easiest solution is to get a print driver for your Clié like PalmPrint, PrintBoy, or one of the solutions from IS/Complete. If you do a lot of printing, get a portable printer and carry it with you. If you can get to a printer, but it isn't IR-capable, you still have options. You can carry the PrintBoy InfraReady Adapter from Bachmann Software, for instance. This is a little device that fits in your pocket (or your travel bag) and plugs into the parallel port of any printer. Its infrared port lets you instantly convert any printer into an IR-ready printer for your Clié. When you're finished printing, remove the adapter and put it back in your travel bag. It's a very cool solution for printing anything anywhere you can find a printer when you travel. As a last resort, you might install a fax program like Mark/Space Fax. Equipped with a modem, you can fax to your hotel's front desk, and then pick up the printout.

10

Software to Bring Along

Don't rely on the software that comes with your Clié to get you through your extended trips away from home. Most of the software we discuss in this next section is available from **palmgear.com**. Experiment and see what applications are useful.

Don't install a new application as you're walking out the door to go to the airport. Some applications might cause your Clié to misbehave. Others can change the way your Clié functions or make it hard to access data you've already created. You don't need to discover those kinds of things on an airplane bound for Topeka. Bottom line: install and experiment with new software well in advance of a trip.

Address and Date Book Enhancements

Sure, you love the Address Book and the Date Book. But, by enhancing these core applications, you might find you can significantly improve the way you work when you're away from home.

Synchronize with the Web

Believe it or not, you can synchronize your Clié's Date Book and Address Book with web-based information managers. Why would you want to do that? Well, when you're on the road, you might want to access your schedule and contacts from a PC that isn't yours. And, if you can get to any web-enabled PC, you can log on to a web-based calendar and address book. Here are some cool reasons to try this:

- Send e-mail from a web-based e-mail system using contact information culled from your Clié.

- Add calendar appointments on the PC and synchronize it to the Clié later.

- If something happens to your Clié on a trip, access all your data from a PC that's connected to the Internet.

The web site **Yahoo.com** offers the best synchronization support on the Internet. By installing a small utility on your home or office-based PC, you can sync the Clié's Date Book, Address Book, and To Do List with equivalent applications on the Yahoo! site. Because Yahoo! also offers free e-mail, you can use the Address Book to send messages without reentering any data.

Share Your Appointments

Let's say that you're meeting with a coworker at a trade show to review the newest, most innovative garden hoses. If your buddy is as busy as you plan to be, how can you reconcile your schedules to meet for lunch?

Try *DualDate,* a program offered for free from Palm and available at **PalmGear.com**. This program replaces your built-in Date Book application and lets you show two calendars side-by-side. Once installed on both PDAs, you can send your calendar to someone else by pointing your Clié's infrared port at the other Palm OS device and choosing Record | Share Calendar from the menu. Your appointments will be sent to the other device and displayed in a second column, as you can see here:

To get your associate's appointments, he or she will have to do the same and beam it to you. While the updates are automatic—you have to manually beam updated calendars to stay in sync— it's an easy way to keep someone else's appointments on your own PDA.

Get Rental Car Phone Numbers

The Clié can hold lots of phone numbers, so why not take advantage of this? Several databases of phone numbers exist to services like rental car companies, airlines, and hotels. Here are some examples of what you can find at **PalmGear.com**:

Topic	What You'll Find
Rental cars	You can find a handful of downloads at PalmGear that include all the major rental car companies. Check out programs called Palm Rent-a-Car and Travel Telephone Numbers.
Golf courses	Believe it or not, we found a slew of downloads at **PalmGear.com** that pour phone numbers to golf courses in locales such as L.A., New York, and Florida into your Palm, so you can easily find the numbers you need when you travel. Search for "phone numbers" at PalmGear for the whole bunch.
Restaurants	Want a guide to restaurants in major cities? You'll find that online as well—The Finer Life Restaurant Guide is available at PalmGear for cities such as San Francisco and L.A. Of course, if you want a really good guide to local restaurants when you travel, you'll want a city guide, which we cover in the section "Have a Better Time with City Guides."

Itinerary Tracking

While you can certainly store your itinerary information in the Date Book, using a specialized program is more efficient for many people. Many applications are at a site like PalmGear that fit the bill. Some of our favorites include TravelTracker and Travel Pal, both seen in the following.

In Search of the Ultimate Alarm Clock

You can set alarms with the Clié, but the somewhat-anemic alarm system built into the Date Book isn't terribly useful in a lot of situations. Instead, you might want to download a copy of a specialized clock application. A program just to tell the time? When your Clié already comes with a clock? Surely we jest.

We don't, and stop calling us Shirley.

Note to selves: That joke simply doesn't work in print.

The Palm OS software universe is filled with some excellent clocks and alarm clock applications. These programs tend to offer more advanced features than those that come with you Clié, such as multiple alarms that aren't tied to specific Date Book events, snooze buttons, countdown and stopwatch modes, and world time displays. Here are some programs worth investigating:

- **BigClock**   *BigClock* is the granddaddy of alarm clock apps. It's free, yet has a wealth of useful features. Not only does it display the time, but it has a timer and four independent alarms. It also lets you easily change time zones—a boon if you're still using an older Clié without OS 5's easy time-zone adjustment. It also lets you change the look of the program and display your own favorite background images behind the clock using the program's themes feature.

- **WorldMate Professional**   This gorgeous program isn't just great for travelers, it's eye candy for your PDA as well. At its core, *WorldMate* lets you compare four world clocks to your local time and features a beautiful map display that animates the day/night terminator. It also synchronizes your Clié with an online atomic clock at each HotSync, retrieves weather forecasts, and includes a currency converter.

- **MegaClock** This is a must-try. *MegaClock* is a multifunction clock app that has a huge collection of alternative views. You can see the time in a variety of analog and digital clock faces, display a world globe with day/night terminator, and more. It has no less than 20 alarms and 4 programmable daily timers.

- **CityTime** Like WorldMate, *CityTime* has a gorgeous color display that graphically shows the day/night terminator as it moves across the globe. CityTime displays four world clocks, and lets you change your location and time easily without entering the Prefs app. It displays sunrise and sunset times, moon phase information, and performs time and distance calculations between locations.

- **Time 2.0** For those who want a simpler, calendar-based view, *Time 2.0* shows the time and a calendar along with a second time zone and upcoming appointments.

Finding Your Way Around

Many Clié tools can help you find your way around in a strange place. In fact, you can connect your Clié to a GPS navigation system (see the section "Navigating with Your Clié")! Most people need more mundane assistance, though, so we've collected a few interesting navigation aids for you here.

Have a Better Time with City Guides

City Guides have become virtually indispensable for frequent travelers. These programs deliver up-to-date, trustworthy information about things to do in cities you travel to—such as restaurant, nightclub, shopping, and sightseeing advice. Here are a few to check out:

■ **Vindigo**   We list *Vindigo* first for a reason: it's become the single most popular city guide in the world. It supports over 50 cities and has categories for food, shops, services, museums, movies, essential services such as banks and ATMs, and more. The program has maps and provides directions to wherever you're trying to go. Vindigo also features reviews to help you make good choices about where to go. Alas, it's not a one-time fee; Vindigo costs $25 per year.

■ **Zagat To Go**   The popular *Zagat* restaurant guide is available for the Palm OS and, hence, your Clié. Its database includes about 65 cities, and has reviews of dining and nightlife in the same familiar form as the paper version.

■ **Qvadis Envoyage**   Looking for a free city guide? Live or travel in Canada? Try *Envoyage,* which has some of the same features as Vindigo and Zagat for a handful of cities, such as Toronto, Vancouver, Montreal, and Ottawa.

Get Metro and Subway Routes

Do train, bus, and subway routes leave you scratching your head? Those maps they put in the train stops aren't exactly intuitive, and finding the best route from one end of Paris to the other can be a nerve-wracking experience. That's why you might want to search a site such as PalmGear for metro aids—these programs help you find your way around strange towns when you travel. The best ones let you enter two stations and simply tell you what train to get on. Others include digital maps and displays to help you navigate. To get started, search PalmGear for terms like "metro" and "subway" to locate apps that interest you. Here are some of the better ones we dug up:

Region	Service	Program Name
200 cities worldwide	Displays best routing information for finding your way by subway or bus.	MetrO
Paris 3.1P	Metro paths among monuments, museums, and stations.	Paris
Versions available for New York, Boston, London, Paris, Chicago, and others	Map that plans the best route between metro stops; combined with a street map for easier route planning.	TUBE
Databases available for select cities in California, Washington, New York, and others	Comprehensive bus and train schedules.	Transit
19 cities, including New York, Paris, and London	Computes the best route between any two stations.	Route Expert
New York	Enter a Manhattan address and the program provides the nearest cross street.	X-Man
Southern California	MetroLink schedule.	MetroLink

Navigating with Your Clié

Have you ever gotten lost in a strange town or some deserted stretch of highway? Have you wished you hadn't seen the *Blair Witch Project* because it reminds you of exactly how bad you are at navigating in the wilderness? If so, you might benefit from a GPS navigation system. Combined with a GPS system, your Palm is perfectly capable of telling you exactly where to go.

If you have a Bluetooth-enabled Clié, such as the NZ90, you can use Emtac's *Bluetooth GPS antenna*—it's a tiny gadget that you can place anywhere, like under the windshield of your car, and then use the GPS data on your PDA anywhere up to 30 feet away. It's a great solution because

10

you don't have to keep the PDA itself in view of the satellites or tether it to an external antenna via a cable. It's all wireless and very convenient. *Socket Also* makes one (seen in the following) that, though it ships with Pocket PC software, works fine with Mapopolis's software, which you must buy separately. You might also want to try Sony's car cradle GPS receiver, which we discuss in Chapter 23.

Another alternative—for the non-Bluetooth among us—is the Holux GPS bundle from Mapopolis. Mapopolis offers a *GPS Bundle*—a receiver, the appropriate connection cable, and car power adapter—which is everything you need to get up and running.

The Mapopolis receiver itself is a "puck" style unit with a strong magnetic base, manufactured by a company called Holus, and it tethers to the Clié's serial port via a six-foot cable. As for software, the system relies on Mapopolis's own viewer and a family of maps that vary by price and features. The Platinum Plus maps, for instance, cost $13 each or $45 for a subscription. Basic maps, which cost $3.95 each, lack such Platinum Plus extras as driving directions and local landmarks.

No matter what option you choose, though, Mapopolis doesn't provide real-time driving directions or on-the-fly routing, which is disappointing if you're used to in-car GPS systems. You can create a route between two points and see the path highlighted on the PDA screen or generate a static list of directions, but the software never advises you about upcoming turns.

Language Translators

In the past, traveling abroad often resulted in serious communication difficulties. Do you know how to ask for the bathroom in French? If not, try one of these applications.

What Is GPS?

GPS stands for Global Positioning System, and it's comprised of 24 satellites flying around the earth in semisynchronous orbit (each trip around the Earth takes 12 hours). These satellites transmit extremely precise timing signals toward the Earth.

On the ground, an inexpensive GPS receiver simply listens for these timing signals. At any given moment, the time broadcast from each satellite in the GPS system's field of view is slightly different because the satellites are at different distances from the receiver and, consequently, some signals take longer to reach the receiver from the satellite. Because the orbit of each GPS satellite is very, very precisely known, the GPS receiver can process the different timing signals and determine its own position through simple triangulation.

The bottom line is this: through this process, a GPS receiver can narrow its position to an accuracy of about 100 feet—not bad for a system that works anywhere on Earth.

For GPS to do its magic, though, you must be able to see enough satellites. You need to see no less than three satellites for accurate position data, which isn't a problem in clearings. In a skyscraper-infested metropolitan area or in a forest with lots of tree cover, though, GPS can have trouble working. Even obstacles like trees can block the GPS signal.

You can find out more about GPS in a wonderful new book, *How to Do Everything with GPS*. The reason we know it's wonderful is not because Rick wrote it, but because Dave is doing the "tech edit," which should eliminate the most egregious of the book's many fantastical errors. In any event, Rick would like you to buy several copies, so he will be able to feed his kids for another week.

10

- **Small Talk**   This program is a real-time, two-way translator. Hold the Clié up to the person you want to communicate with. *Small Talk* presents you with complete sentences organized into situation-based categories such as Basics, Lodging, Emergency, Food, and Entertainment. Select a phrase in English and it's translated into the target language, as you can see in Figure 10-1. The person you're communicating with can then select a response from a menu, which is translated back into English. Small Talk supports French, Italian, Spanish, German, and Japanese.

- **TourMate**   Available in several versions (including English-Spanish and English-Italian, English-French, and English-German), *TourMate* is easy to use. Choose a common greeting, expression, or question in English, and read the phonetically spelled foreign-language equivalent expression to the person with whom you're trying to communicate.

- **Translate**   This application enables you to enter a word and instantly translate it among 18 languages. The translator works in both directions, so you can go from English to Italian or Italian to English, for instance.

Unit Conversions

If you're an American in Europe, you need to contend with an alien set of measurements: not only is the currency different, but even the length, weight, and volume of common items are unusual. Heck, unless you're a scientist or an engineer, you might not know if 40 degrees Celsius is hot or cold. Try Conversions (see Figure 10-2), a calculator utility that lets you instantly make conversions among measurements like currency, temperature, length, area, and volume.

FIGURE 10-1   Choose a phrase from a list, divided by topic (left), and your associate can choose a response (right) that's translated back into English for you.

| FIGURE 10-2 | Conversions makes it easy for an American to get by in a metric world. |

Wilderness Survival Tools

It's not surprising to walk into a fancy hotel and see a dozen executives standing around in fancy suits, checking their schedules via the Cliés. But how often do you go camping in the middle of the woods and see people bring their PDAs? Not that often, we're willing to bet. And that's too bad, because the Clié is a handy survival tool. It does almost everything, except open cans of beans or start campfires.

Use Your Clié as a Compass

While we're quite sure you know a Clié won't open a can of beans, we suspect you wouldn't believe it could be a compass, either. But you'd be wrong. Using a program like *Sun Compass,* you can get an immediate onscreen indication of north any time, anywhere (during daylight hours).

Unfortunately, Sun Compass comes with virtually no documentation, which might make it confusing for new users. To use Sun Compass, all you need to do is input a few pieces of information:

- **Tz**   This is the time zone you're in currently. Time zones are calculated from –12 to 0, and then on up to +12. Your time zone value is simply the number of hours away from Greenwich, England (home of Greenwich Mean Time) you're located. GMT is a time zone of 0. New York is –5, and California is –8. You can find a complete list of time zones in Windows by opening the Date/Time Properties dialog box (in the Control panel) and looking on the Time Zone tab.

- **La**   Enter your latitude. Latitude is measured from 0 degrees (the equator) to 90N and 90S.

- **Lo**   Enter your longitude. Longitude is commonly measured from 0 (at the longitude line that cuts through Greenwich, England) to 180E and 180W.

> TIP   *Looking for your latitude and longitude? Visit **www.census.gov/cgi-bin/gazetteer**. Enter your city or ZIP code to find out your lat/long. Traveling outside the United States? Use this much more cumbersome URL instead: **www.census.gov/cgi-bin/gazetteer**.*

- **DSI**   DSI stands for daylight saving time, and it needs to be set either on or off, depending on the time of year. Daylight saving time is on between the first Sunday in April and the last Sunday in October.

> TIP   *A few locations in the United States don't observe daylight saving time at all. These include Arizona, Hawaii, and parts of Indiana.*

Once you enter these values, point the front of your Clié at the sun (keep the Clié level with the ground) and the compass indicates which way is north. That's all there is to it!

Find Stars

You can also use Sun Compass to find the North Star. Choose Misc | Polarstar from the menu and you see a dark screen with the Big and Little Dipper constellations. By aligning them with what you see in the sky, you can find the North Star and, thus, get a northerly orientation even at night.

That's great, but you can also use your Clié for some real star gazing. Here are a few programs you can try the next time you're far away from city lights with your Clié:

- ■ **Planetarium**   This program calculates the position of the sun, the moon, the planets, and over 1,500 of the brightest stars and deep sky objects in the sky. You can enter any location and any time period—you needn't use the present system clock. In addition to using this program for stargazing, it can also be used as a compass when the Sun or Moon is visible (much like Sun Compass).

- ■ **Star Pilot**   This program lets you specify your location, and then see the planets, the moon, and 500 stars in a compact star map. You can identify objects by clicking them and search for celestial objects by name.

Read Late at Night

When all of your tent buddies are trying to sleep while wondering if that odd sound is an approaching bear, you can relax in your sleeping bag and read a good book—with your Clié. The Clié's efficient backlighting makes it easy to read both in total darkness and in bright sunlight. What you need is a document reader. While you can see Chapter 21 for details on electronic books and document readers, we think it's worth pointing out right now that there's nothing like curling up with a good e-book on a camping trip (among other places). You can store lots of reading material on one Clié, so you can travel right and still have a lot of things to read on those quiet, lonely nights.

10

Where to Find It

Web Site	Address	What's There
Electric Fuel	www.instant-power.com	Instant Power Charger
BigClock site	www.gacel.de/palmpilot.htm	BigClock
Mark/Space	www.markspace.com	Mark/Space Fax
Stevens Creek Software	www.stevenscreek.com	PalmPrint
Bachmann Software	www.bachmannsoftware.com	PrintBoy
IS/Complete	www.iscomplete.com	IS/Print
Yahoo!	www.yahoo.com	Web-based information management that HotSyncs to the Palm
WeSync.com	www.wesync.com	Side-by-side calendaring
SilverWare	www.silverware.com	TravelTracker
LandWare	www.landware.com	Small Talk
Mapopolis	www.mapopolis.com	GPS
Vindigo	www.vindigo.com	City guide software

Chapter 11

Clié Communications

How to...

- Send and receive e-mail with your Clié
- Connect your cell phone to your handheld
- Configure your handheld for Web and e-mail access
- Wirelessly connect your Clié to your LAN
- Work with the Palm Mail program
- Use the Clié Mail program
- Send sketches and drawings with RiteMail
- Access America Online
- Use AvantGo to take the Web with you

Someday, probably in the very near future, you might be able to buy a Clié that doubles as a cell phone. But aside from the Clié UX50, which comes with built-in Wi-Fi, no Sony model offers out-of-the-box wireless communication. Several other Palm OS–based handheld devices double as cell phones and wireless gadgets already. In the meantime, surely there must be some way to use your Clié to send and receive e-mail, and maybe even surf the Web?

Sure—there are several ways. In this chapter, we introduce you to the e-mail software that comes with your Clié, and to the process of connecting your Clié to a cell phone for wireless web browsing and e-mail. We also give you the scoop on a couple of cool web browsers, some of which don't require an Internet connection at all—at least, not in the traditional sense.

Connecting Your Clié

Omniscient authors that we are, we can tell what you're thinking right about now. "E-mail on a Clié? No way! It doesn't have a modem or antenna or carrier pigeon, so how could mail possibly get into or out of the thing?" Silly reader—don't you know better than to ask such doubtful questions by now?

In fact, your Clié can transact e-mail a number of different ways. For starters, most Clié models come with an application called, aptly enough, Clié Mail. If yours doesn't, you can leverage several third-party e-mail programs.

That's the software side of the equation. But the question remains: how to get messages to and from your Clié? We have four answers: with your computer, with a modem, with a cell phone, and with Wi-Fi.

With Your Computer

If none of the other options we write about in this section work, you can still use your Clié to send and receive e-mail through your PC. Basically, new e-mail received on your PC gets transferred

FIGURE 11-1   With Clié Mail, you can send and receive e-mail—complete with photos and attachments.

to your Clié when you HotSync, while messages composed on your Clié get transferred to your PC—and sent. We'll talk more about this in the section "Configuring Mail Settings on the Clié."

With a Modem

As of press time, Sony was continuing to manufacture the PEGA-MD700, a 56 Kbps modem "sled" for N- and S-series models. The modem clips onto the bottom and back of the handheld, and then plugs into an ordinary phone jack (just like the modem inside your computer). You can then dial into your Internet service provider (ISP) to check and send mail (and browse the Web, discussed in the section "Web Browsing with the Clié"). Unfortunately, Sony doesn't offer a modem for any other Clié models, and apparently it has no plans to. What's more, the *N* and *S* series have been discontinued, so the modem is likely to follow before long. If you can't get one from Sony, try eBay. You might also want to try an infrared modem, which doesn't require a physical connection to your Clié and, therefore, guarantees compatibility. Check out the Psion Travel Modem and 3Jtech PP2I-5600B.

With a Cell Phone

You probably already own a cell phone—most people do. And it's already wireless, so wouldn't it be great if you could link it to your handheld for web browsing and e-mail? You can, and it's easier than you might think. Here's what you need:

- **A phone that supports data calls**   Most modern phones do (those that work with CDMA and GSM networks), but check with your ISP to be sure. You might also have to pay extra per month to make data calls, though some companies build the cost into their standard service plans.

11

■ **Cable, infrared, or Bluetooth** You can use a cable to link your handheld to a phone, or connect the PDA to the phone with an infrared port, if your phone has one. For many folks, using a cable is the best bet, as it gives you greater flexibility in positioning the two devices. On the other hand, the cable is one extra thing to carry and lose—so if your phone is IR-capable, you might want to try it and see if you like it. With an IR connection, the phone and handheld need to lie on an even surface and point at their respective IR ports so they can communicate, as in the following illustration of the NX80 and Nokia 3650. The very best option: if you have a Bluetooth-capable Clié (like the NZ90) and a Bluetooth-capable mobile phone, you can connect wirelessly, up to a distance of 30 feet, without the line-of-sight restrictions imposed by infrared.

Finding Connection Cables

Unless you're lucky enough to have an IR-equipped phone, you'll need a cable to make the connection to your handheld. We know of two good sources for them:

■ **Purple Data Cables** www.pcables.com

■ **SupplyNet** www.thesupplynet.com

You might also be able to find cables at your local computer or office superstore, or at one of your cell phone company's outlet stores.

Configuring Your Clié with a Cell Phone

Now that you have all the parts, it's time to set up your Clié to connect to the Internet via your mobile phone. Here's what you need to do:

1. Make sure that the data services on your phone are enabled (you might need to call your ISP to be sure).

2. Connect the cable between the Clié and phone, or point the IR ports at each other if you're going the infrared route.

3. On your Clié, tap the Prefs app in the Home screen and choose Connection (it might be in the Communication category if you have a newer PDA).

4. Create a new connection by tapping the New Button.

5. Give your connection a handy name (like Phone or Cable). Set the Connect to option to Modem, and set Via to Cable or Infrared, as appropriate. If you have an older Clié, this screen is a bit different and you might need to select an option like Serial To Modem. Dialing should be set to TouchTone.

6. Tap the Details button and set the Speed to 19,200 for starters. If this setting works, you can later try increasing the speed to 57,600, and then try testing it again.

7. Tap OK twice, and then tap Done to return to the main Preferences screen.

8. Open the Network Prefs.

9. Create a new network by tapping New, and then enter a descriptive name for this service (such as **ATT** or **Sprint**). Set the Connection to the new connection you created back in Step 4.

10. Enter the user name and password, and then add a phone number to dial. Make sure you enter the number properly; some phones require nine-digit dialing.

11

11. Test your connection using the Connect button. If all is well, tap Done. It's complete!

With Wi-Fi

If you're lucky enough to own a Clié with a CompactFlash slot (like an NX70V, NX80V, or NZ90, for instance), then you have the option of wirelessly connecting to the Internet via an 802.11b network, often called *Wi-Fi*. Put simply, if your Clié is in range of one of these networks (which have become extremely popular in homes, offices, and even public places like Starbucks and Staples), you can enjoy high-speed Internet access in the palm of your hand.

To make this happen, you need an accessory for your Clié: Sony's PEGA-WL100 Wireless LAN Card (shown in the following), which costs about $150. After installing the driver that came on the Wi-Fi card's installation CD-ROM, set up your Wi-Fi connection by opening the Network category in Prefs. Just do this:

1. Insert your Wi-Fi card in the Clié's CF slot.

2. Choose Wireless LAN from the Service menu.

3. Tap the Details button at the bottom of the screen.

4. If this is the first time you've used the Wi-Fi card, create a new profile by tapping the Create button.

5. Give your profile a name—like **Home Network**.

6. Enter your network's SSID. Depending on the router your Wi-Fi network is using, you might be able to leave this blank but, for best compatibility, enter the exact name the network is using. If your network is using WEP encryption, select the appropriate type and enter the WEP key.

7. Finally, tap the Advanced Setup button and deselect PowerSaveMode. You might be able to leave this enabled, but we've found this setting can crash some Wi-Fi networks, and make it impossible for the Clié to connect with others. Stay on the safe side and just turn this feature off.

8. Tap OK to work your way back to the main Preferences screen and test your network by tapping Connect. If all went well, you should now be connected to the Internet via Wi-Fi, and you can check e-mail or surf the Web.

11

The Three Body Solution

Just when you think you understand how the world works, new technology comes along to change everything. In addition to smartphones and connected organizers, a third class of device is out there that's part of what's sometimes called a *three body solution*. A PDA like the NZ90 has integrated Bluetooth, which means it can connect to a mobile phone up to 30 feet away. Imagine leaving your mobile phone in your pocket or brief case, dialing a number on the phone from the Clié's Address Book, and automatically taking the call on a Bluetooth headset. Such solutions will get increasingly popular—especially among folks who already use a headset for their mobile phone anyway, and would like to get rid of the clumsy wire that connects the two.

Working with the Palm Mail Program

It's hard to remember life before e-mail, isn't it? Imagine, having to pick up the *phone* every time you want to communicate with someone. Now we just fire off e-mail messages. And with Mail, we needn't wait till we're sitting at our PC to conduct e-mail business.

NOTE *If your Clié comes with Clié Mail, skip to the next section. For the most part, Palm Mail is found only on older devices.*

What *Mail* does, in a nutshell, is link to the e-mail program on your desktop computer. Just as Memo Pad, Address Book, and other applications synchronize with Palm Desktop (or Outlook), Mail synchronizes with Outlook Express, Eudora Pro, and various other e-mail programs. The end result is that Mail becomes a portable extension of that program, letting you view, delete, and reply to messages and write new ones.

NOTE *Mail isn't a stand-alone e-mail client. That is, it works only when it's linked to desktop software.*

This is not to say that Mail is underpowered—quite the opposite. If you don't need, want, or have a wireless Internet connection, then Palm Mail comes in very handy when you're on the road and suddenly think of a message you need to send. Presto: you can compose it on the spot, knowing it'll be sent the next time you HotSync. Or, suppose you take the train to work every morning. You can HotSync before you leave and read all your e-mail from the night before.

Mail also sports some reasonably advanced features, such as blind carbon copies, signatures, and delivery confirmation. And, because it's a Palm OS program, the interface is streamlined and familiar. Let's get you up and running with this great little e-mail manager.

Setting Up Palm Mail

Although Mail comes preinstalled on most older Cliés, you must set it up for use with your desktop e-mail program. It's possible you did this already while installing the Palm Desktop software, which gives you a choice of configuring your e-mail settings then and there or skipping it till later. If you chose the latter (or need to change your settings), you can access the Mail Setup program in Windows by clicking Start | Programs | Sony Handheld | Mail Setup.

The only real step involved in this setup procedure is choosing which e-mail program you use, as shown here:

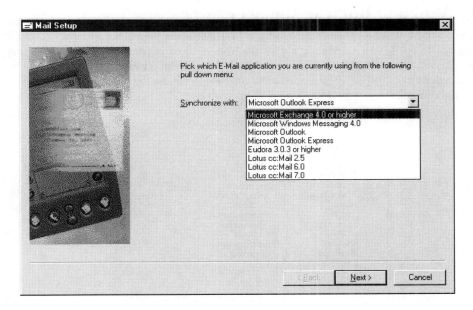

Which Desktop E-mail Programs Does Mail Support?

Mail doesn't work with every e-mail manager on the planet, but it does work with the most popular ones:

- Lotus cc:Mail, versions 2.5, 6.0, and 7.0
- Microsoft Exchange 4.0 or later
- Microsoft Outlook (all versions)
- Microsoft Outlook Express (all versions)
- Microsoft Windows Messaging 4.0
- Qualcomm Eudora 3.03 or later

For the sake of continuity, most of our explanations will center around Outlook Express, one of the most popular e-mail programs. There could be some slight differences if you're using an enterprise-based program like Lotus cc:Mail. Consult your IT manager if you need assistance.

Because of a Windows-related issue, you can't sync your e-mail with Outlook Express if you sync everything else with Outlook. You can, however, use Outlook for outbound HotSync e-mail. And, depending on which version of Windows you use, there might be a solution. Visit **support.microsoft.com** *and search for Fixmapi.exe.*

Palm Mail and HotSync Manager

After you run Mail Setup, check your HotSync Manager settings to make sure they're properly configured. To open HotSync Manager, click the HotSync icon in your Windows System Tray and choose Custom. (You can also access it from within Palm Desktop by choosing HotSync | Custom.) You see a dialog box listing the installed conduits (which handle the actual synchronization for each program) and the setting (that is, action) for each one.

If the action for the Mail conduit reads Synchronize The Files, you're all set. (But don't HotSync yet! We still have to configure the settings on the Clié side.) If, for some reason, it still reads Do Nothing, click the conduit to highlight it, and then click the Change button. In the resulting dialog box, choose Synchronize the Files, and then check the box that says Set as Default.

If you ever decide to stop using Mail, you can simply return to this setup screen and select Do Nothing. Regardless of how you've configured your Clié, this single HotSync Manager setting overrides all others.

Configuring Mail Settings on the Clié

Synchronizing your desktop mail with the Mail applet isn't an all-or-nothing proposition. For instance, you can elect to pull only unread messages into your Clié, or create filters so that only messages tagged as "high priority" will be synchronized. The settings for such options are found in the HotSync Options screen on your handheld, which is accessible by choosing Menu | Options from within the Mail program.

Note that you can configure Mail settings for both local and remote HotSyncs, just by tapping the Settings For arrow at the top of the screen. If you do plan to HotSync remotely, you might, indeed, want to have different synchronization settings to minimize the connection time.

Figure 11-2 shows the HotSync Options screen. Let's take a look at the four choices therein.

All

This option forces all messages to be synchronized between your Clié and your desktop e-mail program. Take caution when selecting this option—if you have more than a couple dozen messages in your PC's Inbox, your HotSyncs could take quite a bit longer (a few minutes instead of a few seconds), and you'll eat up that much more of your Clié's memory.

Send Only

This one-way solution sends any messages composed on your Clié, but it doesn't retrieve messages from your desktop mailbox. Use this if you don't want to view your mail on your Clié.

Filter

The most complex of the e-mail options, Filter lets you choose to ignore messages that meet certain criteria, or retrieve messages that meet certain criteria. Suppose, for instance, you want to retrieve e-mail that comes only from your coworkers. Or you want to ignore messages that originate from a specific address. Filter makes such options possible, all in the interests of giving you greater control over the mail that's retrieved from your desktop mailbox.

NOTE   *If you plan to use filters, plan on experimenting a bit to get them set up right. There's always the concern that you might accidentally miss an important message if, say, the sender misspells the subject name or sends the e-mail using a different-than-expected account. So, use filters with caution.*

11

Unread

Rather than transferring all the e-mail from your Inbox to your Clié, this option transfers only those messages marked as unread. This is an excellent choice if you tend to retain mail on your PC after reading it, as it won't download your entire Inbox.

Truncate   If you find that HotSyncs are taking too long because you often receive lengthy e-mails, or you're just concerned about messages eating up too much of your Clié's memory, you can instruct Mail to truncate (that is, trim) messages that exceed a certain size. By default, Mail truncates messages longer than 4,000 characters, but you can change the value by tapping the Truncate button in the HotSync Options screen.

NOTE   *This has nothing to do with file attachments, which Mail never downloads. If an e-mail in your Inbox has an attachment, it's simply ignored during HotSync.*

The Relationship Between Clié and Desktop

It's important to understand that Mail and your desktop e-mail program are linked together. Thus, when you delete a message on your Clié, it gets deleted on your desktop the next time you HotSync. When you mark a message as read on your desktop, it subsequently gets marked as read on your Clié. Keeping that in mind, consider the following as well:

- In whatever e-mail program you use on your PC, it's not uncommon to have a variety of different mailboxes set up. You might have one marked "personal," another for "work," and so on. This helps you keep inbound messages better organized, rather than lumping them all into a single folder. However, regardless of how you've configured Mail's options or filters, the only place it will retrieve messages from is your main Inbox. Hey—we never said the program was perfect.

- When you compose or reply to a message, the resulting outbound e-mail is sent via Outlook Express (or whatever desktop program you use). Unfortunately, you don't have any control over which desktop e-mail account is used—it's automatically sent via your default account. This might pose a problem if you use multiple accounts and need to send messages using one that's not the default. Again, we never said it was perfect.

Working with Clié Mail

In creating Clié Mail (see Figure 11-1), Sony must have looked at Palm Mail and said, "We can do better." The result is an e-mail program that is, indeed, an improvement. Although Clié Mail can send and receive messages via HotSync, it also supports live Internet connections for e-mail on the go. Translation: if you have a modem or cell-phone connection for your Clié, you needn't be at your computer to send and receive mail. What's more, Clié Mail lets you attach certain items to outgoing messages: an Address Book contact, a memo, a Palm OS program or database (specifically, a PRC or PDB file), or photos stored on your Clié. And certain versions of Clié Mail also let you attach other goodies, like voice memos and movie files captured on the Clié.

Keep in mind that Clié Mail is included only with the newest Clié handhelds, and it's not available to other folks—if you have an older Clié and want Clié Mail, you'll have to buy a new device. Let's look at some of the most important aspects of using Clié Mail:

Installing Clié Mail

Depending on which Clié you own, Clié Mail might not come preloaded on your handheld; in some cases, it's on the Palm Desktop Installation CD-ROM in the section titled "Clié Add-on Applications." If your Clié does include Clié Mail, you'll still have to install the Clié Mail conduit, also found on the CD-ROM (usually in the "Clié Utilities" section).

> NOTE *If you don't plan to synchronize Clié Mail with your desktop e-mail program, but only access e-mail via a wireless connection, you needn't install the Clié Mail Conduit at all.*

The *Clié Mail conduit* does exactly for Clié Mail what the standard Mail conduit does for the Palm Mail program: synchronizes e-mail between your desktop PC and your Clié. Thus, the settings for the Clié Mail conduit can be found in HotSync Manager's Custom dialog box.

Just like with Clié Mail, you need to set the Clié Mail conduit to synchronize with the handheld if you want to get your desktop mail on your PDA, and send PDA mail through the computer's e-mail program.

Working with Attachments

After you compose a new message, you can elect to attach one or more items that will be sent along with the e-mail. If you're using Clié Mail on an NR-series Clié, you can tap the Attach button at the bottom of the screen, and then choose the "Attach Type" from the pull-down list. Your choices include images, Address Book entries, memos, Palm OS apps, and more.

If you have Clié Mail for a newer device, tap the Insert button, and then you can choose any image, voice memo, or video on your Clié for inclusion in the e-mail.

So, just what happens when you attach something to an outgoing e-mail? Address Book entries are automatically converted into a .vcf file, so the recipient can easily import the listing into Palm Desktop or Outlook. Memos become .txt files, suitable for viewing in any text editor or word processor. Photos are automatically sent as JPGs—unless you have an older NR-series Clié, in which case you must first copy them to a Memory Stick in DCF format.

> NOTE *You can receive these kinds of file attachments just as readily as you can send them. Clié Mail gives you the option of previewing attachments and saving them to the appropriate "destinations" on your Clié.*

11

Setting Up Internet E-mail Accounts in Clié Mail

Planning to use Clié Mail with a modem or cell phone? You'll need to set up your e-mail account first. Here's how:

1. Choose Options | Accounts from the Clié Mail menu, and then tap the New button.

2. Follow the instructions on the screens that appear, entering your name, e-mail address, and POP/SMTP server info. If you don't know these last two bits of info, contact your ISP.

3. Enter your account name and password, which are the same ones you use to retrieve mail on your desktop PC.

4. On the Network Setting page, you'll be asked to choose the network settings you want to use with this e-mail account. When you tap the Blank box, you're taken to the Palm OS Network screen, which is normally accessible via the Prefs icon on your Home screen (see Chapter 2 for a refresher). This is where things get a little complicated. Depending on what method you plan to use to connect to the Internet (modem or cell phone), you'll want to have those settings already configured (and tested) in the Network screen. That way, when you get there from within Clié Mail, all you have to do is select the desired service, and then tap Done.

E-mail Alternatives

You don't have to stick with Clié Mail. Many alternatives are available—most of which are commercial applications that cost a small amount of money. This table lists some of the best options currently available:

E-mail Client	Company	Features
Aileron	www.corsoft.com	This outstanding e-mail client's best feature is the capability to send and receive attachments in common word processing and spreadsheet formats.
Basejet	www.basejet.com	An e-mail client that behaves a lot like a desktop program, with lots of cool tap-and-hold menus, 3-D buttons, and drop-down menus. *Basejet* doesn't access your mail server directly. It redirects your PC's desktop e-mail to the PDA, keeping both in sync all the time.
SnapperMail	www.snappermail.com	Our favorite third-party e-mail client, *SnapperMail* has a great interface and can easily handle a wide variety of attachments thanks to "plug-in" applications. It can display JPG images using JpgWatch and sends Word and Excel files to Quickoffice Pro, for instance.

Sending Sketches and Drawings with RiteMail

While Clié Mail lets you attach items like photos and memos, RiteMail goes a step further. *RiteMail* is designed expressly for sending handwritten notes, sketches, maps, or whatever else you care to scribble on your Clié's screen. Indeed, envision your Clié as a blank sheet of paper (or one with gridlines, a feature RiteMail offers), and you get the idea. The software provides some basic tools for writing, erasing, and creating basic shapes.

Just address your note as you would any other e-mail, and then tap the Send icon. RiteMail works much like Clié Mail in that it can send mail when you HotSync or via a live Internet connection. Take it from us: it's a pretty cool product.

Accessing America Online

At last count, America Online (AOL) had something like 70 billion subscribers. Okay, we could be off by a few billion, but there's no debating the popularity of the service. With AOL for Palm OS, you can access your e-mail account(s), as well as some of the service's more popular areas.

11

Get it from within AOL at keyword **Anywhere**, or on the Web at **www.aol.com/anywhere**. You will, of course, need a means of dialing into AOL, via either a Clié modem or your cell-phone connection (see the section "Connecting Your Clié to a Cell Phone for E-mail and Web Browsing").

Web Browsing with the Clié

Did we pique your interest with our discussion of Clié e-mail? As the saying goes, you ain't seen nothin' yet. Your Clié can also double as a portable web browser, though you might need more software than what comes in the box (many newer Cliés do come with *NetFront*, a handy browser).

The Browsers

As we just mentioned, most newer Cliés come with a browser called NetFront. Here's what the program looks like, with a guide to the program's various controls:

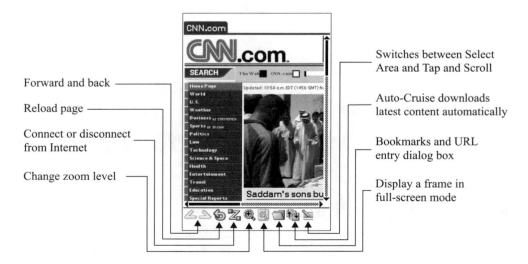

Forward and back

Reload page

Connect or disconnect from Internet

Change zoom level

Switches between Select Area and Tap and Scroll

Auto-Cruise downloads latest content automatically

Bookmarks and URL entry dialog box

Display a frame in full-screen mode

Essential Web Sites

A bunch of web sites are dedicated to the Palm OS family of handheld devices. If you're surfing for good Palm-related content, give some of these sites a try:

- The best collection of downloadable Palm software on the Internet can be found at **www.palmgear.com**.

- Lively discussion forums, news, feature stories, and reviews are at **www.pdabuzz.com**, a site that caters to all kinds of handheld PCs.

- Call it a plug if you like, but we can't help recommending *Handheld Computing* and *Mobility,* two magazines you can subscribe to at **www.hhcmag.com.** Yeah, we're the editors, but we also think these two magazines give you the definitive word on all things Palm OS and Clié.

- Thanks to news and message boards, **www.Cliésource.com** is an interesting place to stop for Clié information.

Don't want to use NetFront—or your Clié doesn't include it? That's okay—you can add your own browser. Several Palm OS browsers are available for the Clié, including AvantGo, Blazer, Eudora, PocketLink, and Xiino. AvantGo and Eudora are free, but the others offer more features.

Surfing Limitations

Once you have a browser installed and some sort of modem (either wired or wireless) attached, you're ready to start surfing. Surfing with your PDA is radically different than surfing with your PC, though. Keep these limitations in mind as you start exploring the Internet with your Clié:

- *Graphics are much more limited.*   It doesn't take a rocket scientist to deduce this one, but you don't have a lot of room to work with. Most browsers can squeeze large graphics to fit on the small screen, but it can make them hard to see clearly.

■ *Connection speeds are much lower.* Your overall Web surfing experience might be a lot more sluggish than you're used to, especially if your desktop PC has a broadband connection. It can take minutes, not seconds, for a web page to display.

■ *Don't download.* The Clié isn't equipped to handle ordinary Windows applications or data files, so don't bother trying to download anything. (One exception: you can download Clié applications using the Xiino browser.)

Channel Surfing with AvantGo

Buy all the modems you want—the Web just doesn't fit on a 2- or 3-inch screen. Enter *AvantGo,* a free service that not only delivers web-based content to your Clié, but also formats it to look pretty (and readable). With every HotSync, the software downloads your preselected channels—everything from news and stock reports to driving directions and movie show times—using your computer's modem to ferry the data. Pretty slick—and did we mention it's free?

Setting Up AvantGo

To get started with AvantGo, visit the AvantGo web site and download the software. Install it per the instructions—you'll need to set up an account, complete with username and password.

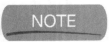

Even if AvantGo is included on your installation CD-ROM, you're better off visiting the AvantGo site and installing the newest software because it's occasionally updated with new features.

To set up the channels you want to transfer to your Clié, go to the AvantGo web site and log in. Your currently selected channels appear in a box called My Account. You can browse the AvantGo web site and click any channel you like to add it to your personal AvantGo hot list.

Editing Your Channel Content

Most AvantGo channels are configured to work well on a handheld device with limited memory. Sometimes, however, you might want to customize the way channel content is delivered to your Clié. Take *The Onion,* for instance—Dave loves to read this news parody each week, but the site is so large that many of the stories often aren't downloaded to the Clié in their entirety. The solution?

How to ...   Use Wireless Channels

AvantGo is mainly known for its offline browsing capabilities, but it also supports wireless channels and real-time web browsing. Visit the "Wireless" section of the AvantGo site and you'll find a collection of channels that are interactive when used with a wireless connection (like your cell phone). You can request real-time stock quotes, find movies playing in your area, get map data, and more. In fact, here are some of our favorite wireless channels:

- **White Pages and Yellow Pages**   The "killer app" for wireless handheld devices! You can look up people and companies using this channel—just enter their name and city to get an address and phone number. Or, if you already have a phone number, but you need the street address, you can search that way, too.
- **Hollywood.com**   This channel lets you find movie listings, theaters, and show times for movies wherever you happen to be.
- **Trip.com**   Want to know details about a flight—like its airspeed, flight path, and arrival time? This channel lets you find that data.

Dave increased the Maximum Channel Size from the default of 100KB to 500KB so it all fits on his Clié. To edit your channels as cleverly as Dave, open the AvantGo web page, log in, and click a channel in the My Account box. You should see the Channel Properties page. Make your changes and click the Save Channel Changes button.

Using AvantGo on Your Clié

While we've spent a lot of time talking about configuring AvantGo channels in your desktop's web browser, all the fun stuff really happens on your Clié. Tap the AvantGo icon and you should see all the channels you selected and configured on the Web.

If you don't see any channels in AvantGo, it's probably because you haven't HotSynced yet. Remember, with AvantGo installed, channel updates are downloaded and transferred to your Clié every time you HotSync. That means you must be online before you press the HotSync button.

To use AvantGo, tap one of the channels in the My Channels list. You can read text, view pictures, and drill deeper into the channel by tapping links. Two navigational tools are built into every channel page:

- Tap the navigational arrows to move forward and backward through the current channel.
- Tap the Home icon to return to the My Channels list.

11

In addition to reading cached channels on your Clié, AvantGo can also be used to open live web pages if you have a cell phone attached. To do that, follow these steps:

1. Start AvantGo.

2. Choose Channels | Connect from the menu. This tells AvantGo to activate your modem.

3. Choose Channels | Open Page from the menu. Enter the URL you want to visit and tap OK.

Some users prefer using a program called Plucker *(available at PalmGear, of course) instead of AvantGo. Another program,* Mobipocket, *offers functionality that's similar to* AvantGo, *but doesn't have nearly as many channels. It does, however, double as an e-book reader, as detailed in Chapter 21.*

All About Bluetooth

As you've no doubt gathered by now, Bluetooth is a short-range wireless technology that allows devices to communicate with each other up to a distance of about 30 feet. That's really just a fancy way of saying that Bluetooth is a technology designed to replace connection cables. By using Bluetooth, handheld gadgets like your Clié and cell phone can communicate with each other without wires and without even getting in line-of-sight with each other.

That said, Bluetooth is a new technology that's just starting to hit the streets. This is obvious from the overall lack of Bluetoothness in the world; only a few Sony Cliés ship with Bluetooth built in.

So, suppose you have a Bluetooth-ready Clié like the NZ90. What can you do with it? Right now, the killer app is connecting your Clié to a Bluetooth mobile phone to get Internet access. That means you need to get a phone with built-in Bluetooth. When we wrote this chapter, only a handful of phones were available with integrated Bluetooth; by the time you read this, no doubt there will be more:

- Sony Ericsson T39
- Sony Ericsson T68i
- Nokia 6310i
- Nokia 3650

Once your Bluetooth adapter is installed, here are some of the things you can do with your Palm:

- *Dial the phone.*   Just tap on a phone number to dial the phone from your Clié's Address Book.

- *Access the Internet for Web and E-mail.*   Once you configure PDA to recognize your Bluetooth cell phone, you can use your Bluetooth connection like any PDA modem to access the Internet.

- *Print.*   Armed with a Bluetooth-aware printer driver from Bachmann Software (PrintBoy) or IS/Complete (BtPrint), you can print to a Bluetooth-enabled desktop or portable printer. Epson, MPI Tech, and HP all sell Bluetooth adapters that work with desktop printers and the Pentax PocketJet 200 portable printer.

FIGURE 11-3   The Prefs app lists all of the "trusted devices" your Clié is paired with.

Pairing Devices

Ready to try your hand at Bluetooth? Once configured, it's easy to use—but you need to begin by "pairing" the two devices that need to communicate with each other. The pairing process is Bluetooth's built-in security. When devices are paired, as in Figure 11-3, both know they have permission to communicate with each other. It's pairing that prevents you from walking down the street and connecting to a total stranger's Bluetooth device.

■ Typically, you'll start by pairing your Clié with a mobile phone. Start with the Sony Mobile Connection Wizard, which should be on your Clié's Installation CD-ROM. You can also get an updated version—with the newest phones and services—from the Sony web site's Service & Support link. This utility runs on the desktop—use it to choose your phone and wireless service, and then HotSync to transfer the settings to your PDA.

Where to Find It

Web Site	Address	What's There
CliéSource	www.Cliésource.com	All manner of software for the Clié
Handango	www.handango.com	Palm OS e-mail programs and web browsers (and lots of other software)
PalmGear H.Q.	www.palmgear.com	Palm OS e-mail programs and web browsers (and lots of other software)
RiteMail	www.ritemail.net	RiteMail
Psion	www.psion.com	Psion Travel Modem
3JTech	www.3jtec.com	PP2I-5600B infrared modem

Chapter 12

Your Clié as a Total PC Replacement

How to...

- Use your Clié as a complete business application computer
- Read and edit Word and Excel documents on your Clié
- Distinguish between Palm Doc and Word .doc files
- Import Clié documents into Microsoft Word
- Generate graphs and charts on the Clié
- View Adobe Acrobat files
- Print to wireless printers
- Print to serial and parallel printers

The core applications that come with your Clié are fine for many people—they offer all the basic functionality you need to stay on top of contact information and schedules while on the go. But, as you've already seen in this book, your Clié can do so much more. In fact, it's possible to use your Clié as a full-fledged alternative PC, capable of running applications as varied as a word processor, a spreadsheet, and a database program.

Why on Earth would you want to do that? Well, which would you rather carry around—a Clié that fits in your pocket or a seven-pound laptop? Which is easier to store in a hotel room? Which is more easily stolen? Which lasts longer on a set of batteries? We think you get the idea. Obviously, using a suite of "office" applications on your Clié isn't for everyone, and it won't work all the time. After all, a Clié has a limited amount of storage space and a much smaller screen than a laptop. Most PDA-sized document editors don't support an extremely extensive array of formatting options, so even if you exchange documents with your desktop apps, your text and format options could be somewhat limited. But if you're intrigued by the thought of leaving your PC at home and traveling only with a Clié, then read on. This chapter is all about creating the perfect Clié office.

Building the Perfect Beast

No, we weren't really big fans of that Don Henley solo album either. But that does describe your Clié if you want to outfit it to be a mobile office, complete with office applications.

The name of the game when it comes to creating a Clié office is convenience and compatibility. What good is it, for instance, to generate documents on your Clié if they're not readable by the word processor on your PC? And why bother trying to do office-style work on your Clié if you can't do it easily, efficiently, and in all the formats you're used to on your desktop? With this in mind, here's a checklist of things to consider if you plan to do serious work on your Clié:

- **Your Clié**   Have memory. Lots of memory. Working with Word documents, databases, and spreadsheets soaks up space, so you should invest in a Clié with plenty of free space. Newer Cliés are starting to appear with 32MB of total system memory, which is a lot better than last year's models—especially some of the NX/NZ Cliés, which came with just 11MB free. And we highly recommend investing in expansion memory, like a 128MB Memory Stick or an even larger Memory Stick Pro (if your Clié supports that variety). Equipped with a large expansion card, you can store lots of files on your PDA without running out of memory. How much memory does your Clié have? Find out by choosing Menu | App | Info from the Home screen.

- **A keyboard**   As much as we love Graffiti, the fact remains you'll hate writing long documents or entering data in a spreadsheet with the stylus alone. Invest in a keyboard. Several compact, yet comfortable keyboards are available for your Clié; see Chapter 23 for a rundown of the best ones.

- **Office suite**   If you want to create new documents or edit files you made in Microsoft Word, then a simple document reader like Palm Reader won't be enough. You should try an office suite instead. Although these applications aren't quite full-featured suites—at least not in the sense that Microsoft Office on the desktop is—a number of them deliver sophisticated tools like spelling checkers, rich text formatting, charting for your spreadsheets, and more. Most important, these programs break through the file-size limit imposed by the Memo Pad and let you edit documents of almost unlimited length that can be shared with Word and Excel. Note, while many Cliés come with Picsel Viewer, that program only lets you view documents, not edit them.

- **Adobe Reader**   If your office makes extensive use of PDF files, you should have a PDF file viewer on your Clié so you can view those documents on the go. Many Cliés come with Picsel Viewer, which is a superb option—if you have it, you're set. If not, see our suggestions in the section called "Adobe Acrobat on the Clié."

- **Database**   Yes, database applications are available even for Palm OS PDAs like the Clié. A slew of them let you create new databases from scratch, and most even let you import existing databases from programs like Access, FileMaker, and other ODBC-complaint applications. Some of the most popular database engines for the Clié include HanDBase, JFile, MobileDB, ThinkDB, and dbNow. FileMaker also has its own PDA "companion" to Filemaker, called (not too surprisingly) FileMaker Mobile. If you're a FileMaker user, FileMaker Mobile could be all you need.

Top Ten Reasons to Use a Clié

Dave: With all the really neat office-like applications available for the Clié, it got us thinking. What are the top ten uses for a handheld computer? So, here it goes (and if you imagine us reading this off blue cards at your local book store, you've pretty much experienced a *How to Do Everything with Your Clié* book signing):

10. New excuse at work: I was writing the weekly status report, but I dropped it and it broke.

9. Something new to lose!

8. Makes you look like a spy.

7. It's smarter than your dog. Wait—that's also true of houseplants and silverware.

6a. As a *Star Trek: The Next Generation* fan, you like to pretend you're an Enterprise crewmember on an away mission.

6b. As a *Star Trek: The Original Series* fan, you like to pretend you're an Enterprise crewmember in a landing party.

You know, for me, the funny thing is you have to be a *Star Trek* fan to even appreciate the difference between those last two items.

Rick: For me, it's funny to hear Dave describe any of his half of the list as "funny."

5. Gives you a great pickup line: "Hey, let's HotSync!"

4. When tipping the pizza guy, now you can calculate 15 percent of $36.87 to the exact penny.

3. No one can tell you're reading Monica Lewinsky's biography.

2. You can look busy in a board meeting when you're actually playing a game of SimCity.

1. They don't put a single penny into Bill Gates's pocket!

Dealing with Documents

If you're like most business travelers, you're used to carting a laptop around with you to edit Word documents. If you have a 14-inch or 15-inch display, then you know what it's like trying to get the laptop screen open in the cramped space on an airplane seat. Heck, sometimes we can't get it open far enough to read what we're typing.

Thankfully, there's an easier solution. Your Clié—combined with a keyboard—can take the place of your laptop for text entry. You can even synchronize specific Word documents with your

Understanding the Doc Format

All Doc files are not created alike. Specifically, when Clié users talk about Doc files—text documents in the Doc format—they're not gabbing about Microsoft Word's .doc format but, instead, about a text format originally popularized by a program called, unfortunately, Doc (we say "unfortunately" because it created confusion that lasts to this very day). These days, programs like TealDoc and Palm Reader are generally considered the de facto standard among text readers today. While any Doc file can be read by almost any Doc reader/editor for the Clié (and vice versa), the Doc format is totally incompatible with the version used by Microsoft Word. On the plus side, you can generally get converters for most of these readers that convert desktop .doc to Palm Doc files and back again.

Clié, edit them on the road, and update your desktop PC with the latest versions of your work when you get home.

Viewing Documents with Picsel Viewer

Sony includes a document viewer with many Clié models that's nothing short of amazing. If you need to view documents—but not edit them—then you owe it to yourself to use Picsel Viewer. It perfectly renders documents in very high resolution, making it easy to read even the most detailed PDF file. Picsel Viewer can display documents in a variety of formats, which include the following:

- Word
- Excel
- HTML (Web pages)
- PowerPoint
- Adobe Acrobat (PDF)
- JPG images

To display these files in Picsel Viewer, you first need to get them onto your Clié. There's no desktop conversion application—just copy them to a Memory Stick via the Install Tool or by copying the files directly using a desktop memory card reader. It doesn't matter what folder the files are stored within; you can even create a new folder called something like Office or Documents and store them there.

TIP *Picsel Viewer didn't come on your Clié? Don't be sad—there's a third-party program that's quite similar. It's called RepliGo, and you can get it from **www.repligo.com**.*

12

When you run Picsel Viewer, you see an interface that looks like this:

There are no menus; the program is controlled from the Carousel icon in the lower right corner. You'll them see the Carousel in the middle of the screen. Here's what each of the icons does.

To open a document, tap the File icon and navigate to the proper folder on the Memory Stick. Tap the document you want to open.

Once a document is open, you can pan and zoom. To pan around a large file, you can drag it with your finger or a stylus by tapping-and-dragging on the screen. You can also pan up and down using

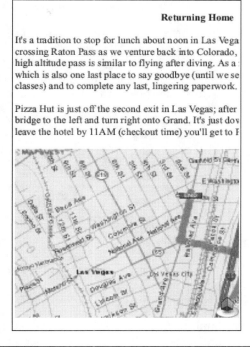

FIGURE 12-1   You can get an overview of the entire document or zoom in for a closer look—and the document remains sharp and easy to read, no matter what the magnification level.

the Jog Wheel on the side of the Clié. To zoom, Press the Jog Wheel in and roll it up (zoom in) or down (zoom out). Check out Figure 12-1 for a look at two views of the same Word document in Picsel Viewer. To cycle through a multipage document (like slides in a PowerPoint presentation), use the up and down buttons on your Clié.

We love Picsel Viewer, but it has a big disadvantage: it can only display documents, not edit them. For editing capabilities, you need an office suite.

Using an Office Suite

Pocket PC users have one teeny-tiny advantage over Clié users—a Microsoft-branded office suite that includes Pocket Word and Pocket Excel. People can trust those apps to be very compatible with Microsoft Office on the desktop.

What a lot of people don't realize, though, is that there are several excellent Office-compatible suites for the Clié as well. Most Cliés come with one right in the box, in fact: Documents to Go,

12

Standard Edition, from DataViz. If your Clié didn't come with an office suite—or you want to try another, you'll be happy to know you can choose from three popular suites:

- **Documents to Go (www.dataviz.com)** Documents to Go is quite popular by virtue of the fact that Palm, Sony, and other Palm OS companies put it in the box of every new PDA they sell. The standard version works with Word and Excel files, and you can upgrade to the 5.0 Professional Edition, which includes additional support for PowerPoint, Adobe Acrobat, and other office tools. Documents to Go supports the full-screen mode on Clié models with a collapsible Graffiti area.

- **iambic Office (www.iambic.com)** Composed of FastWriter and TinySheet, these programs offer Word and Excel connectivity for your Clié. In addition, the suite includes *iambic Mail,* an e-mail Clíent that lets you synchronize messages with your desktop e-mail program or check mail on the go with a modem. iambic Mail uses FastWriter and TinySheet to let you read Word and Excel attachments in e-mail.

- **Quickoffice (www.cesinc.com)** This suite includes Quickword and Quicksheet for reading and editing Word and Excel documents. *Quickword* has its own thesaurus and spell checker, and you can install custom fonts as well. *Quickoffice* supports the full-screen mode on models with a collapsible Graffiti area, and it's Dave's choice for all-around document work on the road.

If you don't want the entire suite, you can usually buy the word processor and spreadsheet separately by visiting the vendor's web site. Cutting Edge Software sells Quickword all by itself, for instance, if you don't need Quicksheet.

Did you know?

If You Only Need Word

Not everyone wants or needs a complete office suite. And, consequently, you can buy any of the suites mentioned in this chapter one piece at a time—instead of the entire Quickoffice suite, for instance, you can just buy Quickword or Quicksheet.

There's another option as well. If you only want a word processor, you can choose Wordsmith or Mobile Word. Both of these are inexpensive word processors designed from the ground up to be great PDA word processors, but they're standalone apps that don't have companion spreadsheet programs.

Wordsmith is a long-time favorite among Palm OS users. It's a great e-book reader (see Chapter 21), has superb font rendering, and retains much of the fancy formatting of desktop Word documents. Stuff like bullets, numbering, and paragraph formatting are fully supported.

12

Mobile Word, on the other hand, is brand new and offers some really cool features not seen on a Palm OS word processor before—like the capability to embed images from a PDA paint program into word documents. It also underlines misspelled words, just like Microsoft Word—a very cool feature.

Transferring Documents Between the Clié and Desktop

No matter which suite you choose, they all work more or less the same way: you use a desktop application to manage the documents you want to work with on the Clié. That's because most office suites don't read and write Microsoft Office documents directly. Instead, they need to convert Word and Excel files, for instance, into file formats that can be understood by the PDA software. That means there's an intermediate "conversion" step to get going.

Just drag the document you want to move into the suite manager (you can see several of them in the following illustration), and it'll be copied to the Clié at the next HotSync. When you make a change to the document on either the Clié or the desktop, it'll be synchronized after the following HotSync, keeping the two documents exactly the same.

If you prefer not to synchronize your Clié documents with their cousins on the desktop, that's fine as well. In each suite manager, you can disable synchronization and select familiar options such as Handheld overwrites, Desktop overwrites, and Do nothing:

What if you create a new document from scratch on the Clié? No problem. On the next HotSync after you create the document, you'll find it's been synchronized with the desktop. To find it, open your suite manager software and double-click on the new file; it'll automatically open in Word.

Editing Native Office Files

There's one important exception to this file conversion process. The newest versions of both Documents to Go and Quickoffice Premier support native Microsoft Office files. That means you just need to drag-and-drop the original Word, Excel, and PowerPoint files onto your Clié's Memory Stick to immediately begin using them—no need for a desktop conversion at all. Even better, you can get Office documents as attachments in e-mail programs and edit them on the PDA:

- **Documents to Go**   To receive and edit Office e-mail attachments on your Clié, you need *DataViz Inbox to Go,* which interfaces with Documents to Go to provide seamless document viewing and editing.

- **Quickoffice Premier**   If you use Quickoffice and want to edit Word and Excel files you receive via e-mail on your Palm, use *SnapperMail* (shown in Figure 12-2), from **Snapperfish.com**.

Working with Documents and Spreadsheets

If you want to leave your laptop at home and just carry a PDA, it's absolutely essential to be able to read and edit Word and Excel files on the go. Any of the suites we've already mentioned will work and, if all you care about is text, you have a fourth excellent option as well—a program from Blue Nomad called WordSmith. WordSmith doesn't come as part of a suite with a spreadsheet. Instead, it's a stand-alone word processor for the Clié that, like Quickoffice, includes font support,

12

FIGURE 12-2   New e-mail programs such as SnapperMail and Inbox to Go let you get native Office files as attachments and edit them right on your Clié, and then forward the completed documents via wireless e-mail back to someone's desktop.

a spelling checker, thesaurus, and sophisticated formatting controls. Many users choose WordSmith as their word processor of choice, especially if they don't also need a spreadsheet.

While most Clié word processors try hard to preserve all the formatting in your document, keep in mind that these programs do it with varying levels of success. You might find, for instance, that group annotations or graphics like "boxes" around text could be stripped out when the files are synchronized back to the PC. As a consequence, word processing on the PDA is often best reserved

 Work with Documents on the Clié

In a nutshell, here's what you need to know to work with text documents on the Clié:

1. To create or edit long documents on your Clié, you need a program like Documents To Go, Quickoffice, iambic Office, or WordSmith.

2. On the desktop, open your office suite's manager application.

3. Click the button to add a file, or drag-and-drop a document into the suite's manager's window.

4. Close the program, and then HotSync to transfer the files to the Clié.

5. Edit the files on your Clié.

6. HotSync to carry the changes you made to the Clié back to the desktop versions of the affected files.

for documents that have fairly conservative amounts of formatting. In addition, some word processors have more formatting features than others. Documents to Go, for instance, could be popular, but it can't hold a candle to WordSmith and Quickword when it comes to features like offering a spelling checker and a thesaurus.

Bottom line: because all office suites have a free trial period, we recommend installing all of them and seeing which one you like best.

Charts and Graphs on the Clié

Spreadsheets are often reported to be the most popular PC-based application in the history of computers (we're not sure who they talked to—personally, we'd vote for games). And, like milk and cereal or guitars and rock 'n roll, nothing goes with spreadsheets quite like charts and graphs. It makes sense, then, that you might want to view your spreadsheet data visually in the form of charts and graphs even on your Clié. You're in luck: both Iambic Office and Quickoffice come with their

Better Software for Bigger Screens

If you feel constrained by the anemic size of the Clié display and can't imagine word processing on such a small screen, you're not alone. That's why Cliés offer dramatically higher resolutions than PDAs of yesteryear—either 320×320 or 320×480. Virtually all office suites take full advantage of all those pixels (at press time, only iambic Office didn't), along with a variety of fonts and font sizes. So you can pack a lot more data on the screen—provided you have strong enough eyesight to see all those little letters.

12

own spreadsheet graphing tools. As you can see in the following, you can make some attractive graphs using these programs.

Adobe Acrobat on the Clié

In most offices, Word and Excel pop up pretty often—but Adobe Acrobat files, also known by their file extension as PDF files, are incredibly popular as well. That's because PDFs are self-contained, fancy-looking text-and-graphic documents that display exactly the same, no matter what kind of computer you view them on. They also can't be edited, so you can distribute a PDF secure in the knowledge that some clown in room 234 won't make changes to your handiwork.

That's great, but how do you view them on the Clié? If your PDA came with Picsel Viewer, use that—it's great. If your Clié doesn't come with that viewer, though, here are two of the most popular two ways to display Adobe Acrobat files on your PDA:

- **Documents to Go Professional** has its own PDF viewer. On the downside, this viewer strips out graphics, so it's only useful for text-based documents.

- **RepliGo** is a multitalented document reader, much like Sony's Picsel Viewer. It has superb Adobe PDF viewing capabilities. Indeed, if you don't have Picsel on your PDA, you should get RepliGo.

- **Adobe Reader for Palm** is a free program from Adobe that lets you download PDF files to your Clié. This program lets you choose to include or strip out graphics, so you can save memory on your PDA by leaving out nonessential graphics or leave them in if they're needed to understand the document.

PowerPoint on Your Clié

The last piece of the puzzle is PowerPoint. If you lug your laptop around just so you can deliver slideshows on the road, well, we have some good news for you. Your Palm is capable of pumping slides directly to a projector—in their entire 1024×768, full-color glory.

- **Margi Presenter-to-Go**   If you want to plug your Clié into a projector, get Presenter-to-Go. This product is available in several versions, including a Memory Stick card for your Clié. You can fit hundreds of slides in memory, they project in high-res and full-color, and you can avoid all the hassles that go with setting up, booting, carrying, and managing a laptop.

■ **iGo Pitch**   Like Margi's line of PowerPoint projectors, *Pitch* lets you display PowerPoint presentations stored on your Clié directly on a VGA screen. Pitch is a small, PDA-sized gadget that connects to your Clié via a HotSync cable (you can use just a HotSync cable or the entire cradle) or even wirelessly via Bluetooth (if you have a Bluetooth-equipped PDA like the NZ90). The Pitch hardware also has a standard VGA connector for attaching it to a monitor or projector.

Printing from Your Clié

The ultimate handheld PC would probably look a lot like the Clié, but with one important difference: it would have a paper-thin printer embedded inside, enabling you to print anything you see on the screen. While that's pure fantasy—kind of like Rick having the ability to beat Dave at any game of skill or knowledge—this doesn't mean you can't print stuff from a Clié. Quite the contrary: armed with a print driver, you can send a wide variety of documents from your Clié to a desktop printer or to a portable, pocket-sized printer.

To print anything from your Clié, you need to add a print driver. Several are available, and selecting one might not be as easy as it sounds. You need to consider these ingredients:

■ **What you want to print**   Some print drivers only print data from the Clié's four core apps, while others can print documents from certain office suites.

■ **What kind of printer you want to print to**   If you have your eye on a compact, battery-operated portable printer, you'll need to find a print driver that works with that printer.

This chart outlines some key data for the most common Clié print drivers:

	Print Methods	Common Software
InStep Print	Infrared	Documents to Go Quickoffice iambic Office Wordsmith
BtPrint Pro	Bluetooth and infrared	Documents to Go WordSmith
PalmPrint	Bluetooth and infrared	Quickoffice
PrintBoy Anywhere	Bluetooth, infrared, Wi-Fi, serial, and TCP/IP	Documents to Go Quickoffice Wordsmith

12

Be sure to visit the web site of each of these print driver vendors to check their latest list of compatible programs and printers.

Infrared Printers for Your Clié

The easiest way to print from your Clié to a nearby printer is via infrared or Bluetooth. Your Clié's infrared port (the same one that you can use to beam apps and data to other PDAs) can communicate directly with compatible printers, and Bluetooth PDAs like the NZ90 can wirelessly send print jobs to nearby printers as well. A small handful of lightweight portable and IR-enabled printers are around. If you like the idea of printing wirelessly from your Clié, or if you travel frequently and want to print from wherever you happen to be, look into one of these:

Manufacturer	Printer	Comments
Canon	BJC-50	Lightweight mobile printer
	BJC-80	Lightweight mobile printer
Datamax	E-3202	Desktop thermal printer
Hewlett-Packard	LaserJet 2100	Desktop laser printer
	DeskJet 450	Portable color inkjet printer (infrared and Bluetooth)
Pentax	PocketJet 200	Lightweight mobile thermal printer (infrared optional)
Sipix	Pocket Printer A6	Handheld portable printer (discontinued, but still available in retail)

Bluetooth Printing

If you have a Bluetooth-equipped Clié, you can print wirelessly to a Bluetooth-enabled printer. As we wrote this chapter, our Bluetooth options in the printing world were somewhat limited, but we expect that will slowly start to change over the next year.

Several desktop-bound printers can accept Bluetooth adapters. Epson sells its own Bluetooth Adapter (a small gadget that plugs into the back of the printer), and you can send print jobs to the printer from up to about 30 feet away. Anycom and MPI Tech sell similar gadgets for a wider range of printers.

Of course, if you get a Bluetooth printer, you'll need a Bluetooth-aware print driver for your Palm as well. There are two, and both worked great in our testing:

- **PrintBoy Anywhere**   bachmannsoftware.com
- **BtPrint**   iscomplete.org

IrDA

Technically, IrDA stands for the Infrared Data Association, which is just a bunch of companies that make IR-enabled products. More important, though, IrDA represents the industry-standard infrared port you can find on most laptops, handheld PCs, and printers with IR ports. If you find a printer with an IrDA port, chances are excellent it'll work with one of the Clié's print drivers.

Where to Find It

Web Site	Address	What's There
Stevens Creek	www.stevenscreek.com	PalmPrint
DataViz	www.dataviz.com	Documents To Go
Blue Nomad	www.bluenomad.com	WordSmith
Cutting Edge Software	www.cesinc.com	Quickoffice
Iambic Software	www.iambic.com	Iambic Office
IS/Complete	www.iscomplete.org	BtPrint, IrPrint
Bachmann Software	www.bachmannsoftware.com	PrintBoy Anywhere
Instep Group	www.instepgroup.com	InStep Print
MPI Tech	www.mpitech.com	Bluetooth adapter
Anycom	www.anycom.com	Bluetooth adapter
RepliGo	www.repligo.com	RepliGo document reader

12

Chapter 13

Hacks and Other Handy Utilities

How to...

- Install and use Hacks
- Make capital letters the easy way
- Automatically correct spelling errors
- Drag-and-drop text
- Use the hard buttons to load multiple applications
- Remove duplicate entries from your databases automatically
- Access "hidden" Clié memory
- Manage and beam applications
- Choose a launcher
- Create your own Palm OS software
- Find and install Graffiti area skins

When you hear the word "utilities," you probably think of your monthly electric bill or those four worthless Monopoly properties (hey, $150 isn't gonna break anybody's bank). In the world of computers and Cliés, however, *utilities* are software programs that add capabilities and fix problems. They're power tools, though not necessarily limited to power users.

In this chapter, we tell you about some cool and worthwhile Palm OS utilities. When we're done, you'll find yourself with a reliable backup that can overcome any data-loss disaster, a way to drag-and-drop text, a timesaving way to write capital letters, and lots more. Utilities might sound boring and technical, but they're fun, easy to use, and extremely practical.

X-Master

The mother of all Clié utilities, X-Master is what separates the men from the boys, the women from the girls. It's a tool Tim Allen would love, as it allows Clié devices to reach beyond their limits, to achieve "more power!" And, it's a tool many users come to find indispensable.

CAUTION *Hacks don't work on the Clié NX/NZ series and other models equipped with Palm OS 5. However, some software developers have introduced OS 5–compatible versions of their products. See the section "OS 5 Hacks" for some utilities specific to your operating system (OS). In the meantime, don't install X-Master (or any Hacks) on your OS 5 device—it could cause major problems. That said, TealPoint Software's TealMaster does offer an OS 5 compatibility mode, but that might be more trouble than it's worth—unless there are some Hacks you absolutely cannot live without.*

What X-Master Does

Technically speaking, *X-Master* is an "operating system extension manager." By itself, it serves no function. But it enables the use of *Hacks*—little programs that extend the capabilities of your Clié. Forget the negative connotations usually associated with "hacking"—these programs are here to help, not harm.

And if you want to run them, you must first download and install X-Master. See Chapter 4 for information on installing programs like this—it's applicable to the Hacks you'll be downloading as well.

 Because Hacks tinker directly with the Palm OS, they can create the occasional glitch. And the more Hacks you have installed and running, the greater the likelihood of some sort of problem. The most common is your Clié device crashing, which is usually more of an annoyance than anything else.

As you venture out into the world of Clié software, you might discover other Hack managers. For instance, there's *HackMaster,* the granddaddy that started this whole crazy Hack business. There's also *TealMaster,* the most robust and feature-rich of all the Hack managers. But we're partial to X-Master because we've used it extensively and it has just the features we need. Plus, it's freeware—unlike TealMaster, which costs $9.95 (still a great deal).

How to Use It

Launching X-Master is no different from launching any other program—you just tap its icon. But, as previously noted, the software is useless without any Hacks loaded. Therefore, to help you learn to use this utility, we're going to walk you through the installation of one of our favorite Hacks.

It's called *MiddleCaps,* and it saves you from having to write the Graffiti upstroke every time you want to create an uppercase letter. Instead, you simply write the letter so it crosses the invisible line between the letter and number sides of the Graffiti area. We find this enables us to write much more quickly and naturally.

NOTE *If your handheld has Graffiti 2, you don't need MiddleCaps. That's because Graffiti 2 works exactly the same way when it comes to uppercase letters: they appear automatically when you write across the middle.*

MiddleCaps is freeware, as many Hacks are, so you can download and use it free of charge. (A note of appreciation e-mailed to the author is always nice.) You can find MiddleCaps at **PalmGear.com**, among other sites. Let's get it running on your Clié device.

1. Download MiddleCaps and install it on your Clié. You won't find an icon for it in the Home screen. The only real evidence of Hacks appears in X-Master.

2. Tap the X-Master icon to load the utility, and you'll see MiddleCaps listed.

13

3. Notice the empty box to the left of the name. Tap it with your stylus and you'll see a check mark appear. That means the Hack is now enabled. If you want to disable it, just tap the box again. (For purposes of our tutorial, please leave it enabled.)

4. Notice the Configure button at the bottom of the screen. Tap it to set up MiddleCaps (a one-time procedure).

5. You're now in the MiddleCaps Preferences screen, where you can tweak a few of the program's settings. For now, check the box marked Caps On Crossing. This means a capital letter will appear whenever you write a character that crosses between the letter and number sides of the Graffiti area. You can test it by tapping to place your cursor on the line near the bottom of the screen, and then doing some sample writing.

Tap OK to return to the main X-Master screen. That's it! MiddleCaps is now enabled and will work in all Clié applications—even third-party ones.

How to ...   Beam Hacks to Other Users

X-Master has the enviable capability to beam Hacks directly to other users (see Chapter 4 for more information on beaming). But before you start, make sure the recipient has X-Master (or HackMaster or another Hack manager). If he doesn't, you'll need to beam a copy of X-Master before you beam any Hacks. However, X-Master doesn't include the option of beaming itself. For that, you must return to the Home screen and tap Menu | App | Beam. Choose X-Master from the list, and then tap the Beam button. Now you can return to X-Master and beam some Hacks. Highlight the one you want to share, and then tap Menu | Extensions | Beam.

What about those other two buttons at the bottom of the X-Master screen? You can tap Details to get version information and other notes about the Hack or tap Info to get the Hack's "splash screen."

Important Notes About Hacks

You need to abide by a few rules of thumb when using X-Master on your Clié, all of them intended to keep things running smoothly:

- If you ever decide to delete a Hack from your Clié, make sure you disable it first! If you try to delete a Hack while it's still running, it could causes errors, crashes, or even data loss.

- If you install two or three Hacks on your Clié, don't enable them all simultaneously. Instead, enable one at a time, making sure each works properly before enabling the next one.

- If you have to reset your Clié for any reason, a message pops up asking if you want to "reinstall your formerly active collection of system Hacks." Tap Reinstall (the equivalent of "yes") only if you're sure it wasn't a Hack that forced you to have to reset in the first place. Otherwise, tap Cancel. Then you can go back into X-Master and manually enable your Hacks again.

World's Greatest Hacks

If you were impressed by what MiddleCaps did for your Clié, wait 'til you get a load of some of our other favorites. Rather than list them by name, which doesn't always express what they do, we're going to list them by function. You can find all these Hacks at **PalmGear.com**.

13

Automatically Correcting Spelling Errors

Giving Graffiti a helping hand, CorrectHack works like the AutoCorrect feature in Microsoft Word, automatically correcting words you frequently misspell. Alas, it doesn't have a database of its own; you have to supply both the words and their correct spellings. But as you compile your list over time, you'll wind up with far fewer mistakes. And you can also use CorrectHack as shorthand for commonly used words. For instance, you write your initials, and the software automatically plugs in your full name.

Fonts…Lots and Lots of Fonts

The Palm OS comes with a whopping three fonts: regular, bold, and large. That's not nearly enough for those of us who grew up with Arial, Century Gothic, Times New Roman, and other font faves. You can have access to a boatload of typefaces if you install *FontHack 123,* which lets you replace the system fonts with fonts of your choosing. FontHack comes with just one—you'll find 20 more in the Alpha Font Collection 1.71. Both products are freeware. Beat that!

Dragging and Dropping Text

Although you can select snippets of text by tapping and dragging your stylus, you can't drag that text to another spot and drop it in (as you can with any word processor). *TextEditHack* adds that capability to text-oriented applications, such as Memo Pad, and even makes it easier to select text. You can double-tap to select a single word, triple-tap to select a sentence, and quadruple-tap to select all the text on the screen. Very handy.

Launching More than Four Programs with the Application Buttons

The more software you have loaded on your Clié device, the harder it becomes to hunt for the desired program icon. Enter AppHack, which use two sequential presses of the application buttons to launch up to 24 programs. You needn't remember the combinations you set up—AppHack displays a cheat-sheet when you press the first button, so you can see which program will load when you press the second one. This Hack is a little confusing to work with, especially because no instructions are provided, but it sure can save time.

Enhancing the Find Feature

FindHack turbocharges the Clié's Find function, remembering the last six searches you performed and letting you define up to four default searches. What's more, you can choose whether to search all installed applications, just the core apps, or only the currently loaded program. It even supports the use of wildcards—searching for "book*" would return "book," "bookmark," "bookstore," and so forth.

Improving Your Graffiti Accuracy

One of our all-time favorite hacks is *TealEcho,* which lets you see your Graffiti strokes as you write them. This "visual feedback" helps you improve your writing speed and accuracy, because it lets you see how your characters really look, as opposed to the way they're supposed to look. TealEcho (**www.tealpoint.com**) costs $11.95, but we think it's well worth the money.

Livening Up Those Sound Effects

Getting tired of your handheld's boring old beeps? TechSounds comes with a handful of nifty audio snippets you can assign to various system functions, and enables you to download even more sound effects (**www.ecamm.com**). It also supports startup and shutdown screens, if you're into that sort of thing.

OS 5 Hacks

Just because Palm OS 5 doesn't support the use of Hacks doesn't mean you can't add some worthwhile utilities. In this section, we spotlight some Hack-like programs no OS 5 user should be without. We found all of them at **PalmGear.com**.

- **Fonts4**   OS 5 doesn't offer much in the fonts department. If you'd like to change the way text looks on your PDA, check out these nifty font collections. Make sure you get the one specific to your model, such as Fonts4NX (for the Clié NX series), and so on. Just search for "fonts" on **PalmGear.com** and you'll find all the collections.

- **PowerOn for OS 5**   It's a common scenario: you slip your PDA into a pocket or purse, only to find it dead a few hours later when you pull it out. The cause? Something was pressing against one of the buttons, causing the unit to power on and the battery to drain. PowerOn reduces the chance of that happening by disabling the hard buttons. Or, more accurately, by requiring two quick presses of one of them to turn on the unit.

- **QLaunch**   Your handheld has just four hard buttons, but there are probably a lot more than four programs you use regularly. *QLaunch* lets you launch up to three applications from each button. You can also use it to access special functions, such as the built-in keyboard or the Bluetooth radio (if your model has one).

■ **ToneDial**   Because OS 5 devices have enhanced audio capabilities, they can dial a phone for you by generating the necessary tones. This can come in handy if you're standing at a pay phone trying to juggle kids, luggage, the phone itself, and so on. *ToneDial* integrates with the Palm OS Address Book, thus enabling you to dial any number in the contact list just by tapping it. Of course, you have to hold the PDA next to the telephone headset, but it's still easier than punching in the numbers by hand. ToneDial doesn't work with cell phones, though.

Other Utilities

X-Master works minor miracles, but it isn't the only tool you should consider owning. No Hacks can create reliable backups of your data, or give you greater flexibility in beaming software to other users, or remove duplicate entries from your databases. And there's certainly no Hack that digs up extra memory for you to use. So read on to learn about some of the other highlights of the Palm OS utility world.

NOTE   *Most of the utilities listed here can be purchased and downloaded from* **PalmGear.com**.

Backup Utilities

One of the cool things about the Palm OS is the way it keeps a complete copy of your data on your PC. Every time you HotSync, it's like you're making a backup of your important info. If something terrible befalls your handheld—the batteries die, or it gets lost, stolen, run over, sat on, or inexplicably wiped clean—at least you know that your data lives on your PC.

Of course, what happens if you're a thousand miles from home and your PDA piffles? To reduce the chance of a major crisis, consider using a backup utility and a Memory Stick card. All Clié handhelds have expansion slots that can accommodate such cards, and there are numerous utilities that can make backups of absolutely everything. If your handheld gets wiped, you simply insert the card, run the backup utility, and press Restore. See Chapter 22 for more information on Memory Sticks.

Backup Software

Once you're outfitted with a Memory Stick, you need a backup utility to go with it. Many Clié models come with MS Backup, Sony's own backup software, so check to see if yours has it before you buy anything. Otherwise, several programs can get the job done with a minimum of fuss. Usually it's just a matter of tapping Backup, then waiting a few minutes for the process to complete. If you need to restore your data, tap Restore and wait again.

That said, you might want to look for certain features when choosing a backup utility:

- **Scheduled backups** Some programs can make backups for you automatically at predetermined times. This can be quite helpful if you're the forgetful sort, because it insures you'll always have an up-to-date backup at the ready.

- **Partial backups** Although it's nice to have a backup of every single bit of data in your PDA, you might want to save time (or storage space) by backing up a select few files. Some programs let you pick and choose which files to copy; others make it an all-or-nothing proposition.

- **Incremental backups** Making a complete backup of everything in RAM takes time. If your software supports incremental backups, only those files that have changed will be copied during subsequent backup sessions. That can save you a ton of time and storage space.

A search of **PalmGear.com** reveals a multitude of backup utilities. We recommend *Botzam Backup,* a full-featured program that supports not only all the features mentioned previously, but also Palm OS 5. At $14.95, it's also reasonably priced. Even if you have MS Backup, you might want to consider Botzam Backup, which offers a lot more features.

The Problem with Prequels

Clié, schmié…let's talk about the really important stuff—namely, treasured sci-fi franchises that have been ruined by prequels.

   Rick: First, there was the colossal disappointment of *Enterprise,* the blandest, most uninteresting *Star Trek* series ever. Now, George Lucas continues to make a mockery of the *Star Wars* trilogy by serving up pabulum like *Attack of the Clones.* Maybe I'm too old, maybe I'm jaded, maybe I just expect fresh writing and decent acting, but these prequels have left me colder than a polar bear in January. They're just not *fun.* The magic is gone. And I think this is a problem inherent to the prequel formula—when you know the outcome, there's no suspense. I *know* Anakin will turn into Darth Vader in *Episode III.* For me, there's no excitement in watching it happen. And don't get me started on all the ways *Enterprise* has violated *Star Trek* canon.

   Dave: You, my friend, have been abducted by mind-controlling body snatchers. First, *Enterprise*: it's fresh, fun, and engaging. I enjoy the show immensely, though I'm sometimes disappointed that the stories are too "*Next Generation*-ish." It's always with the time travel, and there's often not enough "Gee whiz, Batman! We're in outer space!" As for Lucas's *Episode II,* you're just off your rocker. Are you too cool to like stuff anymore? All the million-dollar book royalties gone to your head? What do you expect? To be knocked off your feet like you were watching *Star Wars* when you were 12? Not going to happen—that film is a classic, and you were lucky enough to see it for the first time at the perfect age. *Episode II* is a good film in its own right, though, and it might eventually be judged as the second best of the lot…unless *Episode III* really knocks our socks off, that is. Check back in the third edition to see what we thought of *that* movie.

"Free" Extra Memory with JackFlash

Psst! Don't let this get around, but your Clié has been holding out on you. It has extra, hidden RAM that's just sitting around doing nothing. You see, in addition to its main memory, it has a couple megabytes of Flash memory (aka the Flash ROM) where the OS is stored. But the OS occupies only some of that space, leaving idle upwards of 4MB (the actual amount varies depending on your model). Brayder Technologies' *JackFlash* lets you tap into that memory, using it to store programs, data, even backups of your primary databases.

| TIP | *Some Cliés don't have enough Flash memory free to make JackFlash worthwhile. Fortunately, you can download and install JackFlash Lite—a freebie—to see how much Flash memory is available in your model. Then you can decide if JackFlash is worth purchasing.* |

13

Given that it ventures deep into the guts of your Clié device, JackFlash is admirably easy to use. It provides a list of the contents of main RAM and Flash memory. To move a program or database from one to the other, you simply tap the menu next to it, select RAM or Flash, and then tap the Update button.

Extending the Clipboard with Clipper

Like most computers, Clié devices make use of a "clipboard" for copying and pasting text. And, like most computers, Cliés can hold only one selection of text at a time in that clipboard. *Clipper* turns it into a repository for multiple selections, thereby expanding your copying and pasting capabilities. Everything you copy is retained in Clipper (where you can even go in and edit the text). When you want to paste something, you simply make a special Graffiti stroke to bring up the Clipper window, and then choose which snippet of text to paste.

 Beam Software to Another Clié User

Suppose you're enjoying a game of *Vexed* (one of our favorites), and a fellow Clié user says, "Hey, I'd like to try that!" Generous sort that you are, you agree to beam a copy of the game (which is perfectly legal because *Vexed* is freeware). To do so, return to the Applications screen, and then choose Menu | App | Beam. Find *Vexed* in the software list, tap to highlight it, and then tap the Beam button. Point your Clié at the other person's device, and then wait a few seconds for the transfer to complete. Presto! You've just shared some great software—wirelessly! Just one caveat: some copy-protected programs (which will have a little padlock icon next to their names) can't be beamed.

This can come in extremely handy if you frequently write the same lengthy words or phrases. Doctors could use Clipper to create a little database of diagnoses, lawyers to maintain a selection of legal terms, and so on. Sure, you could use the Clié's own ShortCuts feature (see Chapter 4) to do much the same thing, but then you have to remember the shortcut abbreviations.

Removing Duplicate Entries with UnDupe

If you routinely work with ACT!, Outlook, or some other third-party contact manager on your computer, it's not uncommon to wind up with duplicate entries on your Clié device. This can also happen if you import additional databases into Palm Desktop. Whatever the cause, the last thing you want to have to do is manually delete these duplicates from your records. *UnDupe* does it automatically, ferreting out duplicate entries in Address Book, Date Book, Memo Pad, and To Do List, and then eliminating them in one fell swoop.

Managing (and Beaming!) Your Files with FileZ

The more you work with software, the more you need a good file manager. *FileZ* lets you view, edit, copy, move, delete, and beam virtually any file on your handheld. It's not the most user-friendly program of its kind, but it does have one feature that makes up for it: it's free.

Beaming is one of FileZ's most admirable capabilities. As you might recall from Chapter 4, beaming programs and data to other Clié users isn't only practical, it's just plain fun. But the Palm OS is a bit limited in terms of what it can beam. Specifically, it can't beam Hacks or e-books or certain kinds of databases. That's where FileZ comes in—it can beam just about anything.

TIP   *If you're an advanced user, you can use a program like FileZ to find and delete the extraneous files that are sometimes left behind when you delete an application. The standard Palm OS Delete tool usually doesn't show these "behind-the-scenes" files. Of course, you should take caution when deleting files, because you could accidentally remove something important. Make a complete backup first, so you can restore files if necessary.*

13

The Wonderful World of Launchers

As you know from poring over Chapter 2 (you did pore, didn't you?), the Palm OS enables you to assign applications to different categories—the idea being to help keep your icons organized and more easily accessible. However, a variety of third-party programs take this idea to a much higher level and with much better results. In this section, we introduce you to a few of our favorite launchers—programs that organize your apps, simplify certain features, and, in some cases, slap on a much prettier interface.

What should you look for when choosing a launcher? Consider these key features:

- **Support for memory cards**   If your handheld has an expansion slot (as most do nowadays), your launcher should have direct support for memory cards. That means you can install applications on a card, but still organize them as you see fit from within the launcher.

- **Support for color and/or high-res screens**   A good launcher should take full advantage of your screen's capabilities, meaning it should offer a colorful visage and let you tweak the colors to your liking. If you have a handheld with a high-resolution screen, choose a launcher that supports it directly. You'll be able to fit more icons on the screen at a time (if you desire to) and enjoy a nicer-looking interface.

- **Support for themes**   Part of the fun of using a launcher is customizing your handheld's interface. Some launchers let you install themes (or "skins," to use MP3 parlance) that dramatically alter their appearance (while maintaining the same basic layout and functionality). The standard Palm OS interface looks downright stark in comparison to these nifty themes, which are usually free to download (though the launchers themselves cost a few bucks).

- **Support for jog dials and navigators**   If you have a handheld with a jog dial or navigator, make sure to choose a launcher that supports it. That way, you can still enjoy the benefits of one-handed operation.

A Few of Our Favorite Launchers

We've tried most of the launchers out there, including the one that attempts to re-create the—horrors—Windows desktop on your handheld's screen. Rest assured, that one isn't among our favorites (but if the idea intrigues you, by all means check it out—it's called GoBar). Here are our favorites:

TIP   *As with most Clié software, you can try demo versions of these launchers before plunking down your hard-earned cash. We recommend you use each one for at least a week so you can really get to know it.*

■ **Launcher X**   This update of one of our all-time favorites, LauncherIII, organizes your icons into tabbed windows, thus enabling you to switch categories with a single tap of the stylus. Plus, you can drag and drop your icons between tabs—no irksome category menus to deal with. *Launcher X* is packed with other helpful features, ranging from onscreen memory and battery gauges to a built-in file manager. It's also one of the most expense launchers, priced at $24.95.

■ **MegaLauncher**   In addition to its crackerjack support for memory media and high-resolution color screens, *MegaLauncher* offers a wealth of advanced features (including one-tap beaming, deleting, and copying) and comes with a handful of attractive themes. It costs $19.95.

■ **SilverScreen**   Dave's launcher of choice, *SilverScreen,* offers the most glamorous interface of any launcher and a growing library of way-cool themes. It's also the only launcher to replace the core-app icons with icons of its own, thus creating an even more customized look. In short, if you're big on bells and whistles, this is the launcher for you. However, we should point out that SilverScreen is a bit on the slow side—the unfortunate by-product of its graphics-laden interface.

13

Clié Antivirus Utilities

Unless you've been living under a rock, you know that computer viruses can wreak havoc on a PC and even propagate from one system to another without users' knowledge. Viruses are an unfortunate fact of computer life. They aren't, however, a part of Clié life, at least not at press time. Although a few companies have introduced virus-protection software, do yourself a favor and don't bother wasting any money or energy on them.

Creating Your Own Clié Programs

Ever wonder why so much third-party software is available for Clié devices? Maybe because it's so easy to write programs for the platform. Although the more sophisticated applications do require programming experience and professional development tools, utilities are available that enable you to design basic Clié software with ease. Indeed, if you're willing to tackle a short learning curve, you can create customized applications for your personal or business use.

NOTE   *If you're looking for software to create databases, see Chapter 11.*

Here's a quick rundown of some of the tools available to budding Clié software developers:

- **AppForge**   A powerful development tool (available in Standard and Professional editions), *AppForge* lets you write for the Palm OS, using Microsoft Visual Basic 6.0.

- **CodeWarrior**   Reputed to be the most popular Palm OS-development package, *CodeWarrior* (available for both Windows and Macintosh) requires extensive programming knowledge. It's based on the C and C++ programming languages.

■ **NSBasic/Clié** Remember that BASIC programming class you were forced to take in high school or college? Now you can put the knowledge to practical use. *NSBasic/Clié* (see Figure 13-1) lets you create Palm OS apps with everyone's favorite programming language. Okay, show of hands: who remembers what "BASIC" stands for?

■ **PDA Toolbox** PDA Toolbox doesn't require much in the way of programming knowledge. Rather, the software employs a graphical interface and makes software design as easy as dragging and dropping elements on to a simulated Clié screen. You can even create your own icons for your programs.

■ **SuperWaba** Okay, we don't pretend to understand Java but, if you do, *SuperWaba* is a "Java Virtual Machine" that runs on the Palm OS (among other platforms). It's free, it supports OS 5, and it gives you the opportunity to say "waba" a lot.

FIGURE 13-1 If you can remember your BASIC training, you can program for the Palm OS with NSBasic/Clié.

Where to Find It

Web Site	Address	What's There
AppForge, Inc.	www.appforge.com	AppForge
Botzam	www.botzam.com	Botzam Backup
Brayder Technologies	www.brayder.com	JackFlash
Linkesoft	www.linkesoft.com	X-Master, ToneDial
Little Mobile Creations	www.launcherx.com	LauncherX
Megasoft2000	www.megasoft2000.com	MegaLauncher
Metrowerks	www.metrowerks.com	CodeWarrior
NS Basic Corp.	www.nsbasic.com	NSBasic/Clié
PalmGear	www.PalmGear.com	The vast majority of the Hacks and utilities mentioned in this chapter
PDA Toolbox	www.pdatoolbox.com	PDA Toolbox
Pocket Sensei	www.pocketsensei.com	Silver Screen
Stevens Creek Software	www.stevenscreek.com	UnDupe
TealPoint Software	www.tealpoint.com	TealEcho

Chapter 14

Time and Money Management

How to...

- Track your finances with the Clié
- Keep up with Quicken data entry on your Clié
- Calculate loans using your Clié
- Calculate restaurant tips and divide dining bills with the Clié
- Track your investments on the Clié
- Manage projects and clients with the Clié
- Keep up with time zones
- Calculate the time between any two dates

There's a saying where Dave grew up: you can never have enough time or enough money. Actually, we're pretty sure this expression is common to most places, but Dave tends to ramble on and on about New Jersey. And because there's no reasonable way to discuss authentic New York pizza in this book, we've covering this topic instead.

No gadget that we know of is going to give you more time or money just as a happy consequence of owning it. But many Clié applications are designed to maximize what time and money you have by helping you manage it better. Project management systems help you track your jobs and clients, financial programs manage your checkbook, and portfolio systems let you stay on top of your investments. In this chapter, we round up a few of the best of each.

Managing Your Money with the Clié

"Money," the Swedish rock band ABBA once said. "Money, money," they continued. In all, they said it three times, as in, "money, money, money." Then they sang some other stuff. We couldn't agree more. Your Clié is an ideal pocket-sized tool for keeping track of your money. You can use it as an extension of your desktop financial management program or as a stock tracker—and a lot of little applications in between.

Keeping Up to Date with Quicken

You know who you are. No sooner do you get home from dinner and a movie, than you rush to the PC and enter your receipts in Quicken. It's a habit, it's an addiction. Well, your Clié, together with the right software, can now save you the agony of waiting until you get home: relax and enjoy the movie, because Pocket Quicken lets you enter your expenses into your Clié as they happen.

Pocket Quicken isn't a PDA-based replacement for the entire Quicken application on your desktop. Instead, it's a handheld companion that lets you store payments, deposits, and account transfers in your Clié and synchronize the transactions with Quicken on the desktop at your next HotSync. You can also review your account balances and analyze old transactions. If you're

Rock Bands to Live By

We need to make a strong caveat at this point: neither Dave nor Rick is particularly fond of the recently mentioned ABBA (anymore—Rick boogied to "Fernando" every night through his formative years). Since you're relying on this book for advice anyway, we humbly give you our top choices for music to listen to as you troubleshoot your PC or surf the Web with your Clié:

Dave: The dual art forms of Electric Blues and '60s Rock really constitute the height of Western culture. For the most part, it's all been downhill since then, made painfully obvious by whatever that stuff is Rick forces me to listen to when I visit his office or ride in his car. No, I say, stop the madness. Don't listen to music just because it's popular—you know, like Rick does. Instead, try adding some class and culture to your life. Listen to The Beatles, Pink Floyd, Velvet Underground, Kristin Hersh, Throwing Muses, and The Call, and you're pretty well set. If you have a few dollars left over, pick up some Peter Himmelman, B. B. King, Dire Straits, and Eric Clapton. You won't be disappointed. And, whatever you do, don't buy anything Rick is about to recommend.

Rick: Not unless you have good taste and want to *enjoy* what you're listening to. With the exception of The Beatles, Dave feels all music should be weird or depressing—or both, ideally. Give me Elton John, Green Day, Smash Mouth, Simon and Garfunkel, Alanis Morrissette, Big Bad Voodoo Daddy, and, of course, the *Blues Brothers* soundtrack. Yes, that's right, I don't listen to artists or bands just because they're unpopular or unknown. That's Dave's job. Oh, and for the record, Dave doesn't even like jazz—proof positive that he's a few sandwiches short of a picnic.

a Quicken user and you methodically enter all your receipts into the program, then this is a program you should try.

Before you begin using Pocket Quicken, you should perform a HotSync. This transfers your accounts and categories from the desktop version of Quicken to your Clié. Be sure to do this before you take your Clié on the road expecting to enter any transactions!

Once you have a chance to synchronize the applications and get Pocket Quicken configured with your desktop settings, look at the Pocket Quicken interface. Pocket Quicken has two views: the display toggles between the Accounts view (which lists your accounts and current balance) and the Register view, where you enter and review transactions (both seen in Figure 14-1).

When you want to enter a new transaction, tap the New button at the bottom of the screen and choose whether you're creating a payment, a deposit, or a cash transfer. Then fill out the resulting dialog box as appropriate. Pocket Quicken includes Quicken's *AutoFill tool* (which completes the transaction for you when it recognizes what you're entering). You can also choose to use a "memorized" transaction from a pick list to speed your entry.

TIP *You can lock prying eyes out of your records with a four-digit PIN. To protect your Quicken data, start Pocket Quicken, and choose Options | Security from the menu. Then create your PIN.*

Accounts		
Name	**Type**	**Balance**
Savings	Bank	14,492.15

Balance Total: **14,492.15**

(Edit...) (Register)

Register		▼ All
Date ▼	**Ref & Payee**	**Amount**
12/19	Rick	-130.00
12/19 DEP	Cbrt	1000.00
12/19 DEP	Tap	258.00
12/19	Kris	-15.00
12/19 DEP	Zd	250.00

▼ New Transactions   **14,492.15**

(New...) (Accounts)

FIGURE 14-1   Pocket Quicken's two major views

If you use your Clié frequently to store transactions, the data can add up. It's easy to keep it in check, though, and preserve your Clié's memory. To trim your transactions to a manageable size, choose Actions | Trim History. Then delete old transactions based on date or by the oldest set of entries. Remember, though, don't delete any entries that haven't yet been HotSynced.

Using Other Cash Management Tools

If you aren't a Quicken user or you don't want the capability to synchronize your Clié with a desktop finance program, you might want to try other applications. Specifically, these:

■ **PocketMoney**   An outstanding alternative to Pocket Quicken, *PocketMoney* is a comprehensive personal finance program that interfaces with a handful of other applications and a number of desktop financial programs (including Quicken and Microsoft Money).

- **SplashMoney**   Another superb Pocket Quicken alternative, *SplashMoney* works with Quicken and Microsoft Money, or all by itself.

- **BankBook**   Another great personal finance program; the interface of BankBook is simple enough that you can enter transactions as they happen. You can later synchronize with your desktop finance program.

- **Personal Money Tracker**   This is a popular finance package for your Clié that's ideal for non-Quicken users. *Personal Money Tracker* has a conduit that synchronizes the Clié's data with a standard CSV file on the desktop. You can then import that data into a spreadsheet or personal finance software.

- **Accounts and Loans**   This program lets you track your bank account balances and loan information in one application. *Accounts and Loans* is easy to use and lets you export your financial data to the Memo Pad.

Streamlining Your Day with Other Financial Tools

What is the Clié if not convenient? That's why we love to load up the Clié with tools that make it easier to do mundane tasks like pay bills and calculate loans. Real estate and loan professionals use the Clié to calculate amortizations, and you can, too. In truth, dozens of these kinds of programs are floating around, and you can try them all quickly and easily from **PalmGear.com**. *Financial Consultant,* for instance, turns any Palm-powered PDA into a business calculator that includes many of the most useful features of Hewlett Packard and Texas Instruments calculators. The program comes with 90 preprogrammed functions, including loan payments, interest rate conversions, and onscreen amortization schedules. *Loan Pro,* from Infinity Software, is a similar loan-analysis calculator that can be used by professionals or consumers for any kind of amortized purchase—like houses, cars, and boats (if you can afford a boat, by the way, give Dave or Rick a call. We have some business ideas we'd like to run past you). Finally, *Triloan* takes a different approach to the problem of real estate calculations by displaying up to four loans at once on the same screen, allowing you to visually compare several different financial profiles side-by-side. There's also *LoanUtil,*

14

PayPal's PDA Roots

These days, everyone knows PayPal and the way it makes buying stuff electronically on the Internet easy. You probably even have your own PayPal account to make eBay purchases. But we bet you didn't know that *PayPal* started as a way to exchange money using PDAs like Palms and Cliés. We used to love "beaming" money to each other at restaurants to settle bar tabs, for instance. Alas, PayPal discontinued PDA-to-PDA cash transfers a few years back, so only the true handheld pioneers remember those golden days.

a small application that tells you monthly payments, total amount of loan, or interest rate, depending on what data you enter. Tap the icon marked three at the bottom of the screen and you're taken to a Compare screen that lets you directly compare two different loan offers based on the same principal.

LoanUtil - Primary Loan ℹ

First Pay Date: 12-2003

Last Pay Date: 11-2004

\# of Payments: 48.00

Amount Borrowed: $ 12943.00

Interest Rate: 19.000 %

Monthly Payments: ....

1 2 3   (Calculate)

Have we whetted your appetite for handy financial tools? Here are a few other kinds of programs you might want to try:

■ **Shopping Assistant**   At the top of this little heap is a program called *HandyShopper*. This cool little program is designed, quite simply, to help you shop more efficiently and to save money in the process. It lets you maintain lists of products you want to buy, and you can even tell HandyShopper in which store (and what aisle) you found it. Then, you can later go back and track down the products more easily. For us, one of the most interesting features is its capability to compare the actual price of two similar products. Suppose you're buying tissue paper that costs $4.99 for 10 ounces, while another brand sells 12 ounces for $5.49. Which is the better deal? Find out by choosing Record Best Buy from the menu, and then enter the price and quantity in the Best Buy dialog box. For the record, you should buy the second item because it's cheaper by about 4 cents per ounce.

- **Tip Calculator** Let's be honest—no one really needs a program to help them calculate a restaurant tip or divide a bill among a few people. And to add insult to injury, there must be a hundred tip calculators floating around **PalmGear.com**. But if you really want to try one, give EZTip a spin. EZTip enables you to enter the total amount of a bill, add a tip, and then evenly divide the total among a number of diners.

- **Currency Conversion** Traveling? You might want to know what $50 is worth in yen, euros, or rubles. A few programs can retrieve current exchange rates when you HotSync, and other programs can pull the rates down in real-time via a wireless connection. We suggest you check out Travel Pal.

- **Car Maintenance Tracking** If you want to stay on top of your car's routine maintenance, try TealAuto (on the left) or TotalCar (on the right). These programs also track your gas mileage—or, if that's all you care about, try a program called MPG.

Tracking Your Investment Portfolio

One of the Internet's biggest killer applications, it turns out, seems to be investment web sites. Then the Internet crashed, we all lost our money, and no one really wanted to know what our investments looked like anymore. If you're one of those few people that still have a few stocks with a non-zero balance, you might want to track your portfolio on the go.

That's where your Clié comes in. You can use any one of a number of portfolio management packages to monitor your investments. Most investment programs for the Clié let you check your portfolio's health anywhere, anytime. Suppose you don't get a chance to check the paper's business pages until you get on the subway in the morning. You can update your portfolio right from your seat on the train and instantly know your new positions.

If you like the idea of using your Clié for portfolio management, give either one of these programs a shot:

■ **Stock Manager**   One of the most complete portfolio managers for your PDA, *Stock Manager* is a color application that retrieves your current stock prices, as well as the day's high, low, change, and volume. It also lets you set alerts on all your stocks based on current price, profit, and profit percentage. The program lets you categorize your stocks into different portfolios, and a conduit lets you export your portfolio to an Excel-compatible CSV file.

■ **StockPilot**   Do you love to see your holdings in lots of different ways? Then you'll love StockPilot. While we prefer Stock Manager, this is a good alternative, and it's a little cheaper ($19 instead of $25). *StockPilot* tracks a lot of details about your holdings, including dividends, profits, fees as a percentage of stock value, and total value. StockPilot lets you "watch" a stock even if you don't own it. The elegant display shows your portfolio in three columns, each of which is customizable to show different details, like stock symbol, shares, profit, and more.

Streamlining Your Day

Time management isn't only about getting that spreadsheet to your client on time or tracking how many hours you were on the road delivering two tons of fertilizer to a nearby town. Time management can be little things—like knowing how many days are between two project milestones. Here's a small collection of utilities we think you might appreciate having on your Clié:

■ **Time Traveler**   This program is a fairly comprehensive time zone manager that lets you find the time difference between your current location and major cities around the world. One of the most interesting features of *Time Traveler* is in the Time Travel screen, where you can specify your flight itinerary (including your departure location and time, followed by your arrival location and time), and the program calculates the actual travel time, taking time zone changes into account. This way, you know how many magazines to buy for your upcoming plane flight.

■ **BigClock**   We mentioned this program elsewhere in the book, but it's a winner and deserves mention here as well. Use *BigClock* to display the time (if your Clié recharges in the HotSync cradle and you set it to stay on while recharging, it can be turned into a desktop clock), play up to four different sets of alarms, and serve as a counter or countdown timer.

■ **BlueMoon**   When was the last time you changed the filter in the furnace, checked the oil in your car, or called your mom? These tasks don't always lend themselves to regular To Do List or Date Book entries, largely because they happen infrequently and not always on a predictable schedule. But *BlueMoon* is designed to accommodate just those kinds of recurring tasks.

■ **Timeout**   Do you take enough breaks during the day? If not, you might be heading down the road to stress and heart failure, like our friend Rick. *Timeout* is a simple program that pops a reminder on the Clié screen randomly throughout the day to tell you to take a short break and relax.

■ **Date Wheel**   This clever program lets you calculate the number of weeks, days, or business days between any two dates. You can also specify a duration, like ten business days, and find the necessary start or end date. *Date Wheel* is essential for any manager who needs to assign deadlines or determine if there's enough time between two dates to get a job accomplished.

14

Outlining Your Ideas

We all have a million great ideas every day—and promptly forget them minutes later. What you need is an outlining program that can help you get a handle on all the great ideas flowing through your head. It'll make you more efficient, more productive, and save you valuable time every day.

Typically, outliners use a hierarchical approach to data management. This might sound imposing, but the basic idea is that your ideas are generally related to each other. So, start with a single note, and then nest subnotes within it, as if you had a data tree with branches that grew off the main topic. By grouping related ideas together, it's easier to stay organized and arrange your data in a format that works for you.

The Clié has several excellent idea organizers with which you can experiment:

■ **BrainForest**   This program is perhaps the most complete organizer for the Palm and serves as an action item tracker, checklist manager, outliner, idea keeper, and project planner. *BrainForest* uses Tree, Branch, and Leaf metaphors to enable you to nest notes within each other, thus grouping items in a logical manner. Items are numbered using traditional outlining notation (like 1.2.3, for the third leaf in the second branch of the first tree of data). In addition, you can export specific items to the Palm's To Do List and Memo Pad. BrainForest also enables you to prioritize, sort, and rearrange items by dragging and dropping.

■ **MindManager Mobile** *Mind maps* are nonlinear outlines that show the relationship between related topics. They often look like cascading groups of thought bubbles, with spider-like connections holding them together. They let you take notes or brainstorm in a free-form way, without being restricted to a rigid format. The leading mind-mapping software for the Clié is MindManager 2002 Mobile Edition. *MindManager* lets you create original mind maps on the Clié or synchronize with the desktop version of MindManager. Either way, you start with a central hub concept and branch out from there, adding ideas, tasks, and data in radiating branches. Branches can be nested, long-form notes can be attached, and the program makes use of graphic icons and color to highlight certain areas of a map. Although the program can stand on its own, its real power comes when you synchronize a map made on the Clié and feed it back to the desktop for inclusion in PowerPoint presentations, e-mails, or web pages.

Chapter 15

Graffiti Enhancements and Alternatives

How to...

- Improve Graffiti with overlays
- Replace the Graffiti area with a keyboard
- Use Jot instead of Graffiti
- Find better onscreen keyboards
- Improve Graffiti recognition
- Write faster with WordComplete
- Tweak Graffiti to recognize your own handwriting
- Customize the virtual Graffiti area with skins

Many of us have a love/hate relationship with Graffiti, the handwriting-recognition software used by all Palm OS devices. Some users take to it right away, finding it a speedy and convenient method for entering data. Others just plain don't like it or can't get the knack. For those folks (who have absolutely nothing to be ashamed of, really), we present this chapter on Graffiti enhancements and alternatives. We also introduce you to the wonderful world of skins, which should be of interest for owners of NR/NX/NZ models.

> **NOTE** *This chapter deals primarily with Graffiti 1, which at press time was still predominant in Clié handhelds. If you have an NX73V, NX80V, or another model with Graffiti 2, you might still want to check out the products mentioned herein. Many of them could be updated to support Graffiti 2 by the time you read this.*

Suppose you don't mind Graffiti, but find it too slow to keep up with your thought processes—or too inflexible to recognize your particular style of handwriting. The answer could lie in one of many available "Graffiti assistants," which not only can speed data entry, but also make your handwriting more recognizable.

Maybe you've been using the onscreen keyboard as an alternative to Graffiti, but find it too small or cumbersome. There are keyboard alternatives as well, some of them quite radical. And maybe you're just ready to give Graffiti the old heave-ho and try some other means of data entry. Full-blown replacements are out there, and they let you say goodbye to Graffiti forever.

We divided all these products into four categories: overlays, which actually cover the Graffiti area; assistants, which give Graffiti a helping hand; keyboards, which substitute for the stock onscreen keyboard; and replacements, which send Graffiti packing.

> **NOTE** *In this chapter's discussion of keyboards, we're talking about software options. We look at actual keyboards in Chapter 23.*

Overlays: Wallpaper for the Graffiti Area

One of our favorite tips for Clié users is to apply a piece of Scotch 811 Magic Tape to the Graffiti area. This not only protects the area from scratches, it also adds a tackier writing surface that many people find preferable to the slippery screen. A new breed of plastic overlays takes this idea several steps further, redefining the Graffiti area's functionality and protecting it at the same time.

 If your Clié has a virtual Graffiti area, you definitely don't want to muck up the screen with tape. Therefore, you'll probably want to ignore all this discussion of overlays.

How do overlays work? The entire Graffiti area—buttons and all—is sensitive to pressure. That's why when you tap a button or write something with your stylus, your Clié responds. The overlays simply take advantage of this fact, using special software to reprogram the Clié's responses to your taps and strokes. The products take different approaches to this, as you see in our overview of each one.

Introduction to FitalyStamp

Before we talk about Textware Solutions' FitalyStamp, we have to tell you about Textware Solutions' Fitaly Keyboard—an onscreen-keyboard replacement discussed in the section "QWERTY, Meet Fitaly." It's a fairly unusual product, but with practice it can increase your data-entry speed.

The problem with pop-up keyboards like Fitaly (and the standard keyboard, for that matter) is they occupy a major chunk of the viewable area of the Clié's screen. FitalyStamp offers a solution: an overlay that moves the keyboard from the screen to the Graffiti area.

As you can see from the previous photo, the key layout is quite unusual. The idea is to minimize the distance your stylus needs to travel (more on that in the section "QWERTY, Meet Fitaly," when we look at the Fitaly Keyboard). But FitalyStamp also provides cursor-control buttons, numbers, symbols—even the Clié's ShortCut and Command functions. Thus, while there's a learning curve involved with the keyboard itself, there's also a lot of convenience. And FitalyStamp is a colorful, attractive addition to your Clié device—an important consideration for those who prize aesthetics.

You obviously wouldn't want to paste FitalyStamp (or any other overlay) on a Clié that has a virtual Graffiti area. Fortunately, the company offers a software-only version of the product. FitalyVirtual replaces the standard virtual Graffiti area with the FitalyStamp keyboard, while at the same time adding a handy, user-customizable launcher along the bottom.

15

Having Your Keyboard and Graffiti, Too

If you often hop between Graffiti and the built-in keyboard, and wish you had an easier way to do so, Softava's Silkyboard is the answer. This overlay covers the Graffiti area with a large, easy-to-read QWERTY keyboard that enables full-time tap-typing, but also lets you use Graffiti without having to change modes.

Silkyboard's key advantage is it provides access to a keyboard without sacrificing any screen estate. Its secondary advantage is protection of the Graffiti area. Working with the overlay is as simple as tapping on the letter or number you want to enter, and holding down your stylus for a "long tap" when you want a capital letter or punctuation mark. Accessing Applications, Menu, Calc, and Find requires a stroke instead of a tap, but that's just a matter of simple memorization. Indeed, Silkyboard's learning curve is slight. And, if you get mixed up, you can go back to using Graffiti just by drawing the strokes on top of the letters. (The overlay even has the two little arrows that divide the letter and number areas.)

Given that different Clié models have slightly different Graffiti areas, Silkyboard is available in several varieties. Make sure you order the right one for your model. A simple calibration routine is all that's required to set up the driver software, and a handy applicator strip is provided to make sure the overlay is applied without any air bubbles.

NOTE   *At press time, Silkyboard was not available for any Palm OS 5 models.*

If you prefer to write with a keyboard but don't want to give up Graffiti entirely, Silkyboard is a great best-of-both-worlds solution.

Making Graffiti Smarter

One of the most ingenious overlays is *TapPad,* which doesn't try to replace or revamp Graffiti, but merely gives it a boost. TapPad extends the full length of the Graffiti area, thus providing total protection.

TapPad's benefits can be summed up thusly:

- Protection of the Graffiti area and a tackier surface that makes handwriting more comfortable.

- The addition of a keypad in the numeric half, thus enabling you to enter addresses and phone numbers much more quickly (and more easily, in our opinion).

- One-tap buttons for six commonly used commands: Undo, Cut, Copy, Paste, Delete, and Backspace. The Undo button alone is worth the price of admission.

- Left–right and up–down scroll buttons for easier cursor movement and document navigation. If you ever tried to place your cursor between two letters or at the beginning of a line, you know what a struggle it can be. The left–right buttons move your cursor one space at a time, greatly simplifying its placement. And the up–down scroll buttons are a major improvement over the Clié's skinny scroll bars and tiny arrows.

- A host of shortcut and pop-up tools designed to simplify data entry. Space doesn't permit us to list them all, but we think they're outstanding.

If you want superb protection for the handwriting area, along with some Graffiti-related perks, you're likely to love TapPad.

NOTE   *If your Clié has a virtual Graffiti area, you'll be glad to know there's a software version of TapPad that provides all the same functions without the actual overlay. At press time, the TapPad Virtual Overlay was compatible only with the NR series, but the author was hard at work on an NX/NZ-compatible version. Assuming it's available by now, we highly recommend it.*

15

Graffiti Replacements: A Software Solution

Love the idea of Graffiti, but don't like Graffiti itself? We understand—some of those special characters are just plain tough (Dave can't make a *j* to save his life, and who can remember the stroke for the percent sign?). CIC's *Jot,* born for Windows CE devices but eventually ported to the Palm OS, replaces Graffiti with a more natural—and familiar—character set.

NOTE   *A derivative of Jot was used in the creation of Graffiti 2.*

Our Favorite Graffiti Aids

Rick: Although I never travel without my Stowaway Keyboard, most of the time I prefer to use plain old Graffiti. But my accuracy could always use improvement, which is why I've become a big fan of TealEcho. It reproduces my Graffiti strokes in digital ink as I make them, so I can see what my characters look like (and make sure they're drawn correctly). This is the best $11.95 you can spend on your Clié, if you ask me. Of course, Cliés with virtual Graffiti areas have this capability built right in, so TealEcho isn't necessary.

Dave: Personally, I rarely use Graffiti enhancements (my Jedi Master won't allow me to take the easy way out of any situation, lest it weaken my mind and allow the Dark Side to gain a foothold). For the most part, I use my Graffiti zone just the way God intended it. But I used to use TapPad on my old NR70, and I feverishly await the day it's updated to support OS5, so I can use it on my NX70 as well. In addition, I usually have a keyboard with me on trips so I can write long documents on airplanes and in my hotel room.

And that's only one of Jot's advantages. It also frees you from the Graffiti area, enabling you to write anywhere on your Clié device's screen. Even better, it leaves a trail of "digital ink" beneath your stylus tip, so you can see what you're writing as you write, as with a pen and paper. Finally, Jot recognizes a variety of cursive characters (see Figure 15-1), handy for those who mix script with print. Tricky Graffiti letters such as *q, v,* and *y* are much easier to make with Jot.

Not sure this is the Graffiti alternative for you? Try before you buy. As with most Clié software, you can download a demo for a test drive.

Keys, Please

Like to tap-type? Many users prefer the onscreen keyboard to Graffiti, if only because it has no real learning curve. Of course, some software developers think they can do the keyboard one better, as evidenced by Textware Solutions' Fitaly Keyboard and an interesting Hack.

FIGURE 15-1   Jot can recognize five versions of the letter *A* alone, meaning it's more accommodating to your style of writing.

This material doesn't really apply to Cliés with virtual Graffiti areas, as their pop-up keyboards are less intrusive (merely replacing the Graffiti area instead of occupying space above it) and, therefore, less compelling to replace.

QWERTY, Meet Fitaly

The *Fitaly Keyboard* (so named for the layout of its keys, like QWERTY) proceeds from the assumption that the Clié's own built-in keyboard requires too much hand movement. Because it's so wide, you have to move your stylus quite a bit, leading to slow and often inaccurate data entry. The Fitaly Keyboard arranges letters in a tightly knit group designed to minimize stylus travel. Hence, you should be able to tap-type much more quickly.

Clearly, Fitaly represents a radical departure from the standard QWERTY keyboard, and therefore has a high learning curve. Make that practice curve: it could take you several days to master the layout, and even then you might decide you don't like it. The moderate speed gain might not offset the difficulty in learning an entirely new keyboard.

On the other hand, Fitaly is much more practical than the stock built-in keyboard, in part because it makes most common punctuation marks readily available, without the need to shift modes (or even tap the SHIFT key). And when you do access the Numeric mode (done by tapping the 123 button, as with the standard keyboard), you gain access to a number of extended characters (including fractions, the Euro symbol, and more).

If you like the idea of Fitaly, but hate sacrificing a big chunk of the screen, check out FitalyStamp—a plastic overlay that moves the keyboard right on top of the Graffiti area—previously covered in the section "Introduction to FitalyStamp." And NR/NX/NZ users should check out *FitalyVirtual,* which simply takes the place of the Graffiti area, rather than popping up above it.

A Keyboard Hack

In Chapter 13, you learned all about X-Master and the little OS enhancements (Hacks) that work with it. Let's talk about one that's expressly related to the Clié's onscreen keyboard.

15

If you've spent any time with the Clié's standard onscreen keyboard, you've probably been frustrated at having to switch modes to access numbers and punctuation. Horace Ho's *Keyboard Hack* solves the problem by replacing the standard keyboard with a slightly modified one. His keyboard sports 69 keys, including a numeric keypad and a row of punctuation keys. It also has left/right keys for moving your cursor a space at a time.

The latter feature, the cursor-control keys, was suggested by a Keyboard Hack user. The author of the program incorporated it into the next version. This is part of what makes the handheld community so great: so many software developers are just regular folks who are happy to hear from regular users. You can have a voice in the evolution of Clié software!

Giving Graffiti a Helping Hand

Here's a novel idea: rather than trying to build a better Graffiti than Graffiti, why not simply cut down on the number of letters necessary to write a word? Or make it so you can write anywhere on the screen, instead of just in the Graffiti area? How about tweaking the recognition engine, so it's more accommodating to your handwriting? These are among the goals of Graffiti assistants—software tools that just make life with Graffiti a little easier.

Was This the Word You Were Looking For?

Remember the old game show *Name That Tune*? The host would describe a song, and the contestant would say, "I can name that tune in three notes." Imagine if Graffiti could adopt that precept,

What About a Real Keyboard?

Thumbs, overlays, styluses—whatever you use to enter data on your Clié device, it won't be as fast as an actual keyboard. Fortunately, actual keyboards do exist for Cliés. To find out all about them, see Chapter 23.

Improve Graffiti Recognition

For all its quirks, Graffiti is actually an excellent handwriting-recognition tool. If you plan to stick with it, you can use these tips to improve accuracy. By the way, if your handheld has Graffiti 2, the first three tips still apply.

- *Write big.* If your characters fill up the bulk of the Graffiti area, they're more likely to be accurately recognized.

- *Don't write on an angle.* Many of us do just that when writing with pen and paper, but that's poison to Graffiti. Keep your strokes straight.

- *Take advantage of the built-in Graffiti Help application.* This provides a graphical cheat sheet for all Graffiti strokes. Go to Prefs | Buttons | Pen, and then choose Graffiti Help from the list of available options. Now, whenever you draw a line from the Graffiti area to the top of the Clié's screen, the Help applet appears.

- *Draw the letter* V *backward.* If you're having trouble with the letter *V,* start from the right side and end with the left. You needn't add the little tail (as with the standard Graffiti *V*) and the letter will come out perfectly every time.

- *Write the number 3 for the letter* B. Forget trying to draw a *B* Graffiti's way—write the number 3 instead. Similarly, writing the number 6 gives you a good *G* every time, and the number 8 creates the perfect *Y.* Naturally, you should still make these characters on the letter (that is, left) side of the Graffiti area.

- *Start your letter* R *at the bottom of the letter instead of the top.* That initial downstroke often produces the ShortCut symbol instead of an *R.*

guessing the word or phrase you're writing as you write it. By the time you entered, say, the *e* in "competition," the software would have figured out the rest of the word, thereby saving you six additional pen strokes.

That's the appeal of CIC's *WordComplete,* a utility that helps you write faster by helping you write less. As you enter characters, a box containing possible word matches appears. If you spy the word you're after, just tap it. The more letters you enter, the closer you get to the correct word (if it's in the software's database).

Obviously, for little words like "the" and "to," the program won't help much. But for longer words, it can indeed save you some scribbling. And WordComplete lets you add your own words and/or short phrases to its database, which can definitely save you time in the long run.

15

Goodbye, Graffiti Area!

Ever notice that the Graffiti area is kind of, well, small? Most of us aren't used to writing in such a confined space, and that alone can be a source of Graffiti contention. Fortunately, there's a utility that can liberate your stylus from that tiny box, effectively turning the entire Clié screen into one big Graffiti area.

Graffiti Anywhere enables you to write—using Graffiti characters—anywhere on the screen. What's more, it leaves a trail of "digital ink" beneath your stylus tip, which goes a long way toward helping you produce more accurate characters. You see what you write as you write it, just as you would with a pen on paper. Plus, it's free!

The Best Little Graffiti Tweak in Town

Part of the challenge in learning and mastering Graffiti is that you can't see your characters as you write them. (Actually, if you have one of the Clié models with the virtual Graffiti area, you can—the input area leaves a trail of digital ink beneath your stylus. Very cool.)

That's where TealEcho comes in. This simple utility displays your pen strokes on the main screen as you make them in the Graffiti area. As a result, you can gauge just how accurate (or inaccurate) your characters are. Sounds like no big deal, but trust us when we say TealEcho goes a long way toward improving Graffiti accuracy.

Graffiti, Your Way

Finally, we come to the one product that really manhandles Graffiti, that says, "Look, can't you just learn to understand *my* writing?" It's TealPoint Software's *TealScript,* a utility that lets you tweak Graffiti, so it's more responsive to your hand, or replace it altogether with a customized character set.

If you're willing to battle one of the steepest learning curves we've encountered in a piece of Clié software, the benefits are truly worthwhile. TealScript works its wizardry through the use of custom profiles, which contain the Graffiti character set as you define it. In other words, you teach TealScript how you like to write, and it teaches Graffiti to accommodate your penmanship.

The letter *v* is a good example of how this works. Your profile can include the standard character—the one with the little tail we always forget to add—and a regular *v* you added yourself. Similarly, instead of always having to write capitalized versions of letters like *R* and *B,* you can add lowercase versions.

As confusing as TealScript can be to work with, it's not totally out of the question for novice users. That's because it comes with an already-built profile that helps you overcome the most commonly miswritten Graffiti characters. So, right out of the box it's useful. And even though TealScript might not be the friendliest program around, it's by far the best way to make Graffiti an ally instead of an obstacle.

TIP *If you've upgraded to a Clié that has Graffiti 2, but you miss good old Graffiti 1, TealScript lets you switch back.*

Souping Up Your Clié with Graffiti Skins

In case we haven't made ourselves perfectly clear on this, we love the software-based Graffiti area used by the NR/NX/NZ series. And not just because it's collapsible, either. No, what really makes us all tingly are Graffiti *skins*—user-created artistic replacements for the Graffiti area. Here are a few examples (and just imagine what they look like in color!):

As you can see, these skins can dramatically change the look of your Clié, enabling you to customize it in a very personal way. Dozens of skins are available, so you're sure to find something you like.

The whole "skinning" process is a bit different, depending on whether you have a Clié NR or a Clié NX/NZ model (thank you very much, Sony). Thus, we've divided our coverage into sections.

Using Skins on the NR Series

To install a skin on your NR-series Clié, you first need a *skin manager*—a utility that lets you swap the new skin in place of the old one. Our favorite by far is the aptly named *SkinManager,* which gives you an onscreen preview of the skin before you switch to it. (When you do make the switch, your Clié will reset itself, a process that takes about 30 seconds to complete. That's why the preview is such a nice feature.) SkinManager also enables you to rename and delete skins.

15

The shareware version of SkinManager enables you to work with five skins. If you want more, you'll have to pony up the $5 registration fee (a definite bargain).

TIP *There's also a freeware skin manager called Crs-SkinLoader (aka SilkChanger). However, the author is Japanese, as are the instructions for the utility. Fortunately, it's quite easy to use. Just download and install the PRC file as you would any other (see Chapter 4 if you need a refresher on installing software). The advantage of Crs-SkinLoader is that, unlike SkinManager, it can install new skins without requiring a reset of your Clié. Find it at crspalm.hp.infoseek.co.jp/#crssknld.*

So, where can you find the skins themselves? They're scattered around the Web, but we've got links to some spots with great collections:

- **http://alxinc.netfirms.com/clie.htm**   Neat collection of sports-themed skins
- **www.cliesource.com**   Find Clié skins in the Skins & Backgrounds forum and the Skins section under Clié Files
- **www.graphicbliss.com/GraffitiSkins/graffitiskins.html**   Some absolutely beautiful photographic and fractal skins

When you find a skin you like, just download it to your PC, install it on your Clié like you would any other program or file, and then run SkinManager to select it. While SkinManager does let you preview your skin, it requires a soft reset of your Clié to actually install it. This is a hassle more than anything else—it won't harm your Clié.

TIP *A highly recommend alternative to SkinManager is PhotoSkin, which we discuss in the section "Using Skins on the NX/NZ Series." That's because it's the only viable option for those models, but it's also compatible with the NR series. In fact, it lets you convert photos taken with the NR70V camera into virtual Graffiti skins!*

What About the Status Bar?

Why stop with just the Graffiti area? You can also load up a customized "status bar"—the row of icons at the very bottom of the screen.

Just as users have created some beautiful skins for the Graffiti area, so have they designed some nice alternatives for the status bar. Very often, they're designed to match the Graffiti area, as shown in this nifty Sonipa skin/status bar set:

You can use SkinManager to change status bars just as easily as skins. However, you might want to consider a more practical status bar alternative. It's Stand Alone's *NR Buttons,* which doesn't change the design of the status bar, but instead adds more functionality to it:

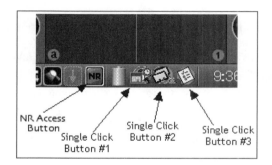

As you can see, it adds application buttons to the status bar, so you can quickly launch up to four of your favorite programs. This is great for when you have your Clié "twisted," so just the screen

PhotoSkin makes it a snap to choose a virtual Graffiti skin and status bar for your NR/NX/NZ handheld.

is showing, as it saves you having to tap the Home button and search for your desired application. It's well worth the $8.95.

Using Skins on the NX/NZ Series

Because NX- and NZ-series Cliés use Palm OS 5, Graffiti skins created for the NR series (which uses OS 4) aren't compatible. While that's kind of a bummer, the good news is there's a program that not only makes for painless NX/NZ skin management, it also supports the use of NR skins. That program is PhotoSkin (see Figure 15-2).

A few tips on working with PhotoSkin:

- The zip file that contains the program includes a large number of files. Make sure you install the correct version for your handheld: *PhotoSkin_EN_OS5.prc* for NX/NZ models, *PhotoSkin_EN_OS4.prc* for NR models. The *Readme_ENG.txt* file contains basic instructions for using the software.

- If you decide to pay the $9.99 registration fee to keep using PhotoSkin, you'll receive a lengthy registration code you need to enter into the program. To do this, you must use your Clié's built-in keyboard. Ironically, PhotoSkin completely deactivates the Graffiti area while it's running, so you can't use Graffiti (or the onscreen keyboard) to enter the registration code.

- In fact, to exit PhotoSkin, you must tap the Quit button (see Figure 15-2). You can't just tap the Home icon in the Graffiti area like you normally would.

So, where can you find the skins themselves? They're scattered around the Web, but we've got links to some spots with great collections:

- **http://alxinc.netfirms.com/clie.htm**   Neat collection of sports-themed skins
- **www.cliesource.com**   Find Clié skins in the Skins & Backgrounds forum and the Skins section under Clié Files
- **www.graphicbliss.com/GraffitiSkins/graffitiskins.html**   Some absolutely beautiful photographic and fractal skins

When you find a skin you like, just download it to your PC, install it on your Clié like you would any other program or file, and then run PhotoSkin to select it. While PhotoSkin does let you preview your skin, it requires a soft reset of your Clié to install it. This is just a hassle more than anything else—it won't harm your Clié.

> **TIP**
>
> *You don't need PhotoSkin to load NX/NZ-compatible skins on your device. In fact, you can simply install one like you would any other program, and then perform a soft reset. Presto: the new skin should appear. Ah, but what if you want to load a different skin or return to Sony's default skin? That's where things get tricky, which is why we suggest that novice users stick with PhotoSkin. To uninstall a skin you've loaded, perform a warm reset (see the Appendix to learn how). Then, using the Clié's keyboard, press* CTRL-H. *Run Clié Files, find and delete the file for the skin you installed, then perform a soft reset.*

Did you know?

What About That Silk Plug-In Button?

As you might have discovered (via natural curiosity, no doubt), the fourth button from the left on NX/NZ status bars loads a little applet called Silk Plug-In. While this would appear to be a Sony-built Graffiti-skin manager, it's not. Well, actually, it is. Sort of. But not really. In fact, this totally undocumented feature is used for virtual Graffiti "plug-ins." One such plug-in is Decuma, which you learned a bit about in Chapter 4. With a little perseverance (and visits to CliéSource and Google), you might be able to find a few other interesting plug-ins—a calculator, a calendar, and more—but at press time we came up fairly empty.

15

Where to Find It

Web Site	Address	What's There
Brochu Software	www.skinmgr.com	SkinManager
CIC	www.cic.com	Jot, WordComplete
PalmGear	www.palmgear.com	Graffiti Anywhere, Keyboard Hack
Raysolutions	www.raysolutions.com	PhotoSkin
Softava	www.silkyboard.com	Silkyboard
TapPad	www.tappad.com	TapPad
TealPoint Software	www.tealpoint.com	TealEcho, TealScript
Textware Solutions	www.fitaly.com	Fitaly Keyboard, FitalyStamp

Part III

The Clié Multimedia Experience

Chapter 16

Showing Digital Photos and Movies on Your Clié

How to...

- Use your Clié camera's settings
- Set white balance
- Prepare Clié photos for the desktop
- Transfer images from the Clié to the PC
- Watch movies on your Clié
- View photos on your Clié

Digital cameras have been around for less than ten years, but they have already dramatically changed the way we think about photography. Almost everyone we know, for instance, owns a digital camera and uses it to take snapshots at family outings. The pictures can be immediately e-mailed to friends and relatives, posted at an online photo site, or mailed out on CD-ROM. Even people who would never haul around a 35mm camera embrace the simplicity and convenience of a digital camera.

What does all that have to do with your Clié? Plenty. A few Cliés—like the NX70V and the NX80V—come with a built-in digital camera; most others can accept Sony's *Memory Stick Camera*—a digital camera mounted on a Memory Stick. Even if you don't have a built-in or MS digital camera, though, you can load your handheld with pictures from an ordinary digital camera and use it like a digital album, filled with your favorite images.

Taking Pictures on a Clié

You can take pictures with your Clié in two ways: use a model that has a built-in digital camera, or purchase Sony's add-on Memory Stick Camera (you can see both in Figure 16-1). If you have the option of using a Clié with a built-in camera, do that. It's better than the Memory Stick camera for a few reasons:

- The Memory Stick Camera limits you to 320×240 pixel images, while Cliés with integrated cameras offer much higher resolutions. The NX70V captures 640×480, while the NX80V offers a 1.3-megapixel camera. The NZ90 is the king of the hill, taking 2-megapixel images.

- The built-in camera doesn't occupy the Memory Stick slot, so you can store pictures and other data on a Memory Stick even while you use the camera.

- The Memory Stick Camera is yet another small gadget that's easy to lose. If it's built in, it isn't going anywhere.

Configuring Your Camera

The Clié camera is quite easy to manage. Depending on which model you have, your options could vary, but you essentially have control over the resolution, storage location, white balance, and color

FIGURE 16-1 Clié cameras typically rotate in their housing, which lets you take self-portraits and shoot from lots of weird angles.

effect of your photos. To see these options, fire up the CLIÉ Camera program, and then tap the wrench icon on the digital camera screen—it opens your options, which will look something (but not necessarily exactly) like this:

Here's a rundown of your key options:

■ **Save to location** If you have an integrated camera, you can save your pictures to the Clié's internal memory or Memory Stick. The Memory Stick is a good place to save your pictures if you want to keep a lot of images around—you won't consume precious system memory—but you can't rename or annotate images stored on a Memory Stick. On older Cliés, you can't include Memory Stick images in the Address Book, but that limitation has been removed on the latest models.

■ **Size** How large do you want your pictures to be? Tiny 88-pixel images are good only for the Address Book, but you might also (depending on the camera) be able to store images in a variety of higher resolutions.

16

- ■ **Date**   Some Clié cameras can record the current date in the picture. We recommend leaving this feature turned off because there's nothing uglier than seeing the date in the corner of a photo.

- ■ **Sound**   You can vary the volume of the "shutter sound" that helps identify when the picture has been taken.

- ■ **Effect**   Many digital cameras offer you color-effect options, and the Clié camera is no different. You can shoot your picture in ordinary color or switch to black-and-white, sepia (an old-fashioned, brown-tinted variation on black-and-white), negative (just what it sounds like—a cool artistic effect) and solarize. *Solarization* decreases the number of colors in the photo, and is commonly used in '80s rock videos and other artistic films. Because the Clié's pictures are kinda low-res to begin with, we generally ignore these fancy options and just take standard color pictures. You can always enhance them later in an image editor on your desktop PC.

- ■ **Scene**   Some Clié cameras have program modes that let you automatically set the camera to take special kinds of pictures. The NX80V, for instance, has a Slow Shutter setting in the Scene menu, which uses a very slow shutter speed to capture detail at night.

- ■ **White Balance**   White balance lets you correct the colors in your photo based on the kind of light in the scene. Sony offers you four options: auto, indoor *A,* indoor *B,* and outdoor. See the sidebar, "Adjusting White Balance," for more info.

- ■ **Brightness**   You can dial in the brightness of your photo to correct for an unusually dark scene (remember, most Cliés have no flash). The Memory Stick camera puts the brightness control on the main screen, under the image preview, while the built-in models put brightness in Settings.

Prepping Your Photos for the PC

Depending on which Clié model you own, the process of working with digital images can be a bit cumbersome. Older Cliés—like the NR70V—didn't make it easy to get your digital images from the PDA to the PC. If you have an older device, you might have seen that your Clié uses two mysterious file formats for its digital images: PGP and DCF. *PGP* is Sony's own format for the Clié (it stands for PictureGear Pocket), while *DCF* is just the JPG format under a different name (Digital Camera Format, to be precise). To transfer images from the Clié to your PC, they must be stored on a Memory Stick in the DCF format. Once there, you can use a Memory Stick reader on your desktop or the PictureGear application (a Windows application that comes on your Clié's installation CD-ROM) to copy them to a computer; see the section "Move Your Pictures to the PC" for details.

 Sony's newest Cliés save files in true JPG format and make it much easier to copy files to the PC. If you have one of those models, you're in luck, and can skip this section!

Adjust White Balance

Your Clié camera has a four-setting control called "white balance." Your old 35mm film camera didn't have anything like it. So what the heck is white balance? In a nutshell, different light sources have different color temperatures, meaning that a scene will appear to have a different color tone depending on how it's illuminated.

You can get a sense of this yourself. Candlelight appears more yellowish than sunlight, for instance. And other sources—like tungsten lights—can cast strange, greenish glows around a room. But in general, our brains automatically adjust for different color sources and make the color correction for us. We usually don't even notice.

Your camera's white balance control works like the human brain. It adjusts the exposure so your pictures have the same color cast no matter what light source you use. When properly balanced, your camera won't apply strange color casts to your pictures even if you shoot indoors, outdoors, in florescent lighting, or in candlelight.

Most of the time, your Clié is fine if you leave it set on auto (as in the following image). If you notice your camera is taking pictures with a weird color cast—everything is coming out greenish or bluish, for instance—try one of the preset white balance settings and see if that improves your shots.

To make the needed conversion, do this:

1. Open the application called PG Pocket on your Clié and make sure you're in the thumbnail view. If you only see a single image, tap the Return button in the lower-left corner to see the thumbnails. Make sure you're currently looking at pictures stored internally by selecting Internal from the menu at the top of the screen.

2. Tap the Import/Export button at the bottom of the screen. The button looks like a PDA with an arrow in it.

3. Select the images you want to move to the Memory Stick by tapping the selection boxes.

4. After you've selected your images, tap Export.

5. On the Import/Export dialog box, choose the DCF format and tap OK. After a short conversion process, the images will be copied to the Memory Stick, ready for the big move to your PC.

It's also possible that you have images on your Memory Stick in PGP format. You won't be able to copy these to your PC until they're in DCF format. To make the change, import the images back to internal memory, and then export them back to the Memory Stick, being sure to choose the DCF option.

 Move Your Pictures to the PC

You'd expect that Sony would include some sort of conduit to automatically transfer your pictures from the handheld to the PC, but that's not quite the case. One of the most common questions people ask us is "How on Earth do I get pictures from the Clié to the computer?"

Good question. And the answer is it's pretty simple (though not particularly obvious). You have two choices. If you have a Memory Stick reader for your desktop PC, just pop the Stick out of your Clié, put it into your reader, and open the DCIM folder on the Memory Stick to see and copy the images.

If you don't have a Memory Stick reader at your disposal, follow these steps instead:

1. Start by moving your digital images to a Memory Stick. If you have an older Clié, you'll also have to convert them to DCF format. See the previous section "Prepping Your Photos for the PC" for info on how to do that. If your Clié is newer, they'll already be in JPG format, so you needn't do anything extra.

2. Place the Clié in its HotSync cradle and turn it on.

3. If you have an older Clié, Start the MS Import on the Clié. Wait until you're connected, and then move on to the next step. If you have a new Clié, on the other hand, start the Data Import application on the Clié. The Memory Stick folder should open automatically on your desktop; just find the DCIM folder and copy your digital images to the desktop, where they'll be ready for their next adventure on your PC. New Clié owners—you're done.

4. On the PC, start PictureGear Lite, which came on your installation disc.

5. In the folder list on the left side of the screen, find the Clié's Memory Stick and open the folder. You should see a folder called DCIM; this is where you'll find your photos.

6. Drag the photos to the Windows desktop or to another folder on your PC. They'll be in good old JPG format.

Watching Movies on Your Clié

Why would anyone want to watch a low-resolution movie on a screen barely larger than a matchbook? This question has been a source of much debate between Dave and Rick. Rick, who dismissed the idea of movies on a Clié out of hand without ever really trying it, recently had a change of heart when he found that he could watch TV shows on his Clié while traveling by plane. Now he's sold—yet another example of Dave being proved right.

The Movie Debate

Dave: Personally, I love the idea of watching a TV show I saved on my VCR on plane trips. But you, Mr. Blows-in-the-Wind, what's your opinion of PDA movies now? For years, you told me that it was silly to watch movies on a small handheld screen and, even when I suggested that faster processors, better screens, and improved sound would someday make watching a movie on your PDA commonplace, you poo-poo'd the idea as insane. But I know you're using Kinoma to watch Spongebob episodes on your Clié, so what's your excuse? What made you decide that video on a Clié was a good idea? I expect to hear a lot of groveling, with the words, "You were right, Dave."

Rick: The day those words escape my lips is the day I've been drugged, beaten, and threatened with having to see Kristin Hersh in concert. Years ago, when you were going ga-ga over postage stamp–sized slideshows playing on your Palm without sound, I did indeed poo-poo the notion of handheld video. And on most Palm-based handhelds, the experience is still extremely lame. But on a Sony Clié—especially one with a high-resolution color screen and enhanced sound—mobile movies are pretty cool. There are still plenty of obstacles, like making space for the video files (a mere half-hour show can eat up over 64MB). But we're getting there, and I can't wait for the day when I can walk into an airport and download *Swingers* to my Clié from a kiosk.

You can get movies into your Clié in a whole bunch of ways. And if you have your sights set on copying a few episodes of *Seinfeld* or *The Simpsons* to your Clié for long commutes, the good news is this: your goal is now easily within your reach.

Using Movie Player

Some Cliés come with a truly excellent movie player called, simply enough, *Movie Player*. It works in conjunction with Sony's Image Converter application for Windows (found on the installation CD-ROM).The *Image Converter* supports a few common file formats, including MPEG, AVI, and QuickTime. To make a movie for your Clié, do this:

1. Place your Clié's Memory Stick in a desktop memory card reader and note the drive letter that Windows assigns to it. Alternatively, if you have a new model like the NX80, place your Clié in the HotSync cradle and start the Data Import application on the Clié, noting the drive letter when Windows recognizes it.

2. Start Image Converter in Windows.

3. Click the Add to List button and find a movie that you want to add to the Clié.

4. Click Output to memory Stick. When you see the Memory Stick dialog box, set the Saving Drive to the correct drive letter of your Memory Stick.

16

5. Click the Settings button. Notice that you can control the Movie Quality, which affects the overall size of the clip. Choose Standard or Long mode if your movie is very large—otherwise, stick with High Quality for shorter films. Click OK.

6. Click OK to start the transfer. The movie will be stored on the Memory Stick automatically.

Using Kinoma

Movie Player isn't your only option. Third-party programs like *Kinoma* (which is included with some Clié models) also make it possible to watch movies on your Clié. Indeed, if you don't have access to Sony's Movie Player—or just want to try a different program—then we definitely recommend Kinoma. Why Kinoma? Because it has an easy-to-use desktop converter program and supports the 480×320-pixel HiRes+ mode for NR/NX/NZ-series Cliés. This means you can turn your Clié on its side and watch widescreen video. Most important, the image quality of videos is outstanding, second only to Sony's Movie Player.

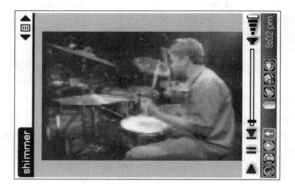

TIP   *Kinoma has the added advantage of supporting CompactFlash memory cards, which are compatible with the Clié NX73V and NX80V. See Chapter 22 for more details.*

Even if you don't want to watch a movie in widescreen, the sideways 480×320 format is great for ordinary television shows. TVs have a 4×3 aspect ratio, making them slightly wider than they are tall. That means you'll get a slightly bigger image if you encode it sideways than if you pack it into the usual 320×320-pixel space on screen.

Get a Big Memory Stick

Of course, you'll want to have a lot of memory for videos. A 128MB Memory Stick is the bare minimum you'll need to get a short television show onto your Clié, and you might need to break up a longer show—like a movie—onto more than one Stick. If you have a new Clié (like the NX70V, NX80V, or NZ90, for instance), you can use a Memory Stick Pro card, which is currently available in capabilities of up to 1GB. See Chapter 22 for more information on Memory Stick Pro and other high-capacity media.

Making a movie with Kinoma Producer is a drag-and-drop affair. It accepts video in a wide variety of formats, including QuickTime, MPEG, and AVI, and it lets you tweak the movie's specs, like frame rate and audio format. You can also rotate the file to play in widescreen mode on compatible devices, and set other details like the background color or still image that frames the movie. Dave has used Kinoma extensively to copy music videos downloaded from the Internet, home movie clips transferred from a digital video camcorder, and even complete TV shows.

Finding and Converting Video for Your Clié

Video players like Kinoma, Movie Player, and even other options like TealMovie all come with desktop converters that you can use to import movies in a variety of formats. TealMovie, for instance, accepts video in AVI and the QuickTime MOV formats. Kinoma has broader support for video formats, working with QuickTime, MPEG-1, MPEG-4, AVI, and even Macromedia Flash.

Having a video player on your Clié is all well and good, but it's a lot like being all dressed up with nowhere to go: where do you get the movies for your PDA to begin with? The reality is that you have an embarrassment of riches when it comes to sources for video. People who watch movies on their PDAs can draw on television and videotape, DVD, their digital camcorder, and even the Internet. Here's the skinny:

■ **Television programs** whether live off the air or stored on videotape—is a common source. You might want to copy this week's episode of *Friends* or *24,* for instance, so you can watch it when you travel. You'll need some mechanism on your computer, like a composite-video-in or S-Video input, to capture analog video and store it on your PC. Some multimedia computers ship with video capture capabilities. If you computer doesn't already have this, you can add an ATI All-in-Wonder card to your PC, which has video inputs and the necessary software to store video on a hard disk. Another alternative: Dazzle's *Digital Video Creator* is a USB hub that sits outside your PC and lets you capture video onto your PC via composite video or S-Video ports.

16

■ **Digital Video** is getting very popular as well. Digital video, from a DV or a Digital8 camcorder, requires a FireWire port (also known as IEEE-1394 or i.Link). Many computers come with at least one FireWire connection, but if your doesn't, you can add one for under $100. Just fire up your video editing software (which often comes with the camcorder or FireWire card) and capture your movie on the computer's hard drive. When you're done, you might need to save or export the video in a different file format—but we'll talk about that in the next section, "Converting Your Video."

■ **DVD** is the way most of us watch our movies these days, so it stands to reason that we'd want to be able to copy DVD to PDA. PDQ. Suppose you just rented *Terminator III,* but you're going out of town before you have a chance to watch it. The problem, of course, is getting the movie off the silver platter and onto your computer's hard disk. Because DVDs are copy-protected, this might initially seem like a hopeless task. Fret not—several programs are around that make this possible. Programs like DVD-to-AVI (**www.dvd-to-avi.com**) and MovieJack (**www.moviejack.org**) can "rip" the content from DVD and store the movie as an AVI or MPEG file on your computer's hard drive. From there, it's a matter of converting the movie for viewing on your PDA.

■ **The Internet** is teeming with movies and television shows if you know where to look. Peer-to-peer services like *Kazaa* and *LimeWire* have many videos you can download from other people's computers.

Converting Your Video

So, you have a movie or two and a video player on your PDA. Think you're done? Think again. In some cases, you might be ready to kick back and watch *Logan's Run* on your Clié. But much of the time, you still need to convert, compress, and synchronize. Not all video players recognize the same file formats, and that's where some video utilities can come in handy.

Consider this: you download a vintage Throwing Muses music video from **Beestung.net** with plans to play it on your Clié via the Kinoma Player. When you inspect the video, though, you find it's in a format called DIVX—and Kinoma's desktop Producer software doesn't recognize DIVX files. Game over? Nope. You just need to convert the file from DIVX to a format that Kinoma understands, like MPEG.

To do that, you'll need an intermediate utility that lets you save a video file in a different format. We recommend two excellent utilities without reservation: EO-Video and TMPGEnc. *EO-Video* is a polished, easy-to-use video tool that lets you load files in a broad range of formats and save them as almost anything else. You can load a QuickTime file, for instance, and save it as an MPEG-1 video. More to the point, you can load WMV files—created expressly for Microsoft's Windows Media Player—and save them as general purpose AVI or MPEG videos that Clié players can understand.

Watch a Movie on Your Clié

So, you're ready to copy an episode of *Friends* to your Clié? The exact method will vary depending on which movie player software you use and what format the original movie is in. But here's a general step-by-step guide to making it happen, in this case with TealPoint Software's TealMovie:

1. Find the movie you want and download it to your PC. You might find it's in MPEG format, which means TealMovie Encoder can't work with this file.

2. Start EO-Video and click on the Converter tab. Drag the movie to the file list on the right side of the screen.

3. Configure EO-Video to make an AVI movie. Choose AVI from the drop-down list atop the screen.

4. Set the movie to a size appropriate to your Clié. Click on Output size and set it from there. Remember, if you create a video that's bigger than your PDA's screen size, you're wasting memory and slowing down the video unnecessarily.

5. Click the convert button.

6. After the movie is finished, load it into TealMovie Encoder and create the PRC file.

7. Add the finished PRC file to your HotSync session using the Install Tool. Be sure to change the file's destination—copy it to the memory card, not your PDA's system memory.

8. HotSync, and then watch the movie!

If you've got a DIVX video—and that's an increasingly popular format on the Web—then EO-Video won't be of much help because the program doesn't have a DIVX decoder. Instead, turn to *TMPGEnc,* which can take DIVX and other file formats, and transform them into common MPEG movies.

16

Build an Electronic Photo Album

Even if you're not interested in taking pictures with your Clié, you might still want to use it as a digital photo album to show off images you took with a different camera. With the right photo viewer software, you'll never be without a picture of your spouse, kids, cats, and other loved ones.

How to Find HiRes+ Applications

Nowhere is the capability to fill the entire 320×480-pixel screen on NR-, NX,-, and other Clié models more important than when working with multimedia applications like digital image and video viewers. Trust us: there's nothing in all the world quite like turning your Clié sideways and watching a widescreen movie. But how can you find programs designed with the Clié's HiRes+ mode in mind? Surf over to **www.clieuk.co.uk/cphires.shtml** for a comprehensive list of programs that fill the whole screen.

The process is quite simple: electronic images on your desktop PC (whether scanned, transferred from a digital camera, or downloaded from the Web) are converted to the right format, and then installed when you HotSync. Then you load up your viewer and, well, view 'em.

Choosing Photo-Viewing Software

Many programs enable you to view images on your Clié, some of them quite similar in form and function. You can use the photo viewer that comes with your Clié, or try an alternative. Here are some of the most popular programs:

- **AcidImage** An excellent photo-viewer for the Clié, *AcidImage* supports HiRes+ 480×320-pixel images—so you can literally fill the screen with your favorite photos. AcidImage also reads plain-old JPG images off the Memory Stick, so you don't have to use a cumbersome desktop conversion program first. Just drag and drop JPG images from the PC onto your Clié.

- **HandStory Suite** This multifaceted program displays e-book doc files, Web clips, memos, and digital images. The desktop transfer process is very elegant; just right-click an image on the desktop and choose Save To Palm from the menu. *HandStory Suite*, too, supports full-screen HiRes+ images.

- **SplashPhoto** A more "traditional" photo album program for the Clié, *SplashPhoto* has a desktop converter that lets you crop and edit images to an appropriate size for the Clié screen and also change them to a special file format for the PDA. It reads pure JPG images as well.

- **Photogather**   Similar to SplashPhoto, *Photogather* supports HiRes+ mode and JPG images, and it has a desktop converter to boot. Beware, though: Photogather sends full-resolution images to the Clié instead of shrinking them to fit on the screen—and that can eat up a lot of Memory Stick space very quickly.

Did you know?

Mapmaker, Mapmaker, Make Me a Map

Wouldn't it be cool if you could have street-level maps handy when you visit unfamiliar cities? You can, and they won't cost you a dime. Point your web browser to *Yahoo! Maps* or one of the many other online cartography sources, generate the map you need, and then save it to your hard drive. Now, run it through your image viewer's conversion software and load it on to your Clié device. If you want something a little more sophisticated (and precise), check out *Street Atlas Pro* from Delorme (**www.delorme.com**), which is designed specifically to display maps on your handheld.

16

Where to Find It

Web Site	Address	What's There
PalmGear	www.palmgear.com	Virtually all the applications found in this chapter
SplashData	www.splashdata.com	SplashPhoto

Chapter 17

Painting and Drawing on Your Clié

How to...

- Paint images on the Clié
- Use Clié Paint to modify digital images
- Copy images from the PC to your Clié
- Share and collaborate sketches with two Cliés
- Use an outliner to organize your ideas
- Capture Clié screenshots

So there you are: at your monthly sales meeting, listening to some guy drone on and on about how you need to more proactively leverage your core competency to win the golden carrot for your department's sales quotas.

Or something like that. You're not really sure what he's talking about because you've been doodling on the top page of your meeting minutes.

Well, cut that out! Instead of drawing on a piece of paper, you can be painting a picture on your Clié. It's high tech, it's in color, and people might even think you're working.

Painting on the Clié

You're probably wondering why you might want to paint on a handheld computer so small that it fits in your pocket. Well, in the world of computers, the answer is often "because you can." Programmers have never let something as silly as a technical limitation get in the way of doing something, so when PDAs first came out, programmers seemed to scramble to become the first to create a paint program for their favorite handheld PC.

Aside from that admittedly flippant answer, the capability to sketch things on your Clié is a handy feature. You can draw a map showing directions to a luncheon, outline a process, or design a flowchart. You can also just doodle—use the Clié as a high-tech Etch-a-Sketch for those boring times when you're waiting for the train or pretending to take notes in a meeting. Perhaps most important, you can draw on top of pictures you've stored on your Clié, giving you the capability to annotate images and add captions.

Painting on your Clié is fun and productive, but you need to remember these limitations:

- While some Cliés have a resolution of 160×160 pixels, your Clié could have a resolution of 320×320 or even 320×480. The more pixels you have, the better, but most paint programs can't utilize the full 320×480-pixel screen. Moreover, even the highest resolution devices don't give you a lot of room in which to draw. After your images are transferred to a PC, you'll find that they're still quite small. So, drawing something on the Clié you later plan to export to, say, a PowerPoint presentation, generally isn't a practical plan.

- Few paint programs support printing directly from the Clié and not all even let you transfer completed art back to the PC. That means, in some cases, what you draw on the screen pretty much stays on the screen. If you *can* print your work of art, it'll print just as rough and jagged on paper as it looked onscreen.

Replacement for a Laptop?

Dave: PDAs like the Clié are handy little gadgets, but they were never intended to be full-fledged substitutes for laptop and desktop computers. Nonetheless, that's just the way I use mine: I have an office suite and add-on keyboard for word processing, Margi's Presenter-to-Go for showing PowerPoint slideshows, a few games for entertainment, and a Memory Stick full of MP3s for music. In fact, with the Clié's digital camera, paint software, e-books, and video playback capabilities, my PDA does the work of two or three portable devices. I haven't carried a laptop on a trip in well over a year, and I have never once wished I had one with me.

    Rick: Amen, brother. I like to travel as light as possible, and even a five-pound notebook is more weight than I prefer. With the Clié and a few lightweight accoutrements, like Think Outside's Stowaway keyboard and the aforementioned Presenter To Go, I can go on a business trip and still conduct business. And now that I can watch a full-length movie on my Clié, I'm in schlep-free heaven.

Doodling with Clié Paint

The good news is that Sony includes a paint program with most Cliés, so you can doodle with your PDA right out of the box. *Clié Paint* gives you a small assortment of painting tools and a choice of what image size you'd like to work with. Using Clié Paint, you can create original art from a totally blank canvas, or you can load digital images created with your Clié camera and paint or annotate right on top of them. In other words, you can take a picture of Dave, and then scribble in a pair of horns and a devil beard—one of Rick's favorite activities.

Creating a New Image in Clié Paint

To get started, tap the Clié Paint icon in your PDA's application screen (by default, it's usually in the Clié category). Your first choice is what resolution you'd like to work with. Depending on which model you have, your options might vary, but the screen will look something like one of these screens:

Not all versions of Clié Paint have all these options, and not all put an option to load a digital image right on this start screen. You can load an image and paint on top of that using one of these two methods:

- If you see an option to Load Image on the Clié Paint start screen, tap it and you'll be taken to the Clié's PG Pocket application, which is a program that displays all the digital images stored on your Clié. It actually displays the digital images taken by your Clié camera. Find the image you want to edit and tap it. Finally, tap the edit icon in the toolbar (it has a pencil in it) and you'll be returned to Clié Paint, ready to work on the photo.

- If you don't have an option to load a photo right from the start, then tap any of the image formats to start Clié Paint. The screen size doesn't matter, because it will have no effect on the image you're about to edit. Then tap the File button (it's the one that looks like a page on the far left side of the screen). Tap the Load Image button and choose a photo from the PG Pocket application. Finally, tap the edit icon in the toolbar (it has a pencil in it) and you'll be returned to Clié Paint, ready to work on the photo.

If you want to work with a blank screen instead of a digital image, just select the starting image size and you're immediately taken to the Clié Paint screen. The paint interface is simple. When you first start the program, you'll see this toolbar:

The toolbar has three modes, each with additional tools. To switch among the three toolbars, tap the right edge of the toolbar. You can see which toolbar is currently active by noting which of the three squares is lit with a red block.

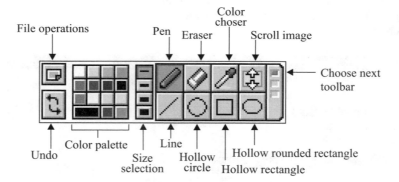

The other toolbars look like this:

Text   Filled shapes   Stamps   Spray   Blur   Mosaic
                                                     paint

Note that the middle of every toolbar lets you change the size of whatever you're painting on the screen. You have a choice of four sizes for painting, text, stickers, and the range of effects like blue and mosaic.

The program also gives you control over the color with a palette control. To switch to the color palette, tap the active color bar, which is the rectangle in the lower-left corner of the color box. When you do, you'll get to pick your active painting color from a hexagon like this one:

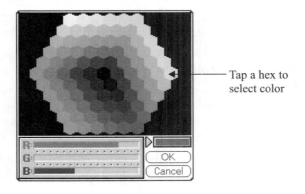

Tap a hex to select color

Clié Paint lets you do some fun and interesting things to your digital images. You can add text and apply "stickers" to your photos, as well as save them to your Clié for use in e-mail messages and other applications.

When you're done with your picture, save it by tapping the File button in the upper-left corner of the toolbar and choose to overwrite the existing image (this will destroy the unaltered image) or save it as a new image. You can transfer the completed image to your PC using the steps outlined in Chapter 16.

Converting a Desktop Picture

Want to doodle on a photo that's currently on your desktop computer? You'll need to get it onto your Clié first. Not a problem: if you have a later model Clie, use the Data Import application on the Clie to open the Memory Stick, and then drag-and-drop images to your heart's content. You're done!

If you have an older Clie, you'll have to use the PictureGear application in Windows. PictureGear probably came with your Clié's installation disk or with your Clié camera's installation disc. Here's what you need to do:

1. Start by converting the image to a pixel size that Clié Paint can work with. On older Cliés, Clié Paint can't handle a typical 3-megapixel image from your digital camera, for instance; it only understands images that come in Clié-standard formats like 160×160, 320×320, and 320×240. So, open your picture in a program that lets you crop the image to a specific pixel size and save a copy in this new format. Dave really likes a program called A Smaller Image (from **www.trivista.com**) for this sort of job (see Figure 17-1).

2. After the image is in a Clié-friendly form, turn on your Clié, place it in its HotSync cradle, and then tap the MS Import program—we're going to copy the picture to the Clié's Memory Stick.

3. Start PictureGear on your desktop PC and navigate to the image in question. Once you find it, select the image and choose File | Output Services | Output Clie Handheld Format To Memory Stick (see Figure 17-2).

4. In the resulting dialog box, choose the drive letter that corresponds to your Clié and click OK. Moments later, the file will be on your Clié's Memory Stick.

Now you can open the image in Clié Paint and fiddle with it to your heart's content!

Other Painting Programs

If you have a hankering to paint, you'll be happy to know that Clié Paint isn't your only option. There's a plethora of painting tools for the Clié—so many, in fact, we decided to narrow the crop for you to only a pair of programs you should evaluate.

■ **TealPaint**   Perhaps the most full-featured paint program for the Clié, TealPaint seems to do it all. *TealPaint* has a complete set of painting tools, including lines, shapes, fill tools, an eraser, and a variety of brushes. TealPaint starts you with thumbnail images of your pictures and lets you view, edit, or animate them. Using TealPaint, you can copy and paste selections of your image, not just within the same picture, but in any picture in your database. TealPaint is also an animation tool; you can use TealPaint to create animations by playing all the images in a particular database in sequence. To make a simple bouncing ball, for instance, draw a series of images in which the ball moves a bit in each successive image. Then tap the Anim button and tap the first picture in your series.

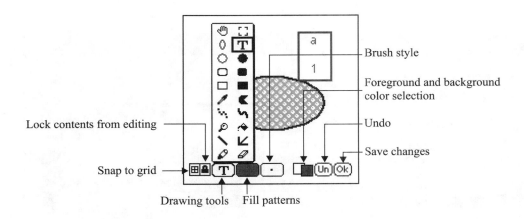

Brush style

Foreground and background color selection

Undo

Save changes

Lock contents from editing

Snap to grid

Drawing tools   Fill patterns

FIGURE 17-1   A Smaller Image is the sort of tool you can use on the desktop to resize an image for your Clie.

17

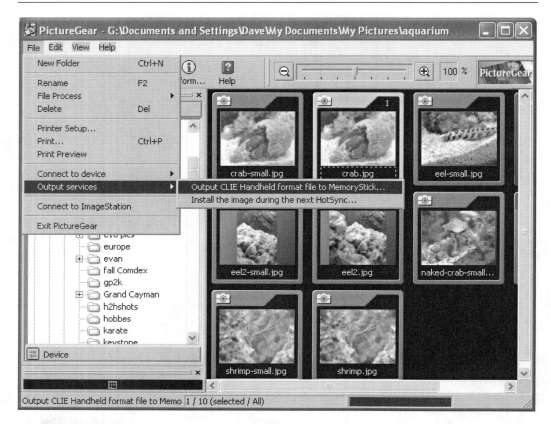

FIGURE 17-2   PictureGear is what you need to send images from the desktop to an older Clie; with a newer model, you can use the Data Import program to drag-and-drop images to the Memory Stick.

■ **Diddle**   *Diddle* is a free, neat little drawing program that enables you to sketch with a minimum of clutter to get in the way of your drawing. The interface is composed of a set of graphical menus at the top of the screen—you can choose from among various drawing styles, line thickness, and text. For the most part, the program is easy to explore on your own—just start drawing.

Collaborating on a Sketch

Drawing on a Clié is usually a solo affair, but what if you're in a meeting trying to lay out office furniture with your business partner? What then, huh? Okay, there might be some better examples, but just work with us for a moment.

Okay, we have a better example! Suppose you're in a long, boring meeting. If you have the right drawing software, you can doodle on your Clié and have it immediately show up on a partner's PDA, who can then add to your drawing and beam it back to you. All the while, your boss is none the wiser.

Anyway, if your buddy, business partner, or intern owns a Clié, the two of you can sketch your ideas on your PDAs. The results can appear simultaneously in both devices more or less in real time. That's totally cool, if you ask us.

Most collaborative sketch programs do their magic via the Clié's IR port. Here are some popular applications you can try:

- **Beamer**   This simple program has just a few buttons, but it's free. You can write short notes in a screen that resembles the Note Pad or draw free-form images in a blank sketchpad. When you're ready, tap the beam button (it looks like a tilde sign) to beam it to another nearby Palm-powered PDA. The recipient can add it to their drawing, and then beam it back.

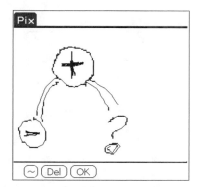

- **Zapster**   Very similar to Beamer, this program has a slightly more elegant interface. On the downside, *Zapster* is' shareware and costs $10. Like Beamer, you use it to draw, and then beam your work to another Clié, where it can be edited and returned.

Capturing Screenshots of the Clié Display

Perhaps you've thumbed through this book, some Clié web sites, or a magazine like *Handheld Computing* or *Mobility* magazine and wondered what it would be like to have lunch with Dave and Rick. (Answer: like keeping a pair of six-year-olds entertained in line at McDonald's.) You might also have wondered how everyone seems to be able to capture screenshots of the Clié display and publish them in ordinary desktop software. As it turns out, capturing Clié screens isn't that hard to do because several tools are available to automate (at least partially) the process for you.

The easiest way to capture a screen from your Clié—and our favorite, by far—is by using *ScreenShot,* a Palm OS application that works with X-Master (see Chapter 13) or on its own if you have a Palm OS 5 Clie. ScreenShot is a great general-purpose tool because you needn't do anything special to activate it. There are no countdowns until the screen is captured (unless you specifically set a capture delay), and no funky menu selections. Just display the screen you want to capture and draw the screen capture gesture in the Graffiti area.

Where to Find It

Web Site	Address	What's There
PalmGear	www.palmgear.com	Virtually all the applications found in this chapter
TealPoint Software	www.tealpoint.com	TealPaint and other Teal products
TriVista	www.trivista.com	A Smaller Image

Chapter 18

Music and Clié Audio

How to…

- Play MP3s on your Clié
- Transfer MP3 files from your desktop
- Manage MP3s using a Clié
- Check free space on a Memory Stick
- Use the Clié to make music
- Tune a guitar with a Clié
- Determine if your Clié has standard or enhanced audio
- Expand your Clié's alarm collection
- Convert WAV files to Clié alarm sounds

There was a time when a computer that could reproduce lifelike sound or make quality video was dismissed as a game machine. People Who Knew Things would sternly deride a computer with even a hint of multimedia prowess as something that serious people shouldn't waste their time or money on. After all, only kids play games.

These days, we wouldn't even know where to begin with an assessment like that. Games, for instance, are for everybody—even the CEO of MegaHugeGigantaCorp probably passes time on a long plane flight with a quick little game of *Bejeweled*. More importantly, even multimedia savvy computers are great for business applications. Take the Clié, for instance. You probably use it to track your schedule and contacts, do some occasional word processing, and maybe even dabble in databases. But some Clié models come with excellent audio and video, making them ideal for stuff like music, watching movies, and playing games. In this chapter, we'll look at the audio capabilities of Clié. Not only can you listen to tunes, but you can customize your alarms and brush up on a musical instrument. Read on and see.

Listening to MP3s on Your Clié

Some Clié models come with a built-in MP3 player. Others are compatible with an MP3 add-on that lets you listen to music while you're on the go. If your Clié doesn't come with MP3 capabilities, feel free to skip this section. We don't mind, and we'll catch up with you later.

By and large, the MP3 player is pretty self-explanatory; to use it, just copy tunes to your Clié's Memory Stick and tap the AudioPlayer application on your Clié.

> NOTE *Don't try to load MP3s via the normal Install Tool, which transfers them when you HotSync. It will take a very, very long time to copy music this way. The direct connection is much faster.*

Install Music

To get your songs on to your Memory Stick, you can use a Memory Stick reader that connects to your PC's USB port, or just put the Clié in the HotSync port and connect with the AudioPlayer program directly. You'll have to have installed the drivers from the installation CD, but once that's done, here's how to install music:

1. Start the AudioPlayer and choose Options | Transfer from the menu. Wait until you see a message on the Clié that says "Status: Transfer" with a warning not to remove the Memory Stick while a data transfer is in progress.

2. On your PC, double-click My Computer and find the removable drive that corresponds to your Clié. Open it, and double-click the folder marked Palm. Then double-click Programs, and open MSAudio. This is where you'll copy your music.

3. Open the folder on your PC with your MP3 files and drag and drop them onto the MSAudio folder. When the files have copied, you can disconnect your Clié from the desktop computer.

TIP   *Instead of venturing into AudioPlayer, you can simply run the MS Import or Data Import utility on your Clié. It establishes a direct connection to your PC, thus letting you proceed directly to step 2.*

Playing Music with AudioPlayer

Once you have a small music collection on your Memory Stick, you're ready to listen to music. Tap the AudioPlayer icon on your Clié and you should see a list of tunes, like this:

In addition to the onscreen controls, you can also use the scroll wheel on the side of the Clié to operate the music player. You can change tunes by rolling the wheel up or down, and you can pause and play music by pressing the wheel. Want to reassign the functions of the Jog Dial? Tap the picture of the jog wheel in the upper-left corner and you'll see the Jog Function Select screen, where you can choose from among five different modes for the jog wheel.

Want to listen to music while you do other work on your PDA? You *can* play music while you type into a Clié word processor but, first, you have to enable "background play." Background play lets the Clié multitask, so it plays music while it's also running another program.

To enable background play, choose Options | Preferences from the menu and tap the option for Enable Background Play. When checked, you can change programs and the music will continue to play. When unchecked, the music player will stop as soon as you try to switch applications.

NOTE *Not all Clié models enable background play—if you have an MP3 add-on that connects via the PDA's HotSync port, you might not have the capability to play music in the background while doing other things.*

As you've no doubt noticed, even a Clié with enhanced audio isn't cut out for playing music through that tiny speaker. Instead, for best results, you should use a headset, like the earbuds that came with your Clié. Remember, though, you don't have to use Sony's; you can substitute your own.

TIP *The MP3 player eats a lot of the Clié's precious battery life. To conserve battery power while listening to music—especially if you're not doing anything else with the Clié—you might want to use the Clié's Hold switch. When you press the Hold button on the side of the Clié, you lock the Clié's controls so you can't accidentally interrupt the music. At the same time, the screen goes off. You need to deactivate Hold to turn the Clié on again.*

Play Modes

You can play your music just by tapping the Play button. But like any good music player, you have options, as shown next:

Tap to change play mode, such as Continue (play all), Shuffle, and Reverse (play all in reverse order)

Tap to repeat all songs, just one song, or turn repeat play off

18

Don't want to listen to all the songs in your Memory Stick? You can also create a custom playlist. To do that, choose Tool | Pickup... from the menu and select just the songs you want to play.

The AudioPlayer also has one other cool—but slightly unusual—feature. You can create a musical loop that plays just a specific part of a song. To play a loop, start your song and, when you reach the point where you want your loop to start, tap the Loop button. You should see the *A* and the arrow illuminate.

When you reach the end of the loop, tap the Loop button again. The *B* will also be illuminated now, and the selected portion of music will play forever until you tap the Loop button a third time to cancel the loop play.

There Are AudioPlayer Alternatives

While Sony's AudioPlayer is a good, simple, and free music player (well, free in the sense that it comes with your Clié), you have alternatives:

■ **eNeRgy**   A small, functional, freeware MP3 player. Downloadable from **PalmGear.com**.

■ **AJVMP3**   A pretty-looking HiRes+ MP3 player, ideal for devices like the NR- and NX-series. Find it at **http://ajvmp3.paradise.net.nz**.

■ **AudioControlcDA**   Play your MP3s through a small pop-up window on the Clié. Available free at **http://isweb41.infoseek.co.jp/computer/crspalm/#acda**.

Your Clié as an MP3 Remote

Here's a novel way to use your Clié—as a remote control for the popular WinAmp music player for Windows. If you're adventurous, check out *MP3Remote*, available from PalmGear. This program uses the Clié's IR port to command WinAmp, turning your Clié into an MP3 remote control. On the downside, it requires you to use WinAmp on a computer (most likely a laptop) that has an infrared port.

Checking Your Memory Stick's Memory

How much free space is left on your Memory Stick? The easiest way to check is to tap the icon of the Memory Stick atop the AudioPlayer screen. You can get the same information by choosing Tools | About Memory Stick from the AudioPlayer's menu. Either way, this is a handy trick to remember, even if you want to know about free space for matters unrelated to music. Wondering if that video or e-book will fit? Tap the AudioPlayer application and check the Memory Stick status.

Remember, you can carry multiple "albums" of music just by bringing more than one Memory Stick. You'll get about two hours of music per 128MB Memory Stick (assuming your MP3s are encoded at about 128 Kbps), so you can have several hours of music on just a few sticks.

Managing MP3s

18

If you've been around the PDA block a few times, you no doubt know that a million database programs exist that track everything from your stocks to your favorite books on your Palm-powered PDA. MP3s are no different. At least half a dozen applications out there promise to make your life a nirvanaesque dream through MP3 micro-management. And, lo and behold, a few of them are pretty good. Here are our favorites:

- **Playster**   Now this program is pretty darn cool. *Playster* searches your hard disk for MP3s and synchronizes the track data—like title, artist, genre, year, and comments—with a database on your Clié. If you're, um, "extremely diligent" (yeah, that's the expression we were trying to think of) about entering all the ID3 tag data for all your music tracks (you know, stuff like artist, track, album title, and so on), you can do it at your leisure on your Clié, and the changes get HotSync'd back to the PC. You can even build custom play lists stored on your PC as M3U files for your favorite MP3 player to play for you. Because Dave is an, um, "extremely diligent" person, he loves this application.

- **Nappy**   If you visit online music sites on a frequent basis, you might want to try *Nappy,* a program you can use to take note of songs you'll download later when connected to the Internet at home. The name comes from the long-defunct Napster, but it's a good tracking program nonetheless.

Nice, but Impractical?

Dave: I love the idea of integrating an MP3 player into a PDA. The thought of listening to music on my NX80 as I read an e-book gives me little chills of excitement. But, in the real world, this is more trouble than it's worth. Sony's Memory Sticks are just too expensive to be practical. It costs around $225 to get a 512MB stick, good for perhaps four hours of music. For the same price, I can buy an MP3 player with a 20GB hard disk, capable of storing hundreds of hours of music. For that reason, my Clié's MP3 player goes unused while I carry my iPod along on lengthy trips.

   Rick: Well, obviously, if you insist on carrying 20GB' worth of music, the Clie isn't the answer. However, I can buy a 512MB CompactFlash card for under $100 (I also need EruWare's $30 driver so AudioPlayer can recognize it), which lets me carry well over 100 songs, plus a few NPR shows like "This American Life." That's more than sufficient audio for most trips I take. Most people don't fly halfway around the world every weekend like you do, so your "real world" doesn't apply. In fact, the world you live in is downright scary.

Making Music on the Clié

When you tire of simply listening to music and, instead, want to be in the band, it's time for some music software. And, believe it or not, you can indeed use the Clié for a large number of music applications. It has a built-in speaker for creating (admittedly, very basic) sounds, and the display is perfectly suited for musical notation in a small space. If you're a musician, be sure to check out some of these applications.

Metronome and Drumming Software

It doesn't take a rocket scientist to figure out the Clié's sound capabilities aren't exactly symphonic in nature. So, one obvious application for your Clié is to keep time, either as a drum machine or a metronome. In fact, this would have come in handy a long time ago—Dave used to carry a guitar around wherever he went, and having a metronome or minidrum machine in a box as small as the Clié would have been really cool.

- ■ **Meep**   This is your standard metronome. *Meep* has a slider for choosing any tempo from 40 to 280 beats per minute, and you can select up to 8 beats per measure, as well. You can also work from onscreen counts or add an audible beep to each beat.

- ■ **Responsive Metronome**   Another simple metronome tool, *Responsive Metronome* enables you to choose any tempo from 35 to 300 beats per minute, and both see (via a pulsing quarter note) and hear the beat. This program is quite simple and, in fact, there's no on/off switch for the beat—you have to disable both the audio and video filters to shut it off.

- ■ **Pocket Beat**   This application simulates a drum kit right on your Clié. *Pocket Beat* can remember two distinct tempos and you can switch between them easily by using onscreen controls or the Scroll button. Pocket Beat can also play straight or shuffle beats, and it can vary between 40 and 196 beats per minute. The best part, though, is you can tap out your own meter on the Clié screen—Pocket Beat memorizes the tempo and plays it accordingly.

Here you can see images from Meep, Responsive Metronome, and PocketBeat:

18

Portable Music Lessons

Budding musicians can carry around the following applications with them to bone up on notes, keyboard positions, and fingering:

- **MusicTeacher** This program can be used as an aid to learning to sing *prima vista*—that is, by reading sheet music by sight. Several tunes are stored in the MusicTeacher database, and you can also enter your own using the onscreen keyboard.

This program is interesting because it's written in Java and uses a Java interpreter on the Clié to run. Because it's only a Java application, the MusicTeacher program can also be found on the Web and runs from within a web browser window. You can find it at **mathsrv.ku-eichstaett.de/MGF/homes/grothmann/java/waba**.

- **GTrainer** If you're learning to play guitar and don't want to be forever tied to "tab" sheet music, try this application. *GTrainer* displays a note onscreen and you need to tap the correct place on the guitar fretboard. It isn't enough just to choose the right note—you have to tap the correct octave, as well.

- **McChords** If you're learning piano, *McChords* is an essential portable tool for working through chord fingerings. It shows you which keys to press to form the majority of chords you need to master basic piano playing.

■ **PChord**   This program, seen next, is indispensable for anyone trying to get the hang of the guitar. In fact, PChord also supports mandolin, banjo, violin, and other stringed instruments. Choose a chord and PChord displays a variety of ways to finger it. PChord includes every chord we could think of, including obscure chords (minor 9th and stacked fourths) you might play only once in a great while. As such, it's a good memory jogger even for experienced players. Similar programs to try include *Guitar Power, FretTrainer,* and *CDB FretBoard Trainer.*

Tools for Musicians

Tuning—bleh. I hate tuning my guitar. If only there were some automated way to….

Well, of course there is. Every guitarist on Earth probably owns a $30 electronic tuner, but did you know you can use your Clié for tuning as well? We've found a bunch of tuners for the Clié—one good example being a program called Guitar Tuner Lt. Dave has used it himself on several occasions. *Guitar Tuner Lt.* comes with standard and alternative tunings. Tap the appropriate onscreen string and the tone plays for several seconds. Or, tap the Auto button to hear each string's tone in turn.

Music Annotation and Recording

You might have experimented with (or frequently use) applications on the Mac or PC that enable you to compose and play music. Those programs generally let you drag notes on to musical staffs or play an onscreen keyboard to construct musical compositions. Well, you can do the same thing on the Clié—the screen is just a bit smaller, and you don't have multiple voices to hear your multitimbral creations. Here are a few applications you can try:

■ **TS Noter**   This unusually named program is an online favorite because it's so good at helping you create music. *TS Noter* features a staff and a set of tools for placing notes and rests. When you create your song, you can save it, play it, or even export it as an alarm for the Clié's Date Book. A desktop companion program lets you play the music you create on your Clié from a PC using a MIDI instrument.

18

■ **miniPiano**   This program enables you to play an onscreen keyboard while the notes you strike get added on a staff. You can then play back your creation. *miniPiano* has a Free Play mode in which the keys are duration sensitive—the longer you hold the stylus on the key, the longer it plays.

■ **Palm Piano**   This simple program records the notes you tap out on a four-octave keyboard and it can play back the results. Palm Piano has some simple editing tools built in, but it doesn't have rests and there's no way to select note lengths—they all play back at the same timing.

■ **PocketSynth** Like Palm Piano, this program enables you to create music by tapping on an onscreen keyboard. *PocketSynth* enables you to select note lengths and rests, though, which gives you more composing flexibility. Unfortunately, you must select the length of the note, and then tap it on the keyboard, which makes the composition process less than entirely fluid.

Adding Sounds to the Clié's Alarms

After all that fancy music stuff, you might think the Clié's alarms are kind of mundane. But think about it: wouldn't you like to be warned about upcoming appointments by the theme to *Superman* or some home-brewed song?

If you have a Clié model with Sony's "enhanced audio," you can enhance the Clié's built-in alarm library in two ways. If you have the ordinary Palm OS audio, you have just one option. How can you tell which you have? For starters, the enhanced audio is an important feature, so it's probably mentioned on the box. Another way to find out: if your Clié has enhanced audio, it'll have a program, probably located in the CLIE category, called Audio Utility.

If you have enhanced audio in your Clié, you can either download new material from the Internet or you can convert MIDI and WAV files you've stored on your desktop PC. If you have standard Palm OS audio, there's no way to convert your own stuff—so let's start by looking at getting those prefabbed alarm tunes.

Getting Prefabbed Alarm Tunes

The few alarm sounds that come with your Clié are all simple tunes that use a chip in your Clié to convert musical instructions (in the MIDI language) into music that plays through your Clié speakers. Because the Clié uses standard MIDI files, several add-on musical libraries are available. For a few dollars, you can get popular movie tunes, pop songs, folk tunes, and other musical pieces to choose from when setting your alarms. If your Clié has enhanced audio, here are some of the available options.

- **CliéSounds 2.0**   Includes several dozen replacement tunes for your Clié. Available on PalmGear and written by Jeffrey VanderWal. It's free.
- **Clié Sounds Collection 1.3**   Offered on PalmGear by a company called PalmGSM, this $10 collection of songs costs a little, but it features no less than 130 songs from TV, movies, and popular bands.

If your Clié doesn't have enhanced audio, you have a lot more options, just because developers have had years and years to release old-style audio. Here are some places to look for Clié models without enhanced audio:

- **GeekSounds**   A free collection of songs that includes many of your classic movie favorites.
- **Alarms for PalmOS**   Over 300 songs for your Clié, including all your favorites from ABBA, sci-fi films, and dance songs. Costs $10.

Converting Songs

If your Clié has enhanced audio, you can also copy your own individual tunes to the Clié's alarm library. The Clié comes with a desktop program for Windows called, simply enough, Sound Converter. *Sound Converter* accepts music in MIDI and WAV format and converts it to a form acceptable to the Clié, and then puts it in the Install queue for the next HotSync.

TIP   *You can find Sound Converter on the installation CD-ROM that came with your Clié.*

Any MIDI file will work in Sound Converter, though you have to make sure your WAV files fit the Clié's narrow range of acceptable specifications. You can only import WAV files with these characteristics:

- 8 kHz, 8 bit, Mono
- 8 kHz, 16 Bit, Mono
- 22 kHz, 8 Bit, Mono
- 22 kHz, 16 Bit, Mono

- 8 kHz, 8 Bit, Stereo
- 8 kHz, 16 Bit, Stereo
- 22 kHz, 8 Bit, Stereo
- 22 kHz, 16 Bit, Stereo

So, suppose you have a 44 KHz WAV file you want transferred to your Clié as an alarm sound? You need to convert it first. The easiest way to do that is with the Windows Sound Recorder, following these steps:

1. Start the Windows Sound Recorder. It's usually in the Start menu, in Accessories | Entertainment.

2. Choose File | Open from the menu and load your WAV file that needs transformation.

3. Choose File | Save As from the menu. Make sure the Save As Type list box is set to WAV, and then click the Change... button.

4. In the Attributes menu, choose a compatible format, such as 8.000 kHz, 8 Bit, Mono. Then click OK.

5. Save the file with these new attributes.

Now you can add the file to Sound Converter and transfer it to the Clié.

18

Remember, while MIDI files take up very, very little space on your Clié, a WAV file is comparatively huge. If you like the idea of using a digital song file as an alarm sound, we recommend you stick to just one or, at most, two at a time. These files can only be stored in the Clié's internal memory (not a Memory Stick), so you can find yourself committing a lot of system memory for something silly like the theme to *Knight Rider.*

Managing Songs on Your Clié

On the other hand, enhanced-audio Cliés come with a very cool little program called Sound Utility, which is essentially a library of all the MIDI and WAV alarm sounds on your device. You can play songs, rename them, and delete tunes that have worn out their welcome. So, when you—or your coworkers—tire of listening to Rod Stewart's *Hot Legs* as your 11:00 A.M. meeting alarm, you can delete the file and make room for more tunes.

Where to Find It

Web Site	Address	What's There
PalmGear	www.palmgear.com	Virtually all the applications found in this chapter
Handango	www.handango.com	Virtually all the applications found in this chapter

Chapter 19

The Clié as a Remote Control

How to...

- Use your Clié as a universal remote
- Work with Clié RMC
- Find other Palm OS remote software
- Decide between Clié RMC and other programs
- Turn your Clié into a TV guide

Is there no end to your Clié's capabilities? When you add "universal remote" to the list, it probably seems that way. The infrared (IR) transceiver that's built into your Clié can be used for more than just swapping programs and contact listings. In fact, with the right software, it can double as a universal remote, capable of controlling everything from TVs to stereos to DVD players.

Okay, but what's the right software? Before we tell you, we need to explain a subtle difference in the IR capabilities of various Clié models. Specifically, many Cliés have roughly the same IR power as other Palm OS-based handhelds—a transceiver with a range of about five feet. Unless you like to sit really close to your TV or stereo, that's obviously not too great. However, some Cliés—most notably the T, NR, and NX series—have enhanced IR ports with roughly triple the range. Now you can plunk down on the couch and get some serious channel-surfing done.

The products we discuss in this chapter will work with any Clié model. But, suffice it to say, unless you have a model with enhanced IR, you might not enjoy them to the fullest. Furthermore, the idea of using your handheld as a remote could seem a little kooky, especially if it doesn't spend a lot of time near your entertainment center, but it can be quite practical at times—and good for a few practical jokes, too.

Our Favorite TV Shows

Rick: I'll take television over the movies any day. Movies are a crapshoot, and most of them are, well, crap. But just look at some of the intelligent, inventive, and entertaining shows TV has given us in recent years: *Alias, 24, Frasier, The West Wing, King of the Hill, Scrubs, Andy Richter Controls the Universe*...the list goes on and on. Even my guilty pleasures—*Boston Public, Survivor, Trading Spaces*—have elements of quality to them. Why spend $8.50 on two hours' worth of drivel when I can enjoy the good stuff in the comfort of my own home?

Dave: What??? Are you seriously comparing two completely different mediums—TV and cinema—and declaring one a winner? Using that logic, I see no reason to build mass transportation, because vegetables are better. It's interesting that you anecdotally find a few good TV shows and use those as examples, but don't mention any life-altering films that have graced the big screen: *Schindler's List, The Sixth Sense, Gone with the Wind, Life is Beautiful, Memento....* Good grief, I don't have room for them all. But that's okay; we don't need to read books, because I have a fridge full of salad dressing.

Rick: As usual, you miss the point entirely. Obviously in the entire history of cinema there have been some great movies. But let's see what's playing as I write this: *Gigli, From Justin to Kelly, Dumb and Dumberer,* and countless other flops. Now let's see what's on TV: nearly every one of the shows I mentioned, and they're all jewels. I find it interesting that you didn't bother to mention any of your favorite shows. Could it be because you don't want people to learn of your secret love of *The Bachelorette*?

Dave: I'm sorry, did I insult your "picture stories?" In truth, and despite your cheerleading, the percentage of good TV to bad is depressingly low. It's hard to tell when you only point out the good TV shows and the bad movies—a little debating trick you must have learned from other Democrats. Here's reality, dude: out of the hundreds of shows on TV each week, there are only a few worth watching—last year, I watched *24* as if my life depended on it. I also looked forward to *Enterprise, Friends, Dennis Miller Live* repeats, and *The Daily Show*. But I try to watch less TV, not more. It's a little something I have called "culture."

Sony's Remote Software: Clié Remote Commander

We didn't hatch the idea of using your Clié as a remote—Sony did. (Actually, turn-your-handheld-into-a-remote software has been around for Palms for quite some time, starting with OmniRemote, which we discuss in the section "Other Remote Control Programs." But Sony was the first hardware maker to write remote software from scratch and include it with a handheld.) If you have one of the enhanced-IR models, you can use it as a remote right out of the box, thanks to a bundled application called Clié RMC (also known as Clié Remote Commander). With it you can control up to four different kinds of devices: TVs, VCRs, DVD players, and stereo components. And you don't necessarily need to squint at the screen every time you want to control something—Clié RMC takes full advantage of the Clié's hard buttons and Jog Dial.

TIP   *How many times have you found yourself in a hotel room with a TV remote that's flaky or just plain broken? Your Clié can come in mighty handy as a substitute, though Clié RMC might not have the right codes for the off-brand TVs found in some hotels. If you travel a lot, you might want to try one of the other remote-control programs discussed in the section "Other Remote Control Programs." Some have much larger code databases, while others can "learn" from existing remotes, meaning you can control just about anything.*

19

You can find complete setup instructions in Sony's Add-on Application Guide, so we won't rehash them here. However, we should point out a few key items before you get started with Clié RMC:

- This is a fairly confusing program to set up, so it's a good idea to read the documentation thoroughly before getting started.

- Clié RMC has a limited database of TVs, VCRs, and so on, plus all the remote control codes that go with them. However, if you own a model that's not in the database, you're out of luck—the program cannot "learn" to control unknown devices (as many regular universal remotes can). What's particularly unfortunate is that many of Sony's best products—like DIRECTV with TiVo—aren't supported.

- Clié RMC has four quick-launch buttons—labeled A–D—across the top of the screen. To set the parameters for each one (that is, to choose which device it should control), tap the desired button, and then tap Menu | Details.

- In the Details screen, one of the available settings is called Mode. Your choices here are usually nothing more descriptive than mode1, mode2, and so on. Here's an explanation by way of example: Panasonic makes dozens of different VCRs, but many of them use the same sets of control codes. Thus, if you choose a Panasonic VCR, but nothing happens when you tap the Test button, choose a different mode and try the test again. Chances are one of them will work.

- You're not limited to four components—just four *kinds* of components. Thus, if you want to use Clié RMC to control, say, two VCRs and three TVs in your home, you can add them all (provided they're in the database).

TIP   *If you find yourself using Clié RMC on a regular basis, it might be practical to reassign one of your Clié's hard buttons to launch the program. That way, you won't have to hunt for its icon every time you plop down on the couch. Refer to the section entitled "Buttons" in Chapter 2 for information on reassigning buttons, or just choose Prefs | Buttons and jump right in. It's not complicated.*

Play a Great Practical Joke

One of the really fun things about Clié RMC is how easy it is to choose a device to control. Just tap Select, then New, and then fill in the appropriate details (Category, Maker, Name, and so on). In about 30 seconds, you can add an entry for, oh, say, a friend's TV set. The next time you're over watching *Alias,* use your Clié to secretly change channels or the volume—and then say, "Dude, what's up with your TV?" Of course, *Alias* is too good to mess with, so wait for a commercial—or just play around during a dumb show like *Dog Eat Dog.*

Other Remote Control Programs

If your Clié didn't come with Clié RMC or you'd like a program that's a little more robust, several solid alternatives are available, including NoviiRemote, OmniRemote Pro, and ProntoLite.

Pacific NeoTek's *OmniRemote* was the first remote-control program ever created for the Palm OS, and the company has refined it quite a bit over the years. The Pro version supports high-resolution screens, jog dials, and an unlimited number of remotes (meaning you can train it to operate virtually any device). Better still, you can design customized button layouts right on the Clié screen, create macros (used to perform a sequence of actions—like turn off the TV, turn on the stereo, and turn on the CD player—with a single button-tap), and set timers (so you can, say, turn the TV into your alarm clock by instructing OmniRemote to turn it on in the morning).

TIP

Like the idea of using your TV or stereo as an alarm clock? Try AirClock, a clock/calendar/ alarm program that enables your Clié to turn on any remote-controlled appliance at a designated time. Just leave your Clié pointed at, say, the TV before you go to bed, and AirClock will send the turn-on signal at whatever time you preset. Wouldn't you rather wake up to Katie Couric than a boring old beep-beep-beep?

19

In short, if you're interested in turning your Clié into a full-featured universal remote, OmniRemote is worth a look. It sells for $24.95—a lot less than the price of stand-alone programmable remotes.

You should also check out *ProntoLite,* which is based on the Philips Pronto remote that's so popular among home-theater enthusiasts. However, whereas the Pronto sells for about $400, ProntoLite costs just $19.95. Plus, it has the most attractive, streamlined, and logical interface of any of the remote programs, so it should be easier for novices to manage. ProntoLite can control up to ten A/V devices, but you're a bit limited in adding devices not directly supported—like, say, a TiVo or Replay recorder. Still, as with OmniRemote, there's a free trial version, so you can put it through its paces before plunking down your cash.

NOTE   *At press time, ProntoLite wasn't compatible with any OS 5 devices.*

Finally, we come to *NoviiRemote,* one of the newest and most sophisticated remote-control programs. In fact, it's so new that, at press time, it wasn't yet compatible with OS 5 handhelds, and most of its most exciting features weren't even functional. Those issues should be resolved by now, so make sure to grab the trial version of NoviiRemote and give it a whirl.

Based on what we've seen so far, NoviiRemote offers a much more attractive interface than OmniRemote and a lot more features than ProntoLite—including support for an unlimited number of devices. It even promises better IR range, courtesy of an enhanced software driver. The NoviiRemote Guide adds customized TV listings to the mix, meaning your Clié will serve as both a remote control and a program guide.

Turning Your Clié Into a TV Guide

Several products take the idea of using your Clié as a remote a step further. Instead of merely letting you flip channels and adjust the volume, these programs download current and complete TV listings to your Clié, thus obviating the need for that *TV Guide* that's always getting lost in the couch cushions. Some of them just provide listings, while others go the full nine yards with remote features as well. Thus, your Clié becomes not unlike the program guides common in digital cable boxes: you sift through programs to find what you want to watch, and then tap a box to switch to that channel.

Of course, that begs the question: why not just use your cable box's own guide? For starters, they're often slow and difficult to navigate. What's more, they commandeer your TV screen, blocking whatever show you were watching. If you have a guide in your hand (you've got a remote there anyway, so why not a guide too?), your screen remains unobstructed. Yeah, we know, we're reaching, but if you weren't such a gadget nut, you wouldn't be reading this section anyway.

Let's take a look at a few TV guide programs, which have proliferated rapidly since last we wrote about them (in the first edition):

■ **ConnectedTV**   ConnectedTV downloads TV listings into your Clié when you HotSync, then presents those listings on the screen as an interactive TV guide. Tap the show you want to watch, and your TV automatically switches to that channel. The software offers a variety of nifty features, including a Favorites page, details about each show, and support for the Clié's Jog Dial and hard buttons (for functions like mute, power, and volume). ConnectedTV also has the distinction of being one of the few subscription-oriented Palm OS programs—it costs $30 per year (a reasonably affordable price tag, in our humble opinions). The only downside is the interface: it's atrocious, meaning you'll expend considerable time and effort getting the software set up properly, then more time learning to navigate it. We hope the creators will refine the interface as time goes by because this is one cool program.

■ **Pocket TV Browser**   *Pocket TV Browser* downloads 14 days' worth of TV listings, complete with descriptions, ratings, VCR+ codes, and a search option that lets you find your favorite shows and actors. It's fairly inexpensive at $9.95, but you have to download and run a separate application—TV Grid Listings, $10—if you want a more traditional grid-like view of the data. What's nice about TV Grid Listings is that it supports the HiRes+ screens found in NR/NX/NZ models—something few other TV-guide programs currently support.

19

And If You're Really Serious About Using Your Clié as a Remote...

As we noted at the beginning of this chapter, different Clié models have different IR strength. If you want to maximize your handheld's infrared capabilities, consider this handy accessory: the TaleStuff IR Blaster. This little module plugs into the bottom of your N- or S-series model and comes with its own IR port—one that has a range of 35–65 feet (depending on the device you're pointing it at). Okay, you're thinking, sounds good, but if the IR Blaster plugs into the *bottom* of my Clié, won't I have to turn it upside down? The answer is yes, you smart reader, you. Fortunately, programs like ConnectedTV and OmniRemote allow you to flip the screen 180 degrees, so you can still use your Clié while it's inverted. The IR Blaster costs $24.95.

Where to Find It

Web Site	Address	What's There
AirSpell	www.airspell.com	AirClock
ConnectedTV	www.connected.tv	ConnectedTV
DoubleBit Software	www.pimcity.com	Pocket TV Browser
Pacific Neo-Tek	www.pacificneotek.com	OmniRemote Pro
Novii Media	www.novii.tv	NoviiRemote
Philips	www.pronto.philips.com	ProntoLite
TaleStuff	www.talestuff.com	IR Blaster

Chapter 20

Playing Games

How to...

- Adjust your handheld's volume for games
- Install new games
- Control games on your handheld
- Play action, board, and card games
- Play sports, strategy, and word games
- Play two-player games on two handhelds
- Use your PDA as a substitute for dice

Spreadsheets, databases, document readers, and memos are all well and good. If that's all you ever plan to do with your PDA, that's fine—you're just unlikely to ever get invited to one of our parties.

Your PDA is a miniature general-purpose computer, and, as a result, it can do almost anything your desktop PC can do—including games. Sure, there are limitations. The display is pretty small and the processor isn't nearly as fast, but the fact remains your Clié is a great game machine for passing the time in an airport, on a train, in a meeting (where it looks like you're taking notes), or any other place you're bored with doing productive activities. In this chapter, we discuss what you should know to get the most out of your handheld as a gaming machine, and we recommend some of the best games for you to try.

NOTE *As Cliés have evolved, so have their capabilities. Some have color screens, some have high-resolution color screens. Some have limited audio hardware, some have rich audio hardware. Some have Palm OS 4, some have Palm OS 5—and so on. As you look around for games (and even check out those we recommend), make sure they're compatible with your particular model. Some games require OS 5; others are optimized for HiRes+ screens like you find on the NR/NX/NZ models. A lot of games are universally compatible, but you should always check the system requirements before installing anything on your PDA. At the same time, be on the lookout for games that have been enhanced to support Clié audio. Many of Astraware's great games (like Bejeweled) are available this way.*

Prepping Your Clié for Gaming

No, playing games isn't exactly rocket science, but before you get started with them, you should learn a few things that'll come in handy. You should know, for instance, how to control your Clié's volume, install applications, and enable beaming (some games let you play against other handheld users via the IR port).

Controlling Game Volume

At the top of the list is the Palm OS sound system, which includes a control for how loud to play game sounds. Logic dictates you'll want to set this loud enough to hear what's going on in your game, but this might not always be the case. As much as we like to play games, we don't always want others to know that's what we're doing. Fortunately, it's possible to set the game sound level low or even off completely. This means you'll play your games without sound (which, if you're at work, is probably a wise decision).

To tweak game sounds, do this:

1. Tap the Prefs icon to open your Preferences application.

2. Switch to the General category by tapping on the category menu at the top-right corner and choosing General.

3. Find the Game Sound entry and choose the volume level you're interested in.

 If you find that a game still squeaks and squawks even if the Palm OS volume setting is set to off, the game must have its own sound preferences. Check its options menu for a control to set the sound volume. Indeed, many games have built-in volume controls that eliminate the need to futz around with the settings in Prefs.

Enabling Beaming

If you know other Palm OS handheld users, you might want to try your hand at some head-to-head games, which are made possible thanks to the devices' infrared ports. It's fun and addictive, and very nearly sociable. For two games on different handhelds to "find" each other, though, you need to make sure the Beam Receive setting in Prefs is enabled.

1. Tap the Prefs icon to open your Preferences application.

2. Switch to the General category by tapping the category menu at the top-right corner and choosing General. (If you have an OS 5 device, choose the Power option.)

3. Look for the entry called Beam Receive and make sure it's set to On. (By default, it is.)

Installing Games

Installing games is a snap. We discussed how to install applications on your handheld in Chapter 4, and working with games is no different. After all, a game is just another kind of Clié application. Need a refresher? We won't make you go all the way back to Chapter 4. Turning pages is such a drag.

Let's assume you're dealing with games you want to download from the Web. (Some computer and office-supply stores sell game bundles, most of which have their own installation programs. You don't need us for those.) If you're new to downloading, you need to know that most apps come compressed in one of two popular formats:

- **Zip** This is the standard way of managing files in Windows. To install a Zipped file, you need a program capable of unzipping it first. Typically, this means using a utility such as WinZip. (Windows XP can automatically extract the contents of Zip files.)

- **SIT** Macintosh files are compressed in the SIT format, which can be uncompressed with a program such as Aladdin Stuffit Expander 5.0.

Once you expand the compressed file, you'll probably end up with a folder containing several files. Installation instructions typically come in one or more file formats:

- **Plain text files** These are usually called something clever like readme.txt or install.txt. These will tell you which file(s) to install.

- **HTML pages** These will probably have an Internet Explorer icon (or whatever Web browser you use), and usually contain the game's instructions. Double-click them to see the instructions in your web browser.

- **PDF files** You need Adobe Acrobat Reader to read these files, though it's probably already installed on your computer. If not, visit **adobe.com** to get this popular document reader.

- **Files with a PRC extension, and possibly PDB as well** These are the actual game files that need to be installed on your Clié. Open the Install tool and use the Add button to mark these files for installation during the next HotSync.

Game Packs

Occasionally, you might find game compilation discs in the store or online. They promise to deliver hundreds of unbeatable Palm OS games for just 10 or 20 bucks. Should you invest in one of these packages?

Our opinion: probably not. The collection might sound promising, but anyone with a halfway decent Internet connection can get all the games they like from a site like **PalmGear.com** or **Palmgamingworld.com** just as easily, without spending a dime. Remember: Clié games are tiny compared to games for the PC, and they download in seconds.

Also, keep in mind that you won't get the full, registered version of shareware games, even though the disc itself cost you cash. Instead, these discs are sort of like samplers for folks who want a guided tour of someone else's idea of the "best" games for the Clié. If you like a game you find on the disc, you'll still have to pay to keep playing it, just as if you downloaded it from the Internet.

 If you use WinZip, a faster way to install the games is simply to double-click the PRC and/or PDB files from within WinZip. That will save you the extra step of having to unzip the files first.

Game Controller Peripherals

As you'll see throughout this chapter, lots and lots of cool games are available for the Clié—more than we could ever fit in this book, in fact. Some are so addictive you might miss a meeting trying to get the high score. But they all have the same basic limitation—you need to use a stylus or the buttons to control the action.

 ## Control Your Jet/Race Car/Submarine/Spaceship

Now you're all set to start playing some games, but where's the joystick? There isn't one, silly. Many games use the handheld's buttons to control the action. While the game is running, the Date Book, Address Book, Memo Pad, and To Do List buttons are typically diverted to game controls and won't switch you to the usual apps. To find out which buttons do what in a given game, you can experiment (our favorite way) or check the game documentation. In most games, you can find basic instructions by checking the game's built-in Help screens (tap Menu to find them). A handful of newer games take advantage of the Navigator control found in newer Clié handhelds.

Depending on which Clié model you own, there might be a better way. Add-on game controllers give you a more authentic arcade experience, complete with joystick or gamepad, instead of mashing the Clié's buttons. Here are two options:

- **Sony Game Controller**   Compatible with most of the newer Clié models, Sony's own clip-on accessory uses buttons to re-create the typical d-pad-style controller found on console game systems. This is' probably the best bet for serious game fans, as it's designed by the same company that made your Clié and sells for the reasonable price of $40.

- **SimpleJet PDA Game Pad**   Designed for the Clié N series, this somewhat hard-to-find clip-on makes your handheld look a lot like Nintendo's Game Boy, complete with a traditional four-way d-pad controller and two action buttons.

A Few (Dozen) of Our Favorite Games

Games account for a pretty healthy chunk of all software sold for Palm OS handhelds, so it should come as no surprise that you can find hundreds upon hundreds of titles spanning every genre. Card games, action games, puzzle games—you name it, it's out there. Of course, we can't list all of them without doubling the size of the book. It's big enough already, don't you think?

Did you know?

Gone, but Not Forgotten

Rick: Frogger, Galaxian, Pac Man—these were household names back in my youth, and they're just a few of the arcade classics that have been resurrected for Palm OS handhelds. Of course, a Clié's buttons don't compare too favorably with traditional coin-op controls, so longtime favorites like Spy Hunter, Joust, and Sinistar are a bit tricky to control. Still, it's a blast to revisit my youth with these favorites of yesteryear—and I don't even need to pump quarters into my PDA.

Dave: I love the old arcade classics as much as the next geek, but it's time to move on, dude! It's the 21st century! I've put childish games like those well behind me and today, I play mainly just the mature, modern classics. Like Bejeweled.

Rick: Don't call me "dude."y

As with other kinds of Clié software, games are easy to try before you buy. Most have a trial period, usually from two weeks to a month, after which the game becomes disabled unless you register it (that is, pay for a code to unlock it permanently). Games usually cost $10–$20, though a few will set you back $30. There's also a treasure trove of great freebies like these (all of them available at **www.freewarepalm.com**):

- **Cribbage 3.0**   Sure, you could pay 12 bucks or so for one of the commercial Cribbage games, but why? Well, the Clié tends to cheat a bit—but, otherwise, this is a freeware gem.

- **Mulg II**   Use your stylus to guide a marble through a maze within a fixed amount of time. Devilishly addictive.

- **Napalm Racing**   Not the greatest racing game we've ever played, but surprisingly robust for a freebie.

- **Patience Revisited** An amazing collection of Solitaire games—21 in all, all in color, all free, free, free!
- **PilOth** A clone of the classic game of Othello.
- **Pocket Video Poker** Why take a trip to Vegas when you can gamble all you want for free? There's also Pocket Video Blackjack if that's more your speed.

- **Sea War** A nice implementation of the beloved game Battleship. There's even a high-resolution version.
- **Solitaire Poker** One of many variations on Solitaire, this one involving poker hands.
- **Vexed 2.1** One of the most addictive puzzle games ever, and a Palm OS freeware classic. The 2.1 version includes multiple puzzle packs with over 600 levels.

These freebies are a great place to start for anyone interested in a little fun on the run. In fact, there are enough freeware games to keep you entertained almost indefinitely. On the other hand, if you're willing to shell out a few bucks, you'll find some of the best mobile entertainment money can buy. In the following sections, we' list some of our favorites, all divided into a few major categories.

Action and Arcade Games

Did you pump an untold number of quarters into arcade machines in the '80s? We sure did. These action games will make you long for the classics of yesteryear—and, in some cases, revisit them.

- **Galax** An excellent retread of the inimitable (but often imitated) Galaxian.
- **Midway Arcade Classics** Five flawless re-creations of arcade greats: Defender II, Joust, Root Beer Tapper, Sinistar, and Spy Hunter.

- **PacMan** You had to know the little yellow chomper would make an appearance on the Clié, right? There's not much in the way of sound, and we'd much rather play Ms. Pac Man, but for pure nostalgia, nothing beats good old Pac-dude.

- **Zap!2016** A scrolling space-shooter with gorgeous graphics and terrific sound effects.

Card Games

Card games transition well to handheld PCs because they don't require fancy graphics or complicated controls. They're games you can relax with, maybe play in the bathtub. (On second thought, the bathtub probably isn't the best place for your PDA. Try the shower.) Poker, Hearts, Blackjack—there are versions of just about every classic card game you can think of.

- **AcidFreecell** Freecell is one of our favorite Solitaire games, and this version includes sound effects, photographic backgrounds, and other nifty perks.

- **KidzTalk GoFish** A memory game not unlike Concentration, the goal is to match pairs of cards from a spread-out deck of 20. As you make matches, a picture is revealed underneath. This OS 5–only game also talks to you in a real human voice. Great for little kids.

- **Texas Holdem Poker 1.2** Rick isn't much of a card player, but he is a big fan of the movie Rounders, hence, his interest in this great little poker game.

- **Vegas Blackjack** Without a doubt the best-looking Blackjack game for the Palm OS, Vegas Blackjack plunks you down at a casino-style table for some serious hands of 21. Double down!

Board Games

There's a reason games like chess, Risk, and Monopoly have been around forever: they're fun, no matter where—or even how—you play them. Lots of the big-name board games are available for the Palm OS. These are the ones we like best:

- **Aggression**   Remember Risk? Aggression is a visually striking re-creation of the beloved board game. It looks best on high-resolution color screens, but you can play it even on grayscale Cliés. Bonus: it even takes full advantage of 320×480 HiRes+ screens like on the NR/NX/NZ models.

- **Monopoly**   This needs no explanation, other than to say that one to four players can partake, human or computer, on the same handheld or on several of them (the game supports play via infrared).

- **Rook's Revenge**   Almost too fast-paced to qualify as a board game, Rook's Revenge is like chess with a jolt of caffeine. Move your pieces as fast as you can (they still have to be legal moves), without waiting for your opponent to make his moves. A great change of pace from boring old chess.

- **Scrabble**   Like Monopoly, no explanation needed here. But how cool to play this old favorite anytime, anywhere, without having to worry about tiles spilling all over the place.

Puzzle Games

Some of the best Palm OS games, bar none, are puzzle games. They're generally easy to learn, seriously addictive, and endlessly entertaining.

■ **Bejeweled**   Like TNT's "New Movie Classics," this game has been around for just a few years, but it's already achieved Tetris-like classic status. It requires zero time to learn to play—and all your free time once you do. If, by chance, you've never heard of it, trust us and give it a try. It might just be the perfect game for PDAs.

■ **Bounce Out**   If you get tired of Bejeweled, try Bounce Out. It's the same game, only with balls instead of jewels, and the chance to work diagonally.

■ **NetWalk II**   An oldie but goodie, NetWalk challenges you to make successful connections between your servers and your computers. Sounds like a tech-support nightmare, but it's a ton of fun.

■ **Triclops**   How best to describe this game? There's a big triangle, see, and lots of little triangles fall into it, and you have to try to remove three or more like-colored triangles with each tap of the stylus. Okay, it sounds a little kooky, but it's a blast.

Word Games

Dave's not much for word games—too much stress on the brain—but Rick loves 'em. Nothing like keeping the old noodle active while you're passing the time.

- **Bookworm**   Make as many words as you can from Bookworm's wall of letters. The trick is, the letters must be adjoining. We're not sure it'll increase your word power as the developer claims, but it's definitely an enjoyable challenge.
- **Crossword Puzzles for Palm OS**   Whether you're a crossword-puzzle fanatic or you haven't looked at one in years, this excellent collection—derived from Washington Post puzzles—is an ideal way to pass the time. Sure beats carrying a big book of puzzles or getting newspaper ink on your fingers!

- **Text Twist**   The first game Rick reaches for when he has five minutes to spare, Text Twist is a bit like Boggle. You're given six scrambled letters and a time limit; try to make as many words as you can from the letters *and* unscramble the six-letter word.

Strategy and Role-Playing Games

You might think a PDA isn't the best place to play a strategy or role-playing game. You might also think Dave is witty and urbane. In both cases, you'd be wrong. Although some strategy and RPG games do benefit from the big screens afforded by desktop computers, those clever Palm OS developers have created some mighty compelling stuff for handhelds. Witness:

- **Dragon Bane**   Remember Bard's Tale? It was a role-playing classic for desktop PCs. Dragon Bane brings the same medieval adventuring to your PDA, complete with monsters, spells, and your choice of character classes. Dungeons & Dragons lives on.
- **Galactic Realms**   Space-based action and strategy that's reminiscent of the great StarCraft.
- **Lemmings**   Show of hands: who remembers the Amiga? Lemmings was one of the all-time great games to emerge from that system. In this perfect re-creation, you must guide the dumb little guys to safety. It supports high-resolution screens, sound, memory cards, and so on—and it's a freebie! (The level packs will cost you a few bucks, though.)

Sports Games

Anyone for tennis? How about racing? Maybe even a little Quidditch? Sports games (even fictional ones based on an amazing book) aren't always ideal for a screen as small as the Clié's, but that hasn't stopped developers from making some admirable efforts. Golf, basketball, football, and even bowling are among the other sports represented as Clié games. Whatever your athletic passion—even if it's darts—you're sure to find a game to match.

Among the most impressive titles we've seen is TableTennis3D, a way-cool Ping Pong simulator. You can play against your PDA or another player via infrared.

Games for Which We Haven't Figured Out a Category

Okay, how would *you* classify a game involving a fish tank? Some games just don't fit a standard mold. Nevertheless, don't miss these amazing titles:

- **Billiards**   If you like pool, you'll love this dazzling interpretation. It's particularly great on HiRes+ screens, like the ones found in NR/NX/NZ models.

- **Bump Attack Pinball**   Pinball is really hard to do right on a PDA, what with the small screen, lack of flippers, and so on. Bump Attack Pinball gets it right, and with several beautiful-looking tables to boot. It even has a few designed for HiRes+ screens.

- **Insaniquarium**   Running a fish tank is hard work. You have to keep all the fish fed, gather up the coins they drop, fend off alien attackers—the usual stuff. Insaniquarium is like no other game we've seen, but it's definitely lots of fun. Your "tweens" and teens will love it, too.

Two-Player Infrared Games

As we already mentioned, two-player games are a cool way to pass the time when you're traveling with another handheld-equipped person. IS/Complete offers perhaps the largest collection of infrared-enabled games, including Palm OS versions of Battleship, checkers, chess, and even Hangman. They all work more or less the same way: you make a move, and then tap a button. Your move is then beamed to your opponent's handheld, where the board is updated to reflect the new data. Then you perform the same process in the other direction.

The games and graphics are nothing spectacular, but they're still kind of cool. And you needn't prearrange a gaming session with another player. That is, if you've got one of the IR games and your buddy doesn't, no problem—just beam it to him. Of course, there might be a few limitations, depending on whether the game in question is commercial or freeware. If it's commercial, the beamed copy will often work only with the one from which it was beamed. Or, it might stop working after a short period of time, like two weeks (this is to encourage "player 2" to buy his own copy).

If you're interested in more sophisticated IR games, check out Handmark's excellent versions of Monopoly and Scrabble. Both can be played either on a single device (with multiple players) or via IR.

Using the Clié as a Pair of Dice

If you like to play board games in the real world, you might be interested in using your Clié as a virtual pair of dice. After all, the Clié is harder to lose (we always misplace the dice that go with our board games). Several apps are available, but many of them have the disadvantage of requiring run-time modules of programming languages, such as Forth or C. We don't care for that approach, because it's just extra stuff you have to install.

Some dice simulators you might want to try include Gamers Die Roller, DicePro, and Roll Em.

Where to Find It

Web Site	Address	What's There
Astraware	www.astraware.com	Bejeweled, Bookworm, Bounce Out, Text Twist, Zap!2016, and many of our other favorites
Freewarepalm	www.freewarepalm.com	Freeware games (and other Palm OS software)
Handmark	www.handmark.com	Midway Arcade Classics, Monopoly, Scrabble
IS/Complete	www.iscomplete.com	Several two-player-via-IR games
PalmGear	www.palmgear.com	Most of the games mentioned in this chapter
PalmGamingWorld	www.palmgamingworld.com	One-stop surfing for all sorts of Palm OS games
SimpleJet	www.simplejet.com	PDA Game Pad
WinZip	www.winzip.com	WinZip file compression tool for Windows

Chapter 21 Reading E-Books

How to...

- Find electronic books
- Understand the differences between Doc files and e-books
- Choose a book viewer
- Work with Mobipocket
- Read e-books on your Clié
- Find free e-books
- Find commercial e-books
- Create your own e-books

You know the future has arrived when a device the size of a Pop-Tart can hold an entire Stephen King novel. Indeed, many users find electronic books (aka e-books) to be a major Clié perk. You can pay nothing at all and read hundreds of literary classics, or pay discounted prices for mainstream titles. In this chapter, you learn everything you need to know about turning your Clié into a world-class library.

A Brief History of E-Books

Before Cliés came along, a huge collection of electronic books—mostly public-domain classic literature, like Voltaire's *Candide* and Sir Arthur Conan Doyle's *Sherlock Holmes* stories—existed on the Internet. Because these works had already been converted to computer-readable text, why not copy them to Cliés for reading anytime, anywhere?

In theory, you could simply paste the text into a memo. But there's a snag: memos are limited to about 500 words, so even short stories are out of the question. Hence the emergence of one of the very first third-party Palm OS applications: *Doc,* a simple text viewer that had no length limitation other than the amount of RAM in the handheld itself. Doc rapidly became the de facto standard, not only for e-books, but also for documents created in desktop word processors and converted for handhelds.

> **NOTE** *In this chapter, we mostly discuss the e-book aspect of Doc files. If you want to learn more about creating and editing text files in a Clié word processor, see Chapter 12.*

We've mentioned this before, but it bears repeating here: The Palm OS Doc format is neither the same as nor compatible with the Microsoft Word Doc format. Thus, you can't simply HotSync your favorite Word files to your Clié and view them there. (Actually, you can, but you need a program like Documents To Go for that. See Chapter 12 for more information.) Yes, this can be a confusing area. We really wish the creators of Palm Doc hadn't chosen that particular name.

Format Wars

In recent years, several document formats have arisen to challenge the Doc standard—kind of like AmiPro vs. Word vs. WordPerfect in the heyday of word processing. The cleverly named TomeRaider, for instance, uses its own, proprietary format. Why work with a format other than Doc, which is almost universally accepted? Cross-platform compatibility, for one thing. The TomeRaider program is also available for Pocket PC handhelds, EPOC-based handhelds (like the Psion Series 5), and Windows. Thus, a single text file can be viewed on a variety of devices and PCs, without having to be converted. The Doc format, in comparison, works only on Palm OS devices, and must be converted back and forth between handheld and PC.

Choosing a Doc Viewer

Many people make this mistake: they download a bunch of nifty e-books from MemoWare (or wherever), load them on to their Cliés, and then spend lots of time trying to figure out why they can't find the books. (When you install software, there's usually an icon for it.) The reason, of course, is they don't have a Doc viewer installed. Without one, there's no way to view Doc files.

Fortunately, plenty of Doc viewers are out there—all free or quite inexpensive. The best place to start is with Palm's own program, Palm Reader, available at **www.palmdigitalmedia.com**. Here's a rundown of some other choices:

Doc Viewer*	Noteworthy Features
CspotRun	Free; supports auto-scrolling
DeepReader	Lots of great features, including automatic scrolling, anti-aliased fonts, and support for HiRes+
Isilo	Supports HTML and .txt files. as well as Doc files
FastWriter, Quickword, WordSmith	These programs, some of which are discussed in Chapter 12, can all double as word processor.
TealDoc	Supports images and links between documents; advanced search options

*All of these programs are available from **PalmGear.com**.

A screenshot of Deep Reader (running in HiRes+ mode, meaning it's taking advantage of the NR/NX/NZ's full screen) alongside one of Palm Reader (going a step further in HiRes+ by rotating the text 90 degrees) is shown next.

TIP

If you have an NR/NXNZ-series Clié, make sure to choose a Doc reader that supports HiRes+—that is, one that will collapse the Graffiti area and display your books using the full length of the screen. Palm Reader is one that does, and it also lets you rotate the text a full 90 degrees. Thus, you get a "wider" viewing area that's more akin to reading a real book. This is, without a doubt, our preferred method for reading books on a Clié.

All about Mobipocket

Depending on when you purchased your Clié, you might already have an e-book reader: *Mobipocket*. This is an interesting product in that it not only lets you view standard Doc files, it also downloads news feeds from the Internet (not unlike AvantGo, which we discussed in Chapter 11), and lets you convert HTML and text files stored on your PC for viewing on your Clié. A Windows utility handles the latter two features, and looks like this:

As for the Mobipocket Reader, this is how it appears:

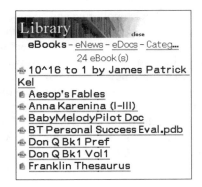

At the Mobipocket web site, you can purchase and download hundreds of commercial e-books, including L. Ron Hubbard's sci-fi classic *Battlefield Earth,* dictionaries and encyclopedias, and even a couple dozen medical texts. For $19.95, you can buy the Mobipocket Office Companion for Microsoft Office, which enables you to export Word, Excel, and PowerPoint documents to your Clié. All told, Mobipocket is a fairly comprehensive e-book solution. And even if it didn't come with your model, you can download it free from the company's web site.

Making Room for the Books

Before we delve into the details of finding, buying, and viewing e-books, you should know that e-books can be extremely large files. Jules Verne's *The Mysterious Island,* for instance, takes a whopping 622K, while the infamous biography *Monica's Story* nabs 500K. Fortunately, not all titles are quite so gargantuan. Most short stories are under 50K, and even Stephen King's novel, *The Girl Who Loved Tom Gordon,* is a reasonable 226K.

The good news is that most of the popular Doc readers support Memory Sticks, meaning you can store your e-books on a stick and not sacrifice any main memory (see Chapter 22). Indeed, with just a 64MB module, you could carry a rather significant library of titles.

An E-Book Love Affair

Many years ago, when Palm OS handhelds were still fairly new, Rick found himself on a train with nothing to do for several hours. Then he remembered he'd loaded an e-book on his PalmPilot just before leaving. He started reading, found the novel totally engrossing, and passed the time as happy as a clam. From that day forward, he vowed never to travel anywhere without an e-book. And when people ask him to explain what that little gadget is he's holding, he says it's a handheld PC—and a portable library.

Free E-Books and E-Books for Sale

There are dozens of online sources for e-books, both free and commercial. The former are works considered public domain: either their copyrights have expired (as in the case of classic literature), or they've been written and released by authors not seeking compensation. Literally thousands of titles are available in the public domain, many of them already converted to the Doc format.

Commercial titles aren't unlike what you'd buy in a bookstore: they've simply been converted to an electronic format and authorized for sale online. Notice we didn't mention Doc: most commercial e-books are created using a proprietary format, meaning a special viewer is required. This is primarily to prevent unauthorized distribution—unlike actual books, commercial e-books aren't meant to be loaned out or given to others. When you buy one, you're effectively buying a license to read it on your Clié and only your Clié.

Finding Free Stuff

If one site is synonymous with Doc files, it's MemoWare (**www.memoware.com**). Here you can find thousands of texts divided into categories such as business, history, travel, biography, sci-fi, and Shakespeare. Whether you're looking for a collection of Mexican recipes, a Zane Grey western, a sappy love poem, or a classic work by Dickens, this is the place to start.

Our Favorite E-Books

Rick: I've become something of an e-book zealot, recommending MemoWare and Palm Digital Media to friends, family, and any strangers who will sit still for five seconds. Among the great titles I've read on my Palm are *Angela's Ashes, Battlefield Earth, The Corrections,* and *Kick the Can.* I also enjoyed rereading *The Most Dangerous Game,* a story I remembered fondly from high school. I got that one free from MemoWare. My only hope is that Dave will one day read something that doesn't involve robots, hobbits, or robot hobbits.

Dave: I have to commend Rick on the progress he's made. When I met him a scant six years ago, he hadn't yet learned to master the written word. Since then, I've seen him get his equivalency diploma, start on "chapter books," and even sign his name in ink instead of crayon. Bravo, Rick! Well done! Nonetheless, I must still pity anyone who only reads books recommended by *Entertainment Weekly.* As for me, I find the best for the buck is the magazine *Fantasy & Science Fiction*—Palm Digital Media has a good assortment of them going back to 1997. I'm rarely disappointed by any of those tales, and there's a month's worth of bedtime reading in each collection.

MemoWare offers a convenient search engine, so you can type in a title or a keyword to quickly find what you're looking for. It also has links to other e-book sites, although none are as comprehensive. Finally, MemoWare provides numerous links to software programs (most for Windows, a few for Mac) that turn computer documents into Doc files. More on that in the section "Making Your Own E-Books."

Finding Commercial Stuff

The thing about public domain e-books is that most of them are, well, old. Somerset Maugham and Jack London are all well and good for catching up on the classics you promised yourself you'd read one day, but sometimes you just want a little Stephen King. Or Mary Higgins Clark. Or Captain Kirk. Fortunately, you can have them all on your Clié, provided you're willing to pay for them.

The top place to go for contemporary, mainstream fiction and nonfiction is, without a doubt, Palm's own online bookstore, *Palm Digital Media* (at **www.palmdigitalmedia.com**). The site offers thousands of books from prominent authors like Stephen Ambrose, Elmore Leonard, and Anna Quindlen.

How to View Palm Digital Media Books

When you purchase a book from Palm Digital Media, you supply your name and credit card number, then receive a Zip file to download. (If you need a utility to expand Zip files, we suggest downloading WinZip from **www.winzip.com**) This file contains the e-book itself (in an encrypted .pdb format), along with the Palm Reader program. If you don't already have the Palm Reader installed on your PDA, be sure to install it.

 When buying subsequent books, you need to install only the books themselves. You needn't install Palm Reader again.

You also receive, via e-mail, a code number that's used to "unlock" the e-book. You need to enter this number on your Clié the first time you open your e-book.

 The code number is usually the credit card number you used to purchase the book. If you don't mind divulging it, you can, indeed, share the book with another handheld user. Just e-mail the file for them to install, then give them the number, so they can unlock the book. This is pretty smart copyright protection, if you ask us, as it allows for sharing among family members and close friends, but prevents you from giving books to strangers.

One more note about Palm Reader: you must use it to view books purchased from Palm Digital Media; no other e-book reader will let you read them. However, Palm Reader will let you view standard Doc files, such as those obtained at MemoWare and Fictionwise. Thus, it's a pretty good all-purpose program.

 If you subscribe to Palm Digital Media's free weekly newsletter, which is distributed via e-mail, you'll receive a code that's good for 10 percent off every e-book you buy. Visit the site for details.

Other Sources for Contemporary E-Books

Palm Digital Media might be the largest source for commercial e-books, but a couple other web sites are gaining notoriety.

- **Fictionwise** Here you'll find a growing collection of fiction and nonfiction stories and novels, all of them discounted. In fact, you can buy short stories for as little as a buck—sometimes even less. One nice thing about *Fictionwise* is the books are provided in the standard Doc format, so you can use your favorite Doc viewing program. (The company also offers Palm Digital Media-format books, so you can read those with Palm Reader as well.) Furthermore, the site includes reader-supplied ratings for each book and story, so you can make more informed decisions on what to buy. Fictionwise also provides a decent collection of free short stories for you to try out, so we highly recommend a visit.

- **Mobipocket** This is not only an e-book content provider, but also a document viewer—one that might have come bundled with your Clié (along with a couple sample e-books). See "All About Mobipocket" earlier in this chapter for more details.

- **PerfectBound**   Individual book publishers are finally getting into the e-book act, as evidenced by this site offering titles from HarperCollins.
- **RandomHouse.com**   Another major-league book publisher offering e-books at discounted prices. At press time, Jon Krakauer's *Under the Banner of Heaven* was selling for $18–30 percent off the hardcover price.

Making Your Own E-Books

Become a published author! Well, not published in the "Stephen King" sense. More in the "kooky old uncle who staples warnings to telephone poles about how mailboxes are alien mind control devices" sense. Nonetheless, if you have your own documents, short stories, novellas, or doctoral theses you'd like to convert to the Doc format, you've got a lot of options. Among them:

- Alexis Lorca's *pDocs* makes it a snap to transfer Microsoft Word documents to your Clié. It converts them to the Doc format, and then adds them to the Install Tool so they'll be loaded the next time you HotSync. It can also pull Doc files from your Clié into Word.
- *Palm eBook Studio* is a $30 program (available from Palm Digital Media) that lets you easily convert text and images to a format that's compatible with both Palm OS and Pocket PC handhelds.
- *MakeDoc* (for Windows users) and *MakeDocDD* (an equivalent program for Mac users) are free, no-frills converters. They turn text and HTML files into Doc files, making them readable using any Doc reader. (For the record, Mobipocket's Web Companion utility does the same thing.)

How to ... Read in Bed Without Disturbing Your Spouse

Since the dawn of time, one seemingly insurmountable problem has plagued the human race: how to read in bed without disturbing one's spouse. Torches didn't work: they tended to set the bed on fire. Battery-operated book lights didn't work: they made books too heavy, leading to carpel reader syndrome. But, finally, there's an answer: the Clié handheld. Just load up a novel and turn on the backlight. You'll have no trouble seeing the screen in the dark, and your spouse will barely know it's on. PDA or marriage-saver? You be the judge.

Where to Find It

Web Site	Address	What's There
Alexis Lorca	www.thinkchile.com/alorca	pDocs
Fictionwise	www.fictionwise.com	A growing collection of short stories and novels
Mobipocket	www.mobipocket.com	The Mobipocket Reader and accompanying software, plus e-books for sale
MemoWare	www.memoware.com	Public domain literature formatted for the Palm OS
Palm Digital Media	www.palmdigitalmedia.com	Huge library of commercial fiction and nonfiction
PerfectBound	www.perfectbound.com	E-books from HarperCollins
Random House	www.randomhouse.com/e-books	E-books from Random House

Chapter 22

Making the Most of Memory Cards

How to...

- Work with Memory Stick media
- Understand the differences between different kinds of Memory Sticks
- Add Memory Stick Pro support to certain Clié models
- Find the best prices on memory cards
- Lock a Memory Stick
- Work with CompactFlash cards
- Manage files on a Memory Stick
- Access a Memory Stick from your PC
- Transfer files to and from Memory Sticks

By now you know the 21st-century spin on the old adage: you can never be too rich, too thin, or have too much memory. Sure, it's grammatically iffy—but it is accurate. What with RAM-devouring e-books, games, photos, productivity software, and even MP3 files, 16MB and even 32MB just don't go as far as they used to. Fortunately, all Clié handhelds offer simple, inexpensive, potentially limitless memory expansion.

And not just memory expansion. Although most Memory Sticks are exactly that—memory—you can also find a Bluetooth networking card (which, at press time, is still being sold only in Japan, but there are web sites that sell it to customers in the United States) and a digital camera mounted right on a stick. There's also an excellent product—Margi Presenter-to-Go (see Chapter 12)—that enables your Clié to run PowerPoint presentations and display them right on a projector. In the future, don't be surprised to see other Memory Stick-based expansion hardware, such as GPS receivers and wireless network adapters.

Meanwhile, a few Cliés—most notably the NX and NZ models—have a secondary expansion slot for a different kind of memory card (CompactFlash, or CF, which we discuss in the section "Cliés and CompactFlash Cards"). This slot can also accommodate Sony's 802.11b Wi-Fi wireless networking card, as discussed in Chapter 11.

Nevertheless, in this chapter, we focus primarily on the memory aspects of Memory Sticks: how to copy files to them, access programs from them, keep them organized, and more. We also show you the finer points of working with CompactFlash media (on those Cliés that support it), which brings its own set of challenges (and advantages).

It's in the Cards

Just what is a Memory Stick? True to its name, Memory Stick (MS) is a small card—about the size of a stick of chewing gum—that contains a fixed amount of Flash memory. *Flash memory* is solid-state storage, meaning everything is electronic instead of mechanical. Think of it as a small hard drive with no moving parts. And, like a hard drive, MS is rewriteable, meaning you can copy data to it over and over again.

You might be familiar with CompactFlash and Secure Digital cards, which are other kinds of Flash storage for handheld PCs. MS is Sony's proprietary format, meaning you won't find the technology used in, say, Palm or Handspring devices. You will, however, find it in other kinds of Sony electronics, most notably digital cameras.

As you might have surmised, Memory Stick cards aren't compatible with CompactFlash, Secure Digital, or other kinds of memory media. That's because they're physically different. However, adapters do exist that would enable you to plug a Memory Stick into, say, your notebook computer's PC Card slot—helpful if you want a quick and easy way to transfer photos, MP3 files, or other data.

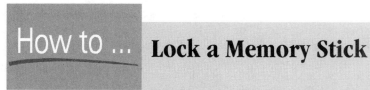

How to ... **Lock a Memory Stick**

If you're worried about the files or data stored on your Memory Stick, there's an easy way to lock the card so no additional data can be written to it—or deleted from it. On the back of every card is a tiny sliding switch labeled Lock. Slide the switch to the right and your MS is secure. Your Clié will still be able to read information and run programs from the card, but there's no danger of anything getting erased or overwritten. This is just like those write-protection tabs on the 3.5-inch floppy disks of yesteryear.

Comparing Memory Stick, Memory Stick Select, and Memory Stick Pro

As you shop for Memory Stick cards, you're likely to encounter three different varieties: Memory Stick, Memory Stick Select, and Memory Stick Pro. They all look more or less identical, but the latter two are relatively new and require a bit of explaining.

What happened was this: the original Memory Stick cards and slots were engineered in such a way that they couldn't accommodate more than 128MB of Flash RAM. Call it a lack of foresight on Sony's part; whatever the reason, it put a practical limit on Cliés (and, for that matter, Sony digital cameras and other Memory Stick-equipped products). You can't fit much music on a 128MB card, and it's not nearly enough space to hold a movie. Even while Sony was touting the Clié's multimedia prowess, the company had to deal with a rather debilitating cap on expansion memory. Competing memory-card products such as CompactFlash and Secure Digital have no such limitations; they quickly surpassed Memory Stick with 256MB, 512MB, and even 1GB capacities.

Sony took two steps to resolve this situation. The first, *Memory Stick Pro,* updates the Memory Stick architecture so it supports higher capacities. However, while it's now possible to buy cards ranging from 256MB to 1GB (with even larger cards planned for the future), MS Pro cards aren't compatible with older Cliés. Kind of a bummer if you purchased, say, an NR70V with the hopes of watching movies, stocking big music libraries, and so on.

That brings us to Sony's second "innovation": Memory Stick Select. Compatible with all Clié models, *Memory Stick Select* packs two or more "banks" of 128MB onto a single card. Thus, a 256MB MS Select has two 128MB storage areas (call them *A* and *B*). You could put, say, a bunch of games and e-books in *A,* leaving *B* free for music or whatever else. It's not a bad stop-gap solution—we'd rather carry one card than two any day—but it's not ideal, either. The memory isn't contiguous, meaning you can't access it in one 256MB chunk. That means if you have a movie file that's even a hair larger than 128MB, you're out of luck.

How to Upgrade Your Clié NX/NZ to Support Memory Stick Pro

Here's some good news for owners of the Clié NX60, NX70V, and NZ90: while your model didn't come with MS Pro support right out of the box, Sony has issued a software patch that enables you to use the newer media. Just visit Sony's support site (**www.ita.sel.sony.com/support/clie/**), choose your model from the list, and then click Drivers and Updates. On the following page, you'll find the Memory Stick Pro Update Program. Follow the instructions on the site to download and install it.

Cliés and CompactFlash Cards

With the introduction of the Clié NX60 and NX70V, Sony added what was essentially a second expansion slot. Thus, in addition to Memory Sticks, you had a spot for CompactFlash (CF) media, see Figure 22-1. Well, actually, no, you didn't. You see, while the slot itself was physically compatible with CF media, Sony didn't modify the Palm OS so it could utilize CF memory cards.

FIGURE 22-1   The CompactFlash slot found in NX- and NZ-series Cliés adds an extra measure
of expansion, but there's a catch.

The reason for that was understandable, if not incredibly annoying. Sony makes money from
the sale of Memory Sticks, but not from CF cards. Thus, restricting the CF slot's compatibility would
force users to continue to buy MS media. So what was the slot good for? One product and one
product only: Sony's PEGA-WL100 (later replaced by the virtually identical WL110), a wireless
LAN card that allows access to Wi-Fi networks. You couldn't even buy physically and functionally
identical third-party Wi-Fi cards—you had to use Sony's pricey version. Bleh.

For many NX60, NX70V, and eventually NZ90 users (that model came later, but it didn't change
anything, CF-wise), access to CF memory cards became something of a Holy Grail. Why such
strong interest? Simple: CF cards aren't limited to 128MB. Plus, they cost a lot less than comparable
Memory Stick Pro cards. Power users wanted to drop inexpensive 512MB and even 1GB CF cards
into their Cliés and carry feature-length movies, multiple record albums, and other space-gobbling
goodies. Fortunately, an enterprising software developer answered those users' prayers.

The EruWare CompactFlash Storage Card Driver

EruWare's NX- and NZ-compatible CompactFlash Storage Card Driver enables you to use 512MB,
1GB, and even Hitachi Microdrive CF cards in place of Memory Sticks. As you might expect, the
programming trickery required to make this possible brings with it some complications and confusion,
which is why we don't recommend the utility for novice users.

NOTE   *At press time, the driver was compatible with only the NX60 and NX70V, but there might
be a version for the NX73V and NX80V (see "CompactFlash Cards on the NX73V and
NX80V") by now. Check EruWare's web site.*

That said, EruWare's documentation is excellent, and the software works fairly seamlessly once installed and configured. Some third-party programs support the presence of two memory cards, but, ironically, Sony's built-in apps (like Audio Player and Movie Player) don't. EruWare's ingenious workaround, *MS Cloaking,* fools the Clié into thinking a CF card is an MS, but it's not perfect—we had troubles with Movie Player and Movie Recorder. There's also a Dual MS Mode, which lets you use CF and MS cards simultaneously.

```
Compact Flash Utility

☐  Read Only  ☐  Auto Mount
☐  Slow Mode  ☐  MS Masquerading
☐  Slow Mount ☐  Cache On

Compact Flash Card Info:
Volume Label: TOSHIBA512M
Volume Size: 499672 KB
Used Space: 220432 KB
Approximately 55% free

[ Mount Card ]      [ Unmount Card ]
```

Regrettably, Sony's MS Import utility (discussed in the section "Access a Memory Stick From Your PC") isn't supported. To stock up on things like MP3 files and movies, you need a CF card reader for your PC—or several hours to complete a HotSync. Still, the driver is a huge asset for Clié power users and a welcome fix for a Sony misstep. It sells for $27, a small price to pay if you want to carry a lot more media on your Clié.

CompactFlash Cards on the NX73V and NX80V

Having heard the cries of frustrated NX60, NX70V, and NZ90 users, Sony decided to add CF memory support to the NX73V and NX80V. However, while you can store applications and data on a CF card, Sony's built-in applications (the important ones, like Audio Player and Movie Player) don't recognize the CF slot. So much for feature-length movies, big music libraries, and so on. We suspect Sony will release updated versions of those programs that do support the CF slot, so check Sony's support site (**www.ita.sel.sony.com/support/clie/**) periodically.

TIP   *Actually, there is a way to play movies from a CF card. You need* Kinoma Player *(see Chapter 16), a third-party video player that supports the Clié's CF slot. Yes, it's ironic (and unfortunate) that Sony's own movie player doesn't, but as Rick likes to say: there is no perfect.*

What Price Memory?

So, what will it cost you to add, say, 32MB, 128MB, or more to your handheld? Prices drop all the time, so the information we've gathered here could be inaccurate by the time you read it—but in a good way. We spent some time shopping at **eCost.com**, our favorite source for memory media like MS cards, and found the following prices:

- 64MB Memory Stick: $34.99
- 128MB Memory Stick: $44.99
- 256MB Memory Stick Select: $64.99
- 256MB Memory Stick Pro: $87.99
- 512MB Memory Stick Pro: $205.99

As you can see, there's a "sweet spot" in the price-per-megabyte ratio. How much space do you really need? If you plan to work with goodies like MP3 files and digital photos, buy the largest card you can afford. If you just want storage for extra programs, games, e-books, and such, a 64MB card would probably suffice.

TIP *You needn't buy media directly from Sony. Lexar Media, I-O Data, and SanDisk are among the companies that also sell Memory Stick cards, and often for less than Sony's equivalent cards. You should also steer clear of Sony's MagicGate-flavor Memory Sticks. They cost more and offer absolutely zero benefit—unless you're buying and downloading copyrighted music content.*

By the way, if you're looking for CompactFlash cards, **eCost.com** also tends to have great deals on those.

What Is MagicGate?

As you shop for Memory Stick media, you might encounter some cards that are purple and some that are white. The latter are labeled *MagicGate,* which refers to a proprietary copyright-protection technology created—and used—by Sony. Put simply, if you were to buy music online from a service like Pressplay (of which Sony is a part), you couldn't copy the music files to a "plain" Memory Stick as you can with ordinary MP3 files. Because the music is copyrighted, it will play only on a Memory Stick—a MagicGate Memory Stick—that supports copyrighted files. Make sense? Yes, it's confusing to us as well. Bottom line: unless you're one of the 27 people who subscribe to Pressplay, you probably won't need to worry about MagicGate. See Chapter 18 for more information on playing music on your Clié.

NOTE *The exception to this "rule" is Memory Stick Pro: all MS Pro cards include MagicGate technology. C'est la vie.*

Memory 101

With the introduction of Palm OS 4.0, Palm also introduced the Virtual File System (VFS)—a way for the operating system (OS) to recognize removable memory cards and access the programs and data stored therein. Thus, you could relocate, say, Palm Reader and all your e-books to a card, freeing a fair chunk of your handheld's valuable internal memory.

More Memory on the Inside

If you're wishing you'd purchased a Clié with more memory on the inside, take heart. It might be possible to increase your model's the internal memory—provided you're willing to part with it for a few days. Just send it to PDA Specialists (**www.pdaspecialists.com**) or Tony Rudenko (**www.palmpilotupgrade.com**). Both can upgrade certain Clié models.

Tony Rudenko, for instance, will upgrade a T615 to 32MB for $109. An S320 can be upgraded to 16MB for $79. (Of course, at that point you're probably better off upgrading to a newer model, which will have 16MB anyway and cost only a bit more.) Check the site for the latest prices and more details.

It's important to note that utilizing either service will void your handheld's warranty, but both vendors offer a 90-day warranty of their own.

Working with Memory Cards

You can get programs and data onto a memory card in two basic ways. First, if you have software that's already loaded in the Clié's internal memory, you can use the Palm OS Copy tool to copy it to the card. (This works both ways: you can copy items from a card back to internal memory as well.) To do this, tap the Home button to return to the main screen, and then tap Menu | App | Copy. Select the program you want to copy (you have to copy them one at a time), making sure to select the correct Copy To and From destinations. Tap Copy to begin the process.

Alas, because there's no move option, the original file remains on your handheld. To claim the extra storage space you were after, you must then delete the software from internal memory. (To do this, tap Menu | App | Delete, and then select the desired file(s) for deletion.)

This is exactly as tedious as it sounds, which is why we strongly recommend either Clié Files (included with some Clié models) or a third-party file manager like FilePoint (**www.bachmannsoftware.com**) or McFile (**www.handango.com**). These programs make it much easier to move, copy, beam, and delete files than the Palm OS.

TIP *If you're an intermediate or advanced user, check out* FileZ *(**www.nosleep.net**), which offers a robust set of file-management tools and cost zilch, zip, zero, nada.*

Better still, get yourself a launcher, which will not only make life easier when it comes to copying, moving, and deleting files, but also provide much better organization of programs stored on Memory Sticks. See the next section for more information.

Installing Applications Directly to a Memory Stick

It's one thing to move a program from internal memory to a memory card. It's a smarter thing to install it there from the get-go. The Palm OS Install Tool lets you specify the destination for new software at the time you install it, meaning you can HotSync apps right onto a memory card.

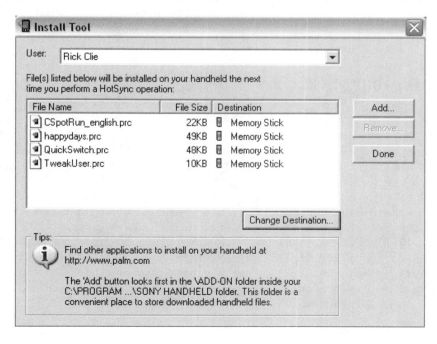

Ah, but what happens to them after that? Novice users often fall into the same trap: they install programs on their memory cards, and then can't understand why they don't see the icons in the Apps screen. The answer lies in a quirk of VFS: all applications stored on a memory card are automatically segregated into a category called Card. Thus, you must look in that category to find your newly installed stuff.

This can be inconvenient, to be sure, especially for users who like to keep their icons orderly. If you wind up with, say, 30 apps on a storage card, now you've got an organization problem—you can't subcategorize the Card category. Fortunately, there's a solution in the form of third-party launchers, most of which now support external storage. That means they treat programs stored on cards no differently than programs stored in main memory, meaning you can categorize and organize them as you see fit. You can find out more about launchers, and see some of our favorites, in Chapter 13.

What's On Your Stick?

Rick: Starving writer that I am, I've yet to pony up for a 256MB—or, better yet, 512MB—Memory Stick Pro card for my Clié NX70V. In the meantime, I make do with a pair of 128MB cards, which is inconvenient, to be sure, but they get the job done. My primary card contains various games, e-books, and applications. The other card contains TV shows that I recorded to my PC's hard drive, and then transferred to the MS for viewing on the Clié. Among other things, I keep an episode or two of *Clifford, the Big Red Dog* for my daughter Sarah. It's handy to have along for extended car trips or unusually long waits in a restaurant.

Dave: I waited patiently for Sony to offer Memory Sticks with capacities beyond 128MB, and they finally have—but a 512MB Memory Stick Pro card costs more than twice as much as a comparable SD or CF card! Whaaaaa???? So, like Rick, I'm sticking with 128MB sticks for now. Because I have a separate MP3 player for playing music on the go, I mainly load up my Memory Sticks with short films, like those from **BMWfilms.com** and KaZaa. I also put music videos on my Memory Sticks. These video diversions come in handy for those long plane rides I must endure every few months.

Access a Memory Stick From Your PC

In the last section, we talked about the intricacies of accessing a Memory Stick via your Clié. But what about accessing one from your PC? Why would you want to? Here's a list of excellent reasons:

- It's much easier to manage the programs and data stored on your MS.

- It's much faster to install large files like MP3s and photos. We mean *much* faster. Suppose you have, say, a dozen MP3 files you want to load onto an MS. You could place them there using the Palm Install Tool, making sure to specify Memory Stick as the destination. But the HotSync process could take upwards of an hour, possibly even longer. If you copy them there via your PC, however, it should take no more than a few minutes.

- It enables you to use an MS as a kind of portable hard drive, capable of storing any computer files you see fit to carry.

To allow direct access to your Clié's Memory Stick via your PC, Sony provides a pair of utilities: MS Import and MS Export. The former runs on your Clié and comes preinstalled on it. The latter runs on your PC and must be installed by you. Here's how to get started.

> **NOTE** *On the NX73V, NX80V, and other newer Cliés, MS Import and MS Export have been replaced with Data Import and Data Export, respectively. The instructions for getting set up with them are pretty much identical, but there's one key difference when it comes to using them: Data Export on the PC consists of a window where you can drag and drop files. That saves you having to load Windows Explorer to navigate to the Clié "drive."*

1. Insert the Sony Installation CD into your PC. The setup program starts automatically.

2. Click Install Clié Utilities, and then Install Memory Stick Export. Follow the instructions.

3. Once the installation is complete, place your Clié into its HotSync cradle (or connect its HotSync cable). Turn it on, and then find and tap the MS Import icon.

> **NOTE** *Obviously, step 3 is all you need to perform on subsequent occasions.*

When you perform this last step, your Clié should beep to notify you that a successful connection to your PC has been made. At the same time, you should now be able to fire up Windows Explorer (or double-click My Computer) and find a new drive letter. Yep, your Clié effectively becomes another drive on your system, meaning you can move, copy, delete, and even rename files just like you would on a floppy disk or hard drive. However, in most cases you won't need to, and you probably wouldn't want to (see the next section for details).

> **CAUTION** *Do not, under any circumstances, remove your Clié from the cradle/cable without first tapping the Disconnect button on its screen. This could seriously harm data, cause weather anomalies, or worse.*

Working With Memory Stick Files and Folders

It stands to reason that if your Clié's Memory Stick becomes another drive on your PC, it should be subject to all the same basic principles of file management. That is, you can create folders to organize your files, and then move and copy files between those folders. If you're thinking, "Oh, no, not *more* confusing file management to deal with," don't worry—there's very little to deal with unless you're a power user, in which case you probably enjoy working with folders and all that. (Dave's been known to spend many a Saturday night organizing the data on his Memory Sticks. Yes, "power user" sometimes equals "lame.")

Indeed, we have a few key bits of information to impart, and then we'll let you go on your merry way.

- When you first insert a blank MS into your Clié, the OS automatically creates a simple folder structure. You don't have to do anything.

- When you use the Palm Install Tool to install programs directly to an MS, they're placed in an automatically created folder called Palm/Launcher. (And they're accessible from the Home screen by selecting the Card category—see Chapter 2 for a refresher.)

- Programs that utilize VFS will often create their own subfolders in a Memory Stick's Programs folder, which also gets created automatically when needed.

- Although the contents of an MS might look like that of a floppy disk or a hard drive, you shouldn't practice the same kind of file management. That is, don't start creating your own folders and shuffling files around. Your Clié knows where everything is stored and, if you move or rename files or folders, you're sure to cause problems. There is, however, one exception to this rule:

- An MS can double as a kind of portable hard drive—a repository for desktop files you might want to back up or transport. Suppose there's a Word document you want to store on your MS. You can just copy it to the root folder or create a folder called Word Files (or whatever you like). In both cases, you'd do this while "connected" to your Clié using MS Import and MS Export, as discussed earlier.

 Copy MP3 Files to a Memory Stick

If your Clié is capable of playing MP3 files and has the AudioPlayer application installed, the Palm OS will automatically create a Palm\Programs\Msaudio folder on a Memory Stick upon its insertion. This is the folder into which you should drag and drop MP3 files from your PC. As noted earlier, it's much faster to load music using this method than with HotSync Manager.

Access a Memory Stick From Your Clié

Easy as it is to explore an MS via your PC, there are times when it's easier—and more practical—to do so on your Clié proper. For instance, suppose you want to move a file from the internal memory to an MS, or vice versa. That's something you can't do from a PC. What you need, then, is a file-management program that supports memory cards (or a launcher that has built-in file-management capabilities).

Sony supplies just such a program: Clié Files (also known as MS Gate on older Cliés). This utility enables you to move, copy, rename, and delete files:

Tap the level-up icon to return to the previous folder in the hierarchy.

Tap the little yellow folder icon to access the files and/or subfolders contained within that folder.

Let's say your Clié is getting a bit short on free space, so you want to move a rather large game to your Memory Stick. Here's the process.

NOTE

Some programs (games included) just plain won't work if placed on a Memory Stick. If you move something over and find it will no longer run, just return to Clié Files and move the file(s) back to internal memory.

1. Insert the MS if it's not already in.

2. Tap the Clié Files icon.

3. Tap the little arrow in the upper-right corner, and then choose Internal. This presents you with a list of all the programs and data files stored in your Clié.

4. Scroll down the list until you find the game.

5. Tap the game to highlight it, and then tap any associated files that need to be moved with it. Clié Files lets you select more than one file at a time. Notice the check mark that appears in the box when you tap a filename. That means the file is selected and whatever action you perform next (such as move, copy, or delete) will happen to that file.

6. Tap the Move button. This will transfer the selected files to the appropriate folder on your MS.

Files that have a little padlock icon next to them are locked, meaning they cannot be moved, copied, or deleted.

If you find Clié Files a bit confusing and underpowered, as we do, you might want to consider one of the many available third-party alternatives. Some recommendations:

■ **FileZ** This file-management utility has nearly every feature you could want, but it's somewhat confusing, and therefore recommended for advanced users only. Why bother with it? It has the appealing distinction of being a freebie.

■ **McFile** Like MS Gate on steroids, *McFile* offers a wealth of file-management features, including beaming and support for HiRes+. It also employs a more traditional method of displaying files and folders, which makes for much easier navigation.

■ **LauncherX** One of our all-time-favorite launchers (see Chapter 13), *LauncherX* includes a good measure of file-management capabilities. Which begs the question: why bother with a separate file manager?

■ **YiShow** Another terrific launcher, *YiShow* also doubles as a file manager. It has certain Clié-specific features that LauncherX lacks, so you should definitely check it out before deciding between them.

Memory 102

While memory cards open the door to carrying much more software than you ever could before, there are a couple hitches. Suppose you have a favorite document reader and a fairly large collection of Doc files that go with it. You decide to move the files to your memory card to free some internal storage space. But the next time you fire up the Doc reader, you discover your Doc files are gone. Why? Because the Doc reader doesn't know to look for them on the memory card. They're still stored there, but the software can't see them. This is true of many older programs (and by "older" we mean those written prior to summer 2001). The good news is that developers are rapidly updating their wares to support VFS, meaning this problem should disappear before long. (For the record, plenty of Doc readers already support VFS, including Palm Reader, TealDoc, and WordSmith.)

To overcome VFS-related issues like this one (and to have an easier time overall working with applications and data stored on memory cards), power users should check out utilities like MSMount (**www.palmgear.com**), PiDirect (**www.pitech.com**), and PowerRun (**www.tt.rim.or.jp/~tatsushi/ powerrun/index-e.html**). In a nutshell, these programs trick the OS into thinking that programs and data stored on a memory card are stored in main memory, so everything is accessible all the time.

Memory Stick Backups

One of the best uses for a Memory Stick is making a backup of your Clié's internal memory. You can perform this invaluable function using Sony's MS Backup utility or one of several more-robust third-party alternatives. See Chapter 13 for more details and MS Backup instructions.

Where to Find It

Web Site	Address	What's There
eCost.com	www.ecost.com	Inexpensive CF and MS cards
Handango	www.handango.com	McFile, YiShow
Little Mobile Creations	www.launcherx.com	LauncherX
NoSleep Software	www.nosleep.net	FileZ

22

Chapter 23

Accessories and Upgrades

How to...

- Choose a case
- Mount your PDA in your car
- Navigate roads with GPS hardware
- Choose a stylus
- Choose a keyboard
- Protect your screen from dust and scratches
- Access WiFi networks with the Wireless LAN Card
- Play MP3 tunes on any stereo
- Recharge your Clié's battery while on the road
- Add Game Boy-style controls to your Clié
- Help a lost Clié find its way home

There's more to the Clié than just software. We're talking gadgets, gear, accessories—the stuff that makes your handheld your own and extends its capabilities beyond what mere software can accomplish. Take the *Targus USB Charge and Sync Cable,* an invaluable travel companion that lets you synchronize—and recharge—your handheld by plugging it into any USB port. Or the *Sony Audio Adapter,* which lets nonmusical Cliés play MP3 files. In this chapter, we look at these and other accessories and upgrades. For starters, let's tackle cases—a subjective category if ever there was one.

This is one area where it's important to make sure the accessory you buy is compatible with your particular Clié model. Many of them are different physically or have different ports and connectors, so not every accessory is compatible with every Clié.

Pick a Case, Any Case

As a new Clié owner, one of the first things you need to determine is how you plan to convey the device. In your pocket? Briefcase? Purse? Clipped to your belt? Backpack? Dashboard? Your answer will help determine the kind of case you should buy.

There are cases for every Clié model and every occasion, and picking one can be a tough call indeed. Do you opt for practical or stylish? (The two are often mutually exclusive.) Do you look for lots of extras like card slots and pen holders, or try to keep it as slim as possible? Do you shell out big bucks for a titanium shell that can withstand being run over by a car? (This happens quite a bit, believe it or not.)

> **NOTE**   *If your Clié came with a plastic or soft-sided screen cover, or it's an NR/NX/NZ model with a rotating screen, you might wonder if you even need a case at all. If screen protection is all you're after, then probably not. But many cases add a measure of drop protection, to say nothing of slots for storing Memory Sticks, business cards, and other stuff.*

Because so many varieties are out there, and because everyone's case needs are different, we're going to start by steering you to the case manufacturers themselves, and then offer a few general tips and suggestions.

Company	URL	Cases Offered
Bellagio Designs	www.bellagiodesigns.com	Various
Case Techworks	www.casetechworks.com	Various
E&B Company	www.ebcases.com	Slipper line
InnoPocket	www.innopocket.com	Metal cases
Piel Frama	www.pielframa.com	Luxury-minded leather cases
Seidio	www.seidio.com	Colorful and contemporary leather cases
Sony	www.sonystyle.com	Various

Here are some things to keep in mind as you shop for a case:

- ■ **Portability**   In the summer, when the tight clothes come out and the jackets get stowed, pockets are hard to come by. That's when something like the E&B Slipper can come in mighty handy.

- ■ **Screen protection**   When your Clié is bouncing around in a pocket, purse, or briefcase, the last thing you want is for some piece of flotsam to gouge or scratch the screen. That's one of the main reasons behind getting a case in the first place. The Seidio *U-Clip Napa Leather Case* offers Velcro-locking screen protection that looks good and doesn't get in the way of buttons and ports.

- **Drop protection**   Gravity—it strikes without warning (especially if you're a klutz like Rick), and it can fatally wound a Clié in a matter of milliseconds. Likewise, we've heard more than a few stories of people driving over their handhelds. Why they're being left in the driveway in the first place is beyond us, but there's one case that's better suited to handle such punishment than any other: InnoPocket's Metal Deluxe.

- **Velcro**   Some cases rely on Velcro to keep your Clié device secured. While we look on this as a necessary evil (who wants a big square of the stuff stuck to the back of their Clié?), we do try to avoid such cases when possible.

Mounting Your Clié in Your Car

Is your car your castle? Your office? Your home away from home? If so, your Clié deserves a place of honor—and a place where you can access it while keeping at least one hand on the wheel.

 In all seriousness, you should never, ever try to use your Clié while driving. If you must look something up or write something down, wait until you've stopped at a light. Or, ask a passenger to do it for you.

Arkon and Seidio are among the companies offering practical and versatile car mounts for your Clié. Their products not only position the handheld within arm's reach (using a variety of mounting methods: windshield, cup holder, air vent, and so on), but also provide power, so you needn't worry about the batteries dying while you're on the road. As icing on the cake, the mounting cradle includes a built-in amplified speaker, thus enabling you to listen to audio and/or audiobook files stored on your Clié—or even navigation directions if you're using a GPS setup that provides voice navigation.

At press time, Seidio was offering a particularly attractive deal on its *Powered Swivel Mount Super Bundle,* which includes three different kinds of mounting hardware (windshield, air vent, and dashboard) and everything you need for charging and audio, all for $49.95. Arkon's similarly equipped Powered Multimedia PDA Mount kit (pictured) was selling for $69.95.

Sony's Do-Everything PEGA-CC5 Car Mount Kit

Mere days before we completed work on this book, Sony took the wraps off the PEGA-CC5 (the company has no shortage of glamorous product names, it seems), by far the most sophisticated car-mount kit we've seen yet. Like the aforementioned Arkon and Seidio products, the *CC5* provides a car-based cradle for your Clié (though its only mounting option is air vents, and it's incompatible with certain types of vents), one that powers and recharges the handheld. However, the similarities end there, as the CC5 offers a raft of extra features—not the least of which is GPS navigation. The cradle includes a wired GPS receiver that magnetically attaches to the roof of your car. Bundled software (Rand McNally's *StreetFinder*) provides driving directions and a real-time moving map.

The CC5 also incorporates an FM transmitter, meaning it can wirelessly transmit MP3 audio to your car's FM radio (which sounds a lot better than any integrated speaker would). Just find an unused frequency on your FM dial, and then fire up the music player. But wait, there's more. When you plunk your Clié into the CC5 cradle, the first thing it does is *read aloud* your current schedule and any e-mail messages you've received in Clié Mail (see Chapter 11). Pretty cool. The package even comes with a wireless remote, so you can operate everything without having to touch the Clié.

Cool as the CC5 is, you should consider a few things before making the investment:

- At $299, it's a lot more expensive than the Arkon and Seidio non-GPS mounts. You could buy one of those mounts, a third-party GPS solution (like one from Mapopolis), and even an add-on FM transmitter, and probably spend less.

- The bundled StreetFinder mapping software is slow and complicated, especially when it comes to plotting destinations. Plus, if you want door-to-door driving directions, you have to create them on your PC, then download them to the Clié—a huge hassle.

- At press time, the CC5 was compatible with only three Clié models: the NX73V, NX80V, and TG50. If you have an older model, you're out of luck.

■   While we love the idea of the Clié reading our e-mail to us, the fact that Sony doesn't offer any kind of wireless option (like a wireless modem) severely limits this feature's potential. You have to synchronize your Clié with your PC so your e-mail is downloaded, and then go get in your car to have it read. In other words, you can't receive e-mail while you're tooling around town. Now *that* would be cool.

Play MP3 Tunes on Any Stereo

As you learned in Chapter 18, most mid-range and high-end Cliés have built-in MP3 players. Wouldn't it be great if you could listen to your tunes on a home or car stereo instead of the Clié's dinky speaker? You can, just by plugging an FM transmitter into the Clié's headphone jack. These nifty little gadgets broadcast the tunes to an unused frequency on the FM dial (not unlike the way Mr. Microphone used to), thus letting you listen in style (and, we hope, static-free—the signal's not always perfect). The CC5 car cradle mentioned in the previous section has this capability built right in, but you can add it to any Clié that has a headphone jack.

Ideally, you want an FM transmitter that can broadcast to whatever FM frequency you choose. Some of the products we've seen limit you to just four frequency choices, and if they're all "used up" (meaning a strong signal is already broadcasting to them), you could be out of luck.

The best one we've tried is Arkon's *SoundFeeder SF121*, which runs off two AAA batteries and supports the FM band between 88–95 MHz. It's $24.95.

The Stylus Decision

Many Clié users are perfectly happy with the stylus that came in the box—until they get a look at some of the alternatives. Indeed, while those bundled plastic and metal pens do get the job done, they're not as comfortable or versatile as they could be. For instance, wouldn't a thicker or heavier writing implement feel better in your hand? And wouldn't it be nice if it doubled as an ink pen? These are just some of the options available to the discriminating Clié user.

As with cases, we wouldn't presume to pick a stylus for you. That's a matter of personal preference. So, here's a look at some of the stylus makers and their offerings.

Product	URL	Comments
Cross DigitalWriter	www.cross.com	Various executive-minded sizes and styles, many with multifunction designs
InnoPocket	www.innopocket.com	Metal replacement styluses
PDA Panache	www.pdapanache.com	Wide assortment of sizes and styles
Pentopia Chameleon	www.pentopia.com	Multifunction replacement styluses
Styluscentral.com	www.styluscentral.com	Giant assortment of styluses
Ttools	www.ttools.com	Nifty multifunction styluses

There are basically two kinds of styluses: those that are too large to fit in a Clié's stylus holder, and those that aren't. The former we'd classify as "executive" styluses: they seem right at home in a suit pocket or briefcase. The Cross DigitalWriter falls into this category—it's big, comfy, and has that classy business look.

Replacement styluses, on the other hand, supplant the stock Clié pen. The *Pentopia Chameleon,* for instance, fits snugly in your Clié's stylus silo and doubles as a ballpoint pen.

If your Clié should happen to crash, the last thing you want is to have to hunt down a toothpick or paper clip to press its Reset button. Thus, look for a stylus that hides a reset pin. Most of them do; it's usually accessible simply by unscrewing one end of the barrel. Same goes for the stylus that came with your Clié.

Keyboards

If you typically enter a lot of data into your Clié device—memos, e-mail messages, business documents, novels—you've probably longed to replace your stylus with a keyboard. After all, most of us can type a lot faster than we can write by hand. Fortunately, a multitude of keyboards are available for Clié devices, all of them priced under $100. In the next section, we give you the skinny on a few of our favorite keyboards.

The TG50 and NR/NX/NZ series have built-in thumb keyboards, obviously, but even those aren't ideal if you need to do a lot of writing.

Full-Size Keyboards

We don't blame you if the notion of carrying around a standard computer keyboard for use with your tiny little handheld PC is making you chuckle. That would be pretty silly, wouldn't it? Still, what better way to do some serious writing than a full-size set of keys? Of the many options now available, there's simply no better solution than the Think Outside Stowaway.

As you can see in Figure 23-1, this amazing keyboard folds up to the size of a small diary, and unfolds to produce a set of keys comparable to those of a notebook PC. It's a bit pricey (anywhere from $69 to $89), but you won't regret the investment. (We've found better prices on eBay, especially

FIGURE 23-1   The Stowaway puts a comfy set of keys beneath your fingers, and then folds up and fits in a pocket.

for versions compatible with older Clié models.) Check out the Stowaway XT, too—it's even more compact than the original (though it lacks dedicated number keys, which is one reason we prefer the original).

TIP   *You can buy the Stowaway direct from Sony, where it sells under the name Compact Keyboard. However, it's not available for all models. Check with Fellowes, the major Stowaway distributor, to find the one that's compatible with your particular Clié.*

The Stowaway does have one disadvantage: limited compatibility. That is, you have to buy the version that's designed to work with your particular handheld model and, if you decide to upgrade someday, the keyboard probably won't be compatible with your new handheld. This is a problem that plagues just about all portable keyboards—but there's a solution.

It's called the *Pocketop Portable Keyboard,* and instead of requiring a direct connection to your handheld, it works wirelessly via infrared ports. That means it's compatible with a wider variety of models (even handhelds that use Microsoft's Pocket PC OS), so it should be able to "stay with you" for the duration.

The Pocketop's keys are smaller and less comfortable than those of the Stowaway, but it also becomes even more compact when folded. It's a truly ingenious product, one that's well worth investigating.

 If you're intrigued by this idea of a "wireless" keyboard, Belkin and Targus now offer similar products—the Wireless PDA Keyboard and Universal Wireless Keyboard, respectively.

Protecting Your Screen

Keeping your screen pristine is the first rule of Clié ownership. Why? One word: scratches. A scratch in the Graffiti area can result in inaccurate handwriting recognition, and a scratch on the main screen can impair its visibility. Fortunately, it's relatively simple to forestall such disasters.

What causes scratches? If your Clié device is flopping around unprotected in a purse or briefcase, any loose item—keys, paper clips, a pen, or pencil—can create a scratch. That's why we highly recommend a case (see the first section of this chapter). More commonly, however, little specks of grit and other airborne flotsam accumulate on your screen, and when you run your stylus over one of them—scratch city.

 Dave is a big fan of tapping his screen with his big grubby fingers. They leave behind oil and smudges, which are more likely to trap dust and grit. Rick, who is much daintier, says that if you must use a finger, at least use your fingernail.

We recommend you buy a lens-cleaning cloth, the kind used to wipe dust from eyeglasses and camera lenses. Every day, just give your screen a little buff and polish to keep it free of dust and grit. Or, consider one of the following products.

ClearTouch

Our new favorite screen protector is the BoxWave ClearTouch. This plastic overlay covers your screen from top to bottom, thus ensuring your stylus causes no damage. It also cuts down on glare and helps keep dust away. Better still, unlike other screen protectors we've tried, which are disposable and must be replaced every month or so, *ClearTouch* is designed to be removed, cleaned, and reapplied. It leaves behind no gummy residue (do we sound like a floor-wax commercial or what?), and it seems to have endless lasting power. We've had one on a Clié NX70V for nearly six months, and it shows no signs of wear.

PDA Screen Protectors

We're not sure this deal will still be around by the time you read this, but it's worth checking out. At a web site called **FreeScreenProtectors.com**, you can order an entire box of CompanionLink PDA Screen Protectors (which are similar to WriteRights, but don't affect contrast) and pay only for shipping. That's right—just enter the coupon code "FREESP" when placing your order, and the sheets are free. Sounds too good to be true, but we placed an order and received our box within about three days. Shipping cost about six bucks. Woo-hoo—free stuff!

Protect Your Screen with Scotch Tape

The Graffiti area is where most stylus contact occurs, and therefore it's where scratches are most likely to result. If you want simple, inexpensive protection, buy yourself a roll of 3M's Scotch Magic Tape 811. It's almost exactly the right height for most Graffiti areas, and one roll will last you a lifetime. Plus, its slightly rough surface makes for less-slippery handwriting—always a plus. Just cut a piece to cover the input area and replace it every month or so. You'll never see a single scratch. (Of course, this tip applies only to those Cliés with silk-screened Graffiti areas. If yours has a virtual Graffiti area, don't cover it with tape, silly!)

Navigating the World with a GPS Receiver

Dave is a huge fan of the *Global Positioning System,* the network of orbiting satellites used to pinpoint one's exact position on the planet. That's because he tends to get lost in his own driveway. Still, GPS is undeniably valuable if you're driving on unfamiliar roads or trying to find your way to, say, a new client's office. And many Clié devices can take full advantage of GPS, thanks to products like Delorme's Earthmate.

Earthmate is a pocket-sized GPS receiver that uses a special cable to connect to your Clié. Street Atlas USA 2004 Handheld is a Palm OS map viewer that lets you download and display street maps created on either Delorme's web site or their Street Atlas U.S.A. software. The result: you can enjoy real-time street-level positioning right on your Clié.

We also recommend checking out *Mapopolis,* a company that offers Clié-specific GPS bundles. What we don't like is that you have to purchase maps piecemeal—the Delorme product comes with street maps for the entire United States. But the actual Mapopolis mapping software that runs on your Clié is superior, so you'll have to weigh the pros and cons.

NOTE *In case you missed it, Sony's PEGA-CC5 car-mount kit (discussed earlier in this chapter) adds GPS navigation to certain Clié models.*

Recharging Your Clié's Batteries While on the Road

A Clié handheld with a rechargeable battery is a mixed blessing. Sure, you don't have to keep a pocketful of fresh Duracells on hand, but what happens if you're on the road and the Clié runs out of juice? Fortunately, there are several clever solutions exist to this little travel problem.

One of the most practical is a cable that charges your Clié just by plugging into a desktop or notebook USB port—no AC adapter required. Check out the Belkin USB Sync Charger and Targus USB Charge and Sync Cable. The former is by far the better deal, as it costs $10 less ($19.99) and comes with a cigarette-lighter adapter for use in your car. For easy recharging just about anywhere, the $39.95 Sony Battery Adapter utilizes four AA batteries, making it the perfect traveling companion.

The Cool Way to Recharge

Another excellent power-supply option is the Instant Power Charger. Instead of charging your batteries from a wall outlet, *Instant Power* tops off your Clié with a disposable power source. The charger is a sort of fuel cell that combines a safe embedded fuel with oxygen drawn from the air. Stored in its aluminum pouch, the charger has a shelf life of about two years. Once you open the pouch, it's good for about three months. That means you can put one in your travel bag and have the peace of mind that you'll have power anytime you need it.

To get started with Instant Power, you need to buy an *Instant Power Charger kit* that includes a single disposable power cartridge and a connection cable for whatever model handheld you own. There are versions for just about every Clié model, as well as wireless modems, digital cameras, Pocket PCs, and even camcorders. Because the power cartridges are interchangeable, you can charge up your entire mobile arsenal without worrying about carrying three different kinds of batteries or chargers.

You should be able to charge your PDA about three times with a single Instant Power cartridge. After you deplete it, just toss it in the trash, but keep the cable—you need to replace only the interchangeable cartridges.

Our Favorite Accessories

Rick: It's not really an accessory, but I wouldn't be caught dead without my 128MB Memory Stick, which has a permanent home in my Clié and holds a boatload of games, e-books, and other essentials. But the real star is my *Stowaway XT keyboard,* a marvel of modern engineering that lets me write while traveling without having to schlep a notebook. They'll have to pry it out of my cold, dead fingers when I shuffle off this mortal coil.

Dave: Using my Sony NX80 is like a refreshing walk through a sun-dappled forest, a cool stream gurgling off to my side, and coyotes playfully wrestling over a bone in the distance. It's a sheer delight; a blissful interlude betwixt the hustle-bustle workaday world. Hence, I consider my Clié to be nearly perfect; little could be done to improve it. That said, a Stowaway keyboard is essential for letting me write on the road. And I often plug in Sony's Wi-Fi CompactFlash card so I can check e-mail. And a big, fat Memory Stick for watching movies. So all that stuff, and whatever I can pry out of Rick's cold, dead fingers.

Recovering Lost Handhelds

No one ever means to lose anything, but it happens. The only thing worse than losing your PDA would be realizing that whoever found it probably wouldn't know how to go about returning it to you. Sure, an address label pasted to the back might do the trick, but we have a better solution: **StuffBak.com**.

For as little as $1.95, you can buy a specially coded StuffBak label to paste on the back of your handheld. The finder need only call a toll-free number or visit the StuffBak web site to arrange for its return, which requires little effort and includes a reward. You pay a $14.95 transaction fee, plus shipping charges and any cash reward you care to offer. (StuffBak's own reward is a pack of its labels, valued at $20.) If you believe people are generally honest, this is an inexpensive and potentially painless way to help a lost handheld find its way home.

If you like the idea behind StuffBak, be sure to check out Boomerangit, which offers a similar set of products and services.

Sony's Accessories

As you've already learned in this chapter, Sony makes quite a number of accessories for the Clié: keyboards, cases, battery chargers, and so on. We think you should know about a few other Sony-made products:

- **Audio Adapter**   Some Cliés have built-in MP3 players, some don't. If yours falls into the latter category, you might want to check out the Audio Adapter. It's a wired remote/headphone jack that plugs into the HotSync port, thereby enabling you to listen to MP3 files (and video clips) stored on Memory Sticks. It also comes with a nice pair of ear-clip headphones. Just one catch: Cliés with built-in MP3 players let you do other things while listening to music, but the Audio Adapter takes over—you can't do anything else until you stop da music.

- **Game Controller**   This is one of our all-time favorite accessories. It adds a Game Boy-like set of buttons to your Clié, making certain action games (like Sinistar, Zap!2016, and Galax) much easier to play and a lot more enjoyable. It also comes with a game: the Tetris clone Columns.

- **Screen Protector**   We discussed these a few pages back, but thought you'd like to know that Sony offers its own protective sheets for certain Clié models.

- **Wi-Fi Adapter**   As discussed in Chapters 11 and 22, you can add 802.11b (also known as Wi-Fi) wireless networking capabilities to those Clié models that have secondary expansion slots (namely, the NX and NZ series). Sony's PEGA-WL110 card sells for about $150 and provides high-speed access to Wi-Fi networks, which are getting to be quite the big deal these days. When connected to such a network, you can browse the Web and send and receive e-mail.

Where to Find It

Web Site	Address	What's There
Arkon	www.arkon.com	SoundFeeder
Belkin	www.belkin.com	USB Sync Charger and other accessories
Boomerangit	www.boomerangit.com	Boomerangit labels
Delorme	www.delorme.com	Earthmate
Fellowes	www.fellowes.com	Stowaway Keyboard
Instant Power	www.instant-power.com	Instant Power Charger
Mapopolis	www.mapopolis.com	GPS hardware and mapping software
Pocketop	www.pocketop.net	Pocketop Portable Keyboard
Sony	www.sonystyle.com	Various Clié accessories
StuffBak.com	www.stuffbak.com	StuffBak labels
Targus	www.targus.com	Charger, Sync Cradle, and other accessories

Appendix

Problems and Solutions

How to...

- Reset your Clié
- Fix a Clié that appears to be dead
- Avoid battery-related problems
- Prevent and fix scratched screens
- Fix a screen that no longer responds properly
- Resolve Hack conflicts
- Deal with a handheld that suddenly won't HotSync
- Troubleshoot HotSync glitches
- Manage two Cliés on one PC
- Manage one Clié on two PCs
- Obtain non-warranty or accident-related repairs
- Find answers to problems on the Web

No computer is perfect. Windows is about as far from the mark as you can get, Macs have problems of their own, and even Cliés suffer the occasional meltdown. Usually it's minor: a Memory Stick that's not recognized, or a wayward Hack that causes the occasional crash. But, sometimes, something downright scary happens, like a sudden and inexplicable lockup that wipes the Clié's entire memory. In this chapter, we help you troubleshoot some of the most common Clié maladies and, we hope, prevent the worst of them.

 Many common problems are addressed on Sony's web site. We're not going to rehash them here, but we are going to suggest you check there first if you have a problem we haven't addressed. Chances are good you'll find a solution.

Curing Clié Problems with a Reset

Just as rebooting a computer will often resolve a glitch or lockup, resetting your Clié is the solution to many a problem. And it's usually the first thing you need to do if your Clié crashes—or even just acts a little strangely.

Just What Is a "Crash," Anyway?

When a computer crashes, that generally means it has plowed into a brick wall—software-wise—and can no longer function. Fortunately, whereas a car in the same situation would need weeks of bump-and-paint work, a computer can usually return to normal by being rebooted. In the case of Cliés, a "reset" is the same as a "reboot."

When a Clié crashes, one common error message is "Fatal Exception." Don't be alarmed; this isn't nearly as deadly as it sounds. It simply means the Clié has encountered a glitch that proved fatal to its operation. Very often, an onscreen Reset button will appear with this error, a tap of which performs a "soft reset" (as we describe in the next section). Sometimes, however, the crash is so major, even this button doesn't work. (You know because you tap it and nothing happens.) In a case like that, you have to perform a manual reset.

Different Ways to Reset a Clié

On the back of every Clié, there's a little hole labeled RESET. Hidden inside it is a button that effectively reboots the unit. When that happens, you see the Clié startup screen, followed a few seconds later by the Prefs screen. That's how a successful reset goes. About 98 percent of the time, everything will be as you left it—your data, your applications, everything.

Technically speaking, there are three kinds of resets: soft, warm, and hard. (Mind out of the gutter, please.) The details:

- **Soft**   Only in rare instances do you need to perform anything other than a soft reset, which is akin to pressing CTRL-ALT-DELETE to reboot your computer. You simply press the Reset button, and then wait a few seconds while your Clié resets itself. No data is lost.

- **Warm**   This action, performed by holding the scroll-up button while pressing the Reset button, goes an extra step by bypassing any system patches or Hacks you might have installed. Use this only if your Clié fails to respond to a soft reset, meaning it's still locked up or crashing. No data is lost, but the Clié will start with a lot of essential software features disabled, like hi-res support on appropriate Cliés. Use this mode to restart a Clié that won't boot any other way—and then delete the offending software and reset it again to enable all the goodies.

- **Hard**   With any luck, you'll never have to do this. A hard reset wipes everything out of your Clié's memory, essentially returning it to factory condition. In the exceedingly rare case that your Clié is seriously hosed (meaning it won't reset or even turn off), this should at least get you back to square one. If it doesn't, your handheld is toast and might need to be replaced (more on repair/replacement options in the section "Obtaining Service and Repairs"). The good news is this: even after a hard reset, all it takes is a HotSync to restore all your data and programs. It's like magic!

The Toothpick Story

Many years ago, Rick was having lunch with a couple of his buddies when he pulled out his PalmPilot Personal (one of the Clié's PDA ancestors) to jot a few notes. To his horror, it wouldn't turn on (a problem he later attributed to the extremely cold weather, which can, indeed, numb a pair of batteries). A press of the Reset button was in order, but Rick didn't have the right tool—namely, a paper clip. So he asked the waitress to bring him a toothpick—the other common item that's small enough to fit in the reset hole. Presto: the PalmPilot sprang back to life.

Perform Warm and Hard Resets

There's a bit of a trick to doing a warm or hard reset successfully. With your Clié on or off (it doesn't matter), hold down the Scroll-up button (for a warm reset) or the Power button (for a hard reset), and then press and release the Reset button on the back of the unit. Now, here's the trick: *wait until the Sony logo appears onscreen* before releasing the scroll or power button. If you release both buttons simultaneously, before the logo appears, all you get is a soft reset.

The moral of the story: be prepared. If your Clié crashes and you need to reset it, the last thing you want is to have to embark on a desperate scavenger hunt for a paper clip or toothpick. Fortunately, many styluses have "reset tips" hidden inside them. And now, a tip about tips.

 If your Clié has a metal stylus (most of them do), it might surprise you to learn that it's stowing a reset tip. Where's it hiding? Unscrew the top (or, in some cases, the bottom) from the barrel to find out.

Fixing a Clié that Appears to Be Dead

So, you fish your Clié out of your pocket, press the Power button, and voilà: nothing happens. Sweating, you press one of the application buttons—again, *nada*. You start to panic. You press the reset button—the screen flashes for a moment, and then goes blank. You start making deals with the man upstairs.

Then you remember that your Clié has a built-in MP3 player, and that if you slide the Hold switch on the side of the unit, it disables the screens and buttons to prevent accidental interruption of your music. In short, it makes your Clié appear to be dead. You check, and sure enough, the Hold switch is in the on position. You slide it back and your Clié springs to life. Whew!

This has given us more than a few scares, so don't feel badly.

Fixing a Comatose Clié

Another kind of dead-Clié problem can scare you to death—unless you know how to fix it, that is. Suppose you install a beta version of some new program and it causes your Clié to crash. When you reset it, though, the screen stays blank, the power light stays on, and no amount of fiddling, whimpering, or screaming to the gods can get it to return to life. Dave has had this happen to him, and trust us: it's not a fun experience.

If that happens to you, all is not lost. Leave the Clié out of its cradle for a day. After the battery drains completely, press the Reset button, place it in the cradle, and let it charge again. After a few hours, press the Reset button again and let it restart. You should have your Clié back, though all the data will be lost—a good reason to HotSync and back up your Clié before you install new software.

Nine Great Tips and Tricks

These handy little secrets will help you on your way from novice user to Palm pro.

A

1. **Find the latest freeware**   At **PalmGear.com**, click the Software link at the left-hand side of the main page, and then find Latest Freeware Software near the top of the Software Categories page that appears. Presto: nothin' but freebies.

2. **...And download it quick**   To save yourself the hassles of downloading, unzipping, and queuing Palm software (freeware and commercial apps alike) for installation, grab PalmGear's StreamLync utility. It's free, and it lets you download and install software from PalmGear with just a few easy clicks.

3. **Hotwired HotSync**   Can't HotSync all of a sudden? Try a soft reset of your handheld. More times than not, this solves the problem.

4. **HotSync with the Web**   Did you know you can synchronize your handheld with Yahoo! Address Book, and then access your calendar, contacts, and memos from any Web-enabled computer? Just visit Yahoo! Mobile (**mobile.yahoo.com**), click the PDA Downloads link, then look for Intellisync for Yahoo! It's free, as is the account you'll need to set up with Yahoo! Follow the instructions carefully, however, because you could accidentally wind up unable to HotSync with your PC.

5. **Multiple-personality buttons**   Your handheld's four application buttons needn't be limited to launching four applications. Utilities such as QLaunch and SmartLauncher let you program the buttons to launch multiple programs with multiple presses.

6. **Sync with your spouse**   It's one thing to sync two handhelds to the same PC. It's another to have access to each other's schedule. *DualDate,* a Palm freebie, puts your calendar side by side with a spouse, friend, coworker, and so on for at-a-glance comparison.

7. **Happy holidays**   Want to add all the holidays to your Date Book? Just download 2004 USA Holidays 1.1 (**www.freewarepalm.com**). It contains 36 United States and religious holidays. While you're at it, get the 2005 through 2010 calendars as well. Just import the file(s) into Palm Desktop, and then HotSync.

8. **Louder alarms**   If you've set the alarm volume to "High" in Prefs, but your alarms still aren't loud enough, try switching to a different alarm sound. In Date Book, tap Menu | Options | Preferences. Tap the arrow next to Alarm Sound, and then choose a tune. You'll hear it played immediately. Find the one that's loudest, then tap OK.

9. **Graffiti at a glance**   Swipe the stylus from the bottom of the screen to the top and a handy Graffiti reference chart will appear.

Fixing a Comatose Clié, Part Two

If you perform a hard reset, HotSync to restore everything, and your Clié continues to crash at the same place that got you into trouble the last time, there's an easy fix: Delete the Saved_prefs.prc file in the Backup folder on your hard drive (the easiest way to find it is with Windows' Search function), and then repeat the reset/HotSync process on your handheld. Unfortunately, you'll have to manually reenter all the registration/unlock codes for your various programs, e-books, and so on, but you should at least have an operable Clié again.

Avoiding Battery Problems

Batteries are the lifeblood of any Clié. When they die, they take your data with them, effectively returning your Clié to factory condition. That's why it's vital to keep a close eye on the battery gauge shown at the top of the Applications screen (see Figure A-1), and to take heed when the Clié notifies you that your batteries are low.

Of course, if you HotSync regularly, a wiped Clié isn't the end of the world. Once you've recharged (or replaced) the batteries, a HotSync is all it takes to restore virtually everything. Still, there's no reason to let things reach that point. The following are some tips to help you avoid most battery-related incidents.

- **Keep 'em fresh**   Suppose you head off to Bermuda for a two-week getaway (you lucky vacationer, you), leaving your work—and your Clié—behind. When you return, don't be surprised to find the Clié dead as a doornail. That's because it draws a trace amount of power from the batteries, even when off, to keep the memory alive. If the batteries were fairly low to begin with, the long period of inactivity might just polish them off. The obvious solution is to keep your Clié with you as much as possible. (It's great for games, e-books, and other leisure activities, remember?) Alternatively, if you know you're going to be away from it for a while, just leave it in the cradle (if it's a rechargeable model).

- **Keep a charger on hand**   You've been on the road for weeks, your handheld has warned you repeatedly that the battery is low, and there's not a charging cradle in sight. That's the Catch 22 of the rechargeable battery: no Duracells to buy, but no easy way to recharge on the road. That is, unless you have one of the many portable charging accessories now available. See Chapter 23 for more details.

Fixing Scratched Screens

Scratches happen. They happen most often when your stylus hits a piece of dust or grit. That's why it's important to keep your screen as clean as possible (we recommend a daily wipe with a lint-free, antistatic cloth). Better still, take a few preventative steps:

- **Tape**   A piece of Scotch Magic Tape 811 placed over the Graffiti input area (where most scratches occur) not only makes existing scratches less tangible while you're writing, but also prevents future scratches and provides a tackier writing surface.

- **Screen protectors**   As discussed in Chapter 23, products such as the *BoxWave ClearTouch* are plastic overlays that protect the entire screen. They won't remove scratches, but they will prevent them and, like the tape, make them less pronounced. Sony makes a similar screen-protection product, and be sure to check out the sheets at **www.freescreenprotectors.com**.

- **PDA ScreenClean**   Fellowes' wash-and-dry system might remind you of those wet-nap packets you get in those greasy-spoon restaurants Dave likes to eat in. One packet contains a wet cloth you use to wash and wipe the screen, the other a dry cloth used for drying and buffing. These won't repair scratches, but they will remove all the dust and grit that can lead to them, and leave your screen looking pristine.

Fixing a Screen that No Longer Responds Properly

As noted in Chapter 2's discussion of the Digitizer option, it's not uncommon to experience some "drift" in the screen's response to your stylus taps. An example: you have to tap just a bit to the left or right of your desired target for the tap to be recognized. This occurs over time, when the accuracy of the digitizer (the hardware that makes the screen respond to your input) degrades.

Unless the digitizer has gotten so off-kilter that you can no longer operate your Clié, the solution is to tap the Prefs icon, and then choose Digitizer from the right-corner menu. Here you can reset the digitizer, effectively making your Clié good as new. If you can't even manage to tap Prefs, you can do a soft reset (as described earlier in this chapter). That gets you to the Prefs screen, where you should at least be able to select the Digitizer option.

The battery gauge tells you how much juice your Clié has left

FIGURE A-1   All Cliés have this handy—and fairly accurate—battery gauge at the top of the screen.

Cure "Mad Digitizer Syndrome"

What happens when the digitizer gets so out of whack your Clié essentially becomes inoperable? This problem, which some have dubbed "Mad Digitizer Syndrome," can strike even if your handheld is only a year or two old. One very effective way to cure MDS is with a utility called *AutoDigi,* which automatically recalibrates the digitizer after a reset. You can buy the $15 program at PalmGear (**www.palmgear.com**). If your screen is really giving you trouble, check out *OnDigi,* a Hack that automatically recalibrates the digitizer each time you turn on your handheld. If neither utility solves the problem, then it's probably a hardware issue that will require service.

Resolving Hack Conflicts

It bears repeating (see Chapter 13 for the first time we said it) that as marvelous as Hacks are, they can wreak havoc on Cliés. This is especially true if you run more than two or three simultaneously, as these little bits of code can conflict with one another. If you find that your Clié is crashing on a regular basis, you might have to investigate your Hacks. Here's what you should do:

1. Start X-Master, and then uncheck the box next to each Hack to disable it.

2. Go back to using your Clié. If you find that the crashes no longer occur, a Hack is the likely culprit. To help pin down which one, go to Step 3.

3. Launch X-Master again, and then enable just one Hack. Use your Clié normally, and see if the crashes return. If not, enable a second Hack. Through this process of elimination, you should be able to figure out which one is causing the problem. When you do, stop using it.

Fixing a Clié that Won't "Wake Up" for Alarms

It's easy to fall out of love with your Clié when an alarm you set fails to go off (meaning the Clié doesn't "wake up" and beep). This can happen for several reasons, from low batteries to a corrupted alarm database to a conflict with third-party software. The first is easy to resolve by making sure your Clié is adequately charged. For the other two problems, try a soft reset, which often does the trick.

If you use a third-party program that has anything to do with alarms (such as ToDo Plus or DiddleBug), it's possible this is causing the snafu. To troubleshoot it, try doing a warm reset (hold the Scroll-up button while pressing the Reset button). This will disable any Hacks or third-party applications that tie into the operating system (OS). Set an alarm in Date Book and see if it works. If so, then another program is likely to blame. A process of elimination should help you determine which one. In any case, you might have to discontinue using that program if it keeps fouling up your alarms.

If none of these options work, it's possible your Clié is damaged. Contact Sony for service.

Beaming Problems

Having trouble beaming? Chances are good the problem is caused by one of four factors. First, if your Clié is brand new and won't beam, you're not alone. Both Dave and Rick have noticed that some Cliés don't beam properly right out of the box. Perform a reset. It should work just fine after that.

Second, make sure the two handhelds aren't too close together. People often make the mistake of holding their Cliés right next to each other, which can give the infrared transceivers trouble. Keep the units at least a foot or two apart.

Third, make sure the Beam Receive option is checked in the Prefs | General screen. While you might not have unchecked it yourself, sometimes it just seems to happen.

Still no luck? Try moving to a darker area. Beaming doesn't always work if you're in a brightly lit room or outdoors on a sunny day. If all else fails, perform a soft reset on both Cliés. More often than not, that does the trick.

The Last Chapter

Dave: Well, this is the last chapter…and it's almost complete. It was a blast to write this book, but I have to admit that I'm kind of burnt out on all this tech writing stuff. I think I'll take my half of the advance (a cool half-million or so) and move to Bermuda. There I'll build a cottage on the beach and let my army of trained monkey butlers bring me cool drinks all day long. I'll pass the time staring at the waves as they gently break onto the sandy, white beach, and occasionally dabble at writing a best-selling novel on my Clié with a Stowaway keyboard. My MP3 player will be loaded up with Kristin Hersh music and my cats will be napping in my lap. Yep, that's what I'm going to do….

Rick: Always with the monkey butlers. As for me, now that the yoke of another book has been lifted, I'll be returning to the soup kitchen where I volunteer three times a week, though not before I finish the urban-beautification program I spearheaded, along with that fundraiser for Greenpeace. Now I just have to decide which charities will be getting my royalty checks this year—always a tough choice. Honestly, there's no better reward for months of hard work than good old philanthropy. Oh, but, uh, your plan sounds really good, too….

Dealing with a Handheld that No Longer HotSyncs

It worked fine yesterday, but today your handheld just refuses to HotSync. We hear your pain—this drives us up the wall, too. We wish we could blame Windows, because it's just the kind of nonsense we've come to expect from it, but this is usually due to a Clié software, hardware, or cradle problem.

Best bet? Start with a soft reset. Use the end of a paper clip (or unscrew the barrel of your metal stylus to find a hidden tip) to press the Reset button on the back of your handheld. In many cases, this will solve the problem outright, and you can get back to playing Bejeweled. If it doesn't, consider reinstalling Palm Desktop. This action won't affect your data, but it will provide a "fresh" version of HotSync Manager—which often solves HotSync problems. If you're not comfortable with that step or it doesn't work, consult Sony's web site for other remedies.

Troublesome USB Ports

USB is usually pretty reliable and any potential problems that crop up generally boil down to just a few things. For starters, you might not have anywhere to plug in your cradle, especially if you already have a few other USB devices. If that's the case, you need to run over to a local computer store and buy a USB hub. This device plugs into a USB port on your PC and gives you several extra USB connectors for additional devices.

But if you plugged in your HotSync cradle and it doesn't seem to work, there are likely causes:

■ Your USB port doesn't have enough power to run the cradle. If your USB port has several devices connected to it, such as through a hub, it might be unable to handle the power requirements of the connected devices. Make sure you're using a "powered" hub (it will come with its own AC adapter) and that it's plugged into the wall. If that checks out, you might need to swap some devices around between your PC's USB ports. This might take a little experimentation.

■ A related problem: your USB port might have run out of bandwidth—in other words, the capacity to transfer data. This can happen if you have some high-performance USB devices connected to the same port. Again, the solution is to move some things around between the ports. Dave found he simply couldn't run all the USB devices he wants to on his PC because they demand more total bandwidth than his PC's USB ports could deliver.

■ Another possibility: something we like to call Windows Funkiness. Reboot your PC and it could work just fine. Heck, if you're having trouble, try rebooting the PC right away, because that might very well solve your problem.

■ Finally, you could run into trouble getting two or more Palm devices installed and properly HotSyncing on the same PC. It will work—you just need to install the software in a certain way. Specifically, you need to install the oldest Palm first, HotSync, and then install the next newer one and HotSync it, and so on. See Chapter 16 for details.

Solving Memory-Related HotSync Failure

If you try to install a new program or database and your Clié doesn't have enough memory, the HotSync will fail—and fail again every time thereafter. Assuming you can't free up enough space on your handheld to accommodate the new item(s), you have to venture onto your hard drive. Specifically, locate the *c:\program files\Sony Handheld\yourusername\install* folder (the "holding tank" for software waiting to be installed during HotSync), and delete everything in there. Now you should be able to HotSync successfully.

Deleting programs and data from the Install folder doesn't permanently delete them from your hard drive. When you choose items to be installed on your Clié, copies are placed in the Install folder. The original files remain.

Solving the Most Common HotSync Problems

A few pesky problems account for about 90 percent of all the HotSync issues we've ever encountered—and they're all pretty easy to diagnose and solve.

The Clié Aborts a HotSync Immediately

If you press the HotSync button on the cradle and the Clié immediately insists that "the COM port is in use"—so quickly that it doesn't seem possible for the Clié to have even checked—the solution is to perform a soft reset on your Clié. After it resets, the HotSync should work fine.

When HotSyncing, the Clié Displays the HotSync Screen but Nothing Else Happens

This problem is usually caused by HotSync Manager: it's either not running, or one of its dialog boxes is open. If you open the Custom dialog box to change conduit settings, for instance, the HotSync won't run—but you won't get an error message, either. Look on the desktop for an open dialog box, and then close it and try the HotSync again. You might have to first tap Cancel on your Clié, and then wait a minute or two for it to respond.

When HotSyncing, this Message Appears: "An Application Failed to Respond to a HotSync"

This one is easy to fix. When you started the HotSync, an Address Book or Date Book entry was probably left open in Palm Desktop. Your Clié can't successfully HotSync with one of those entries open for editing, so you should close the entry and try again.

Outlook HotSync Problems

As you learned in Chapter 3, most Cliés come with a special conduit for synchronizing with Microsoft Outlook. It's called PocketMirror, and we could fill a separate book with information on using and troubleshooting it. Fortunately, you can get lots of helpful assistance from Chapura, the company that makes it (**www.chapura.com**).

Working with Windows 2000

If you're a Windows 2000 user, you'll be glad to know the OS gets along with Clié Desktop just fine. However, at press time, there were a few known issues you should consider:

- Windows 2000's "hot undock" feature, usually found on notebook systems, might not work with HotSync Manager running. Solution: shut down HotSync Manager before performing the undock.

- Infrared HotSyncs won't work. Solution: download the HotSync 3.1.1 update from Palm's web site.

Working with Windows XP

As with every new version of Windows, XP brought with it a plethora of problems: synchronization and otherwise. Some Clié users reported they couldn't HotSync with the new OS, while others encountered problems with XP's multiple user profiles. If you run into something similar, you might need a patch, a new version of Palm Desktop, or some other solution entirely. Visit Sony's web site for more details.

Palm Desktop doesn't support Windows XP's "switch user" option, which allows multiple users to log on to their PCs at the same time. If you have multiple user profiles set up, each person needs to log out at the end of their session, while the next person logs in.

Managing Multiple Cliés or PCs

The Palm OS lets you HotSync the same Clié to more than one PC, or to HotSync several Cliés to the same PC. It's easier than you might think, so feel free to HotSync at home and the office, or to hand out Cliés to every member of the family.

Two Cliés on a Single PC

If you have two Cliés and only one computer, you're not alone. In fact, it's a pretty common scenario: many married couples have their own Cliés and want to HotSync to the household computer.

Here's what you need to do:

1. Be absolutely sure that both Cliés have different usernames. Check this by tapping the HotSync icon on each Clié and looking at the name in the upper-right corner. Identically named Cliés, HotSynced to the same PC, will irretrievably trash the data on the PC and both Cliés.

2. Put the Clié in the HotSync cradle and go. The first time the second Clié is inserted, your PC will ask if you want to create a new account for the other Clié. Click Yes.

CAUTION *If both Cliés have the same username for some reason, do not attempt to HotSync them to the same PC! In fact, change their names before you HotSync at all to prevent accidentally HotSyncing the Cliés in the wrong PC. There's a freeware utility that lets you change your HotSync name after you've chosen one: ChangeName, available from **PalmGear.com**. But that's for making the change right on your handheld; if you want an easier, desktop-based method, just do this: select the Edit Users function in Palm Desktop, choose Rename, and then HotSync the Clié.*

TIP *As long as you're using two Cliés in the same family—like a pair of T665Cs—you can use one HotSync cradle for both handhelds. However, you can't always mix and match. An S360, for instance, won't work with an NR70V cradle, and vice versa. However, it's possible to have multiple cradles connected to the same PC—just plug them into available USB ports. And be sure to install the Palm Desktop that came with the newer of the two models.*

Two PCs for a Single Clié

A Clié can keep two different PCs straight just as easily as one PC can keep a pair of Cliés straight. When you HotSync, the Clié updates the second PC with whatever data it previously got from the first PC, and vice versa. This is a great way to keep your office PC and home computer in sync, or even a PC and a Mac—the Clié can serve as a nonpartisan conduit for keeping all the data current.

Of course, the most efficient way to use a dual-PC system is to acquire a second HotSync cradle. You can buy an additional one for about $40, or you can get a HotSync cable instead, which is a little more streamlined for traveling.

Upgrading from an Old Clié to a New One

To those of you still living with a Clié S320, we salute you. But when you finally decide you're ready for a nicer screen, more memory, and a bunch of cool accessories that won't work with your old model, we'll be here for you. Specifically, we're here to help you make the move from an older

Clié to a new one—an increasingly common task these days, now that the devices have been around for several years.

Unlike upgrading to a new PC (which requires an obnoxious amount of effort), upgrading to a new Palm device is shockingly easy. Here's the process in a nutshell:

Before you perform Step 1, take the time to "clean out" the old handheld by deleting applications and data you're no longer using. At the same time, disable any Hacks that might be running—especially if you're upgrading to a model with Palm OS 5. In fact, as you learned in Chapter 13, Hacks are incompatible with OS 5, so you should not only disable the Hacks from your old model, you should delete them—and your Hack manager as well—before your "final HotSync." Finally, search your computer's hard drive for a file called Saved_prefs.prc, and delete it. The end goal here is to avoid transporting old, unnecessary, and potentially incompatible stuff from the old device to the new one.

1. Do one last HotSync of your old Palm device.

2. Turn off your PC, unplug the old HotSync cradle, and plug in the new one. (Chances are good the new handheld won't be able to use the old cradle. *C'est la vie.*) If your new cradle has a USB connector, install the new version of Palm Desktop *before* plugging in the new cradle.

3. Turn on your PC and install the Palm Desktop software that came with your new handheld. Go ahead and place it in the same C:\Palm directory (or whatever's appropriate) where the previous version was installed. Don't worry—all your data will be preserved!

4. HotSync your new handheld. When you do, a box appears listing your username from your old model. Click it, and then choose OK. This will restore all your data.

Most of your third-party applications will be reinstalled along with your data, but a few might not. Thus, you could have to manually reinstall some programs. At the same time, you might have to reenter registration codes for any software you've paid to unlock.

Obtaining Service and Repairs

Clié problems, while relatively infrequent, come in all shapes and sizes. Yours could be as simple as an alarm that won't go off or as dire as a device that won't turn on. Fortunately, technical support and repair services are available from Sony. Here's the info you need.

- **Tech Support**   (877) 760-7669
- **Web**   www.ita.sel.sony.com/support/clie/
- **E-Mail**   www.ita.sel.sony.com/support/clie/email.html

Obtaining Non-Warranty or Accident-Related Repairs

Right up there with the awful sound of your car crunching into another is the sound of your Clié hitting the pavement. A cracked case, a broken screen, a dead unit—these are among the painful results. And, unfortunately, if you drop, step on, sit on, or get caught in a rainstorm with your Clié, your warranty is pretty much out the window.

All is not lost, however. If your Clié is damaged, or develops a problem after the warranty has expired, you could still have options. For a fee (usually a rather steep $150), Sony will usually replace a broken or out-of-warranty unit with a refurbished one. It's not cheap, but it's probably cheaper than buying a brand new Clié. The bottom line is, if something terrible happens to your device, it's worth a phone call to Sony to see what options are available. You might be able to pay for repairs or buy a refurbished one for less than the cost of a new unit.

A

Other Sources for Help

As we've noted many times already, you can find oodles of help on Sony's web site. In addition, several independent sites offer tips, tricks, hints, and technical solutions. If you're looking for answers that aren't in this book or on the Sony site, try some of these.

Site	Description
www.pdabuzz.com	This site has a message board area in which you can post questions and read answers to common ones. It also contains handheld-related product news and reviews—and just happens to be manned by the authors of this book.
www.cliesource.com	An all-Clié web site with extensive message forums categorized by model.
alt.comp.sys.palmtops.pilot comp.sys.palmtops.pilot	These newsgroups are available to anyone with a newsreader like Outlook Express. They are threaded message boards that contain questions and answers about Palm OS-based handhelds like the Clié. You can post your own questions, respond to what's already there, or just read the existing posts.

Where to Find It

Web Site	Address	What's There
Fellowes	www.fellowes.com	PDA ScreenClean and other accessories
PalmGear	www.palmgear.com	DualDate and a zillion other Palm OS programs

Index

Symbols

INTERNATIONAL CONTACT INFORMATION

AUSTRALIA
McGraw-Hill Book Company
Australia Pty. Ltd.
TEL +61-2-9900-1800
FAX +61-2-9878-8881
http://www.mcgraw-hill.com.au
books-it_sydney@mcgraw-hill.com

CANADA
McGraw-Hill Ryerson Ltd.
TEL +905-430-5000
FAX +905-430-5020
http://www.mcgraw-hill.ca

GREECE, MIDDLE EAST, & AFRICA
(Excluding South Africa)
McGraw-Hill Hellas
TEL +30-210-6560-990
TEL +30-210-6560-993
TEL +30-210-6560-994
FAX +30-210-6545-525

MEXICO (Also serving Latin America)
McGraw-Hill Interamericana Editores
S.A. de C.V.
TEL +525-1500-5108
FAX +525-117-1589
http://www.mcgraw-hill.com.mx
carlos_ruiz@mcgraw-hill.com

SINGAPORE (Serving Asia)
McGraw-Hill Book Company
TEL +65-6863-1580
FAX +65-6862-3354
http://www.mcgraw-hill.com.sg
mghasia@mcgraw-hill.com

SOUTH AFRICA
McGraw-Hill South Africa
TEL +27-11-622-7512
FAX +27-11-622-9045
robyn_swanepoel@mcgraw-hill.com

SPAIN
McGraw-Hill/
Interamericana de España, S.A.U.
TEL +34-91-180-3000
FAX +34-91-372-8513
http://www.mcgraw-hill.es
professional@mcgraw-hill.es

UNITED KINGDOM, NORTHERN,
EASTERN, & CENTRAL EUROPE
McGraw-Hill Education Europe
TEL +44-1-628-502500
FAX +44-1-628-770224
http://www.mcgraw-hill.co.uk
emea_queries@mcgraw-hill.com

ALL OTHER INQUIRIES Contact:
McGraw-Hill/Osborne
TEL +1-510-420-7700
FAX +1-510-420-7703
http://www.osborne.com
omg_international@mcgraw-hill.com

Sound Off!

Visit us at **www.osborne.com/bookregistration** and let us know what you thought of this book. While you're online you'll have the opportunity to register for newsletters and special offers from McGraw-Hill/Osborne.

We want to hear from you!

Sneak Peek

Visit us today at **www.betabooks.com** and see what's coming from McGraw-Hill/Osborne tomorrow!

Based on the successful software paradigm, Bet@Books™ allows computing professionals to view partial and sometimes complete text versions of selected titles online. Bet@Books™ viewing is free, invites comments and feedback, and allows you to "test drive" books in progress on the subjects that interest you the most.

Know How

**How to Do Everything
with Your Digital Camera**
Second Edition
ISBN: 0-07-222555-6

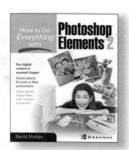

**How to Do Everything
with Photoshop Elements 2**
ISBN: 0-07-222638-2

**How to Do Everything
with Photoshop 7**
ISBN: 0-07-219554-1

**How to Do Everything
with Your Sony CLIÉ**
ISBN: 0-07-222659-5

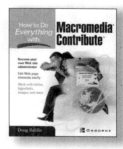

**How to Do Everything
with Macromedia
Contribute**
0-07-222892-X

**How to Do Everything
with Your eBay Business**
0-07-222948-9

**How to Do Everything
with Your Tablet PC**
ISBN: 0-07-222771-0

**How to Do Everything
with Your iPod**
ISBN: 0-07-222700-1

**How to Do Everything
with Your iMac,**
Third Edition
ISBN: 0-07-213172-1

**How to Do Everything
with Your iPAQ Pocket PC**
Second Edition
ISBN: 0-07-222950-0

McGraw

Subscribe Today!

Handheld Computing Magazine
The #1 Guide to Handheld Devices

Get all the information you need on Handheld Devices, software and accessories including PDAs, MP3 Players, Smartphones and Digital Cameras. You'll make smarter buying decisions and get more from your handheld after reading news, reviews, tips and advice from the most respected writers in the field.

Handheld Computing Mobility
The Premier Resource for Mobile Professionals

Mobility covers the products and solutions that make today's businesses successful. From PDAs to Laptops, from Smartphones to Tablets, we'll provide you with the information you need to implement an integrated mobile solution including all you need to know about the latest wireless technologies including Bluetooth, 802.11x, 3G Cellular and more.

Handheld Computing™ Weekly

Get the latest and most up to date information on new products and services. It's Free! Sign up at: www.pdabuzz.com/SubscribeCenter.

Mobility Weekly

Get the scoop on the latest in Palm Powered Enterprise news and services. It's Free! Sign up at: www.pdabuzz.com/SubscribeCenter

Subscribe Now!
Visit **www.pdabuzz.com/SubscriberCenter**
For fastest service call **888-406-4048**